The Screening of America

Of Related Interest
from Continuum

The Screening of America

Movies and Values from *Rocky* to *Rain Man*

Tom O'Brien

A Frederick Ungar Book
CONTINUUM • NEW YORK

1990

The Continuum Publishing Company
370 Lexington Avenue
New York, NY 10017

Printed in the United States of America

Library of Congress Cataloging-in-Publication Data

O'Brien, Tom, 1949–
    The screening of America : movies and values from Rocky to
Rain Man / Tom O'Brien.
        p.   cm.
    "A Frederick Ungar book."
    Includes bibliographical references.
    ISBN 0-8264-0472-3
    1. Motion pictures—Moral and ethical aspects. 2. United States-
-Popular culture. I. Title.
PN1995.5.027 1990   89-20979
306.4'85—dc20   CIP

In Memory of W. C. O'Brien
1896–1985

We don't read. We don't care about who's running our country, we don't care about our neighbors. We don't care about anything. We're so interested in ourselves we don't remember why this country started. What it means. Nobody can read, nobody can write. Everybody watches *Wheel of Fortune*. And I perpetuated that for a long time. I am a victim and a perpetrator of that.

I think if you look at *Moonstruck*, it's a different set of values. And if everybody was like that, maybe we would still be able to unlock our doors and not have, you know, some asshole push a pregnant woman under the subway. Or that people might care if they have to step over someone who's frozen in a doorway.

I think that's kind of a thread in my characters; they're all very old-fashioned in their morals.

—Cher, *Film Comment*, February 1988

Contents

Preface

This book is not intended for film critics, cineasts, or film historians. As a teacher and only part-time movie columnist, I don't really fit into one of these categories myself. No doubt experts will find my theories off, my interpretation arguable, my range what used to be called "middlebrow." These flaws result in part from my own limits. They also result from my approach, a choice that I make because of my views of and hopes about the relation of the media, art, and society.

My judgments in this book are based on my politics and aesthetics. A cornerstone of both is a kind of populism. The book is intended for the common reader because I believe we need works that broaden conversation about our culture and values. It is for people who see movies for fun, escape, or enlightenment, and possibly more. They may know the names of three or four directors and maybe a dozen major stars. They recognize other faces perhaps, but can't always put names to them. They think about movies, and, at times, worry about their influence on our culture and society. I can only define them as my fellow citizens. This book is for them.

Its strengths are due to the help I have received from many friends and colleagues, beginning with my editors and friends at Continuum, Michael Leach and Evander Lomke. At *Commonweal*, I am primarily indebted to editors Peter and Peggy Steinfels; and to Edward Skillin, David Toolan, Karen Smith, Patrick Jordan, the late Anne Robertson, Patricia Mazzola, and others who provided valuable encouragement and guidance; Paul Baumann was also helpful in pinch-hitting at my column while I finished this book. Editors John Koch at the *Boston Globe* and Ken Ringle at the *Washington Post* also deserve my thanks for encouraging features from me that led to some of the chapters below.

11

I also wish to thank Sister Nancy Malone of the *Journal of Religion and Intellectual Life* at the College of New Rochelle, which printed some early versions of some of my chapters; her enthusiasm for my theme pieces played a key role in giving birth to my whole plan. Friends and fellow writers Steven Englund, Greg Abbot, and Elena Sigman also deserve my thanks, as does my toughest critic, biggest fan, and one-time teacher, Paula Bernstein. Katherine Thomas, Fred Rosenberg, and Lura Bane Howes were also greatly encouraging.

At Manhattan School of Music, I wish to thank past and present members of the Humanities Department (Maxine McClintock, Ed Green, Elinor Richter, and Janice Papolos) all of whom spent valuable time in reading and commenting on this text; my thanks also to Bill Fink, who helped on the title. Pianist Zenon Fishbein and composer Elias Tanenbaum also helped by prodding me with their constant interest in movies. Many students were also helpful (Mike, Tara, Scott, Jeff, Hilda, Adrienne, Joanna, Allegra, Michelle) with hot tips on films and plenty of encouragement in my writing project. Goodness knows, I bothered them enough about theirs.

Let me finally thank members of the family, especially my mother, brothers and sisters, nephews and nieces, especially Lisa, who aided me greatly with her advice on word processing and help with printing.

My biggest thanks go to my wife and best friend Alden, for her patience, her knowing comments on movie costumes, and her wise efforts to get me to censor my favorite phrases.

Since this book was primarily completed by December 1989, it can only touch on major releases since then, such as *Driving Miss Daisy, Glory,* and *Born on the Fourth of July.*

Tom O'Brien
December 1, 1989

1

Introduction: The Unusual Suspects

Movies have been in a "feel good" phase lately, but it isn't easy to feel good about it: the first temptation of anyone surveying the last decade of American movies may be to scream. Zany comedy bestrode the time like a colossus. Cartoon styles didn't begin with *Roger Rabbit*, but *climaxed* there, after long nursing not just in children's films but also pop pap like *Ghostbusters* and *Rambo*. Movies like *Lethal Weapon* and *Robocop* relied on fantastic violence to exploit (but rarely explore) anxiety about crime. Films on serious social issues seemed taboo; even satire, once a preserve of serious thought, turned silly. "Always look on the bright side of life," ended *Life of Brian* in 1979. The movie may have offended some religious groups, but it certainly seems a prophecy of things getting jolly and juvenile in years ahead.

What we saw on screen was, perhaps, a country losing its mind. Everything suddenly involved special effects. The Joker was the age's spokesman when, outwitted by Batman, he could only smile in envious delight at his "wonderful toys." Toys above all ruled Hollywood—toys in the form of movies, not just the creative tie-ins dreamed up by marketing geniuses. As George Lucas said about the *Indiana Jones* series, "They're like old 1940s B movies. In fact, those old B movies *are* our A movies." No longwinded study could better describe the film history of our times.

To "feel good" or make other people "feel good" is no sin—traditional, or "cineast" puritans, to the contrary. There is nothing wrong with feeling good, especially if it is periodically connected with other modes of human fulfillment such as doing good and thinking deeply. But these combinations have not been the usual results of watching recent movies. Indeed, many recent films have aimed instead at making audiences feel

13

good by resorting to the least common denominator delights of sex and violence, and, most worrisomely, mixtures of both. It would be easy, but tedious, to detail all the excessess in this vein, especially the newer, gorier depictions of violence against women on screen; to paraphrase Claude Rains in *Casablanca*, all you have to do is round up the usual suspects. Each year of chain-saw, powerdrill, nail-gun, or toxic waste massacres yields another bundle.

But complaints about screen violence are passé; the real cutting edge in Hollywood today is vulgarity. Consider some early scenes from *adult* movies in the later 1980s. In *Working Girl*, Melanie Griffith has to find her boss in the men's room, then has to hand him toilet paper. In *Big Business*, hospital patients are mistakenly given urine samples to drink. In *Tucker*, pet dalmatians leave dog-do for the hero to step on as he traverses his front porch. In *Cousins* (1989), a man moons his own wedding reception. In each film, a terrible new idea of beauty is born: every comedy must dose us with immediate vulgarity. The producers must worry that stray fourteen-year-olds might wander in and need quick reassurance about a movie's quality; hence, the need to amuse early and easily with something familiar. You wouldn't want anyone to leave, would you, because they *hadn't* been grossed out?

The examples are only the tip of an iceberg; remember, they come from "adult" movies. There is no need to detail *Police Academy, Porky's* et al.; their vulgarities are legion. One peak in civilization was certainly reached in *Revenge of the Nerds* (1984) when two characters named Ogre and Booger squared off in a campus belching contest. Yes, I enjoyed it; extremism is always entertaining. But maybe we are getting just too much of a good thing.

Consider, finally, *The Witches of Eastwick*. You can tell things are going to break down quickly in the film; the set is a New England village with a white picket fence and a tall Congregational Church—the kind of place doomed to disaster via au courant irony. Jack Nicholson plays Satan—what is termed "an average horny little devil" to get democratic viewers to empathize. Nicholson brings to his role a whirlwind of bawdy energy; anticipating *Batman,* his eyebrows already look permanently stuck up in wicked insinuation. Masquerading as a rich landowner, he has three ladies to entice into being "witches" (Cher, Susan Sarandon, and Michelle Pfeiffer); he's also got an enemy at the local church (Veronica Cartwright) who smells a rat. The movie rambles along, mixing confused satires on male chauvinism, feminism, and puritanism; naturally, the church lady gets it worst—death by barf-out. The movie parallels many recent movie treatments of religion. Anatomically, it outdoes them, surpassing even *Revenge of the Nerds* or any *Booger Meets Ogre II*. Isn't that special?

The Shape of Things to Come

Granted such excesses exist. Still, this book's purpose is to encourage thinking about the social implications of movies in ways different from those found in the standard diatribes against Hollywood. This introductory chapter is intended to spell out my goals, define key terms (especially "values"), suggest how they might be valid in discussing the film industry, and outline some of the themes that later chapters develop at greater length.

My main goal is to show that the subject of values and movies is larger than the clichéd themes of sex, violence, and vulgarity—debates about which have led us in a loud circle nowhere. Screen mayhem, sudden whirlwind controversies over sex in *The Last Temptation of Christ*, the now near-univeral recourse of comedy to the bathroom—these topics are important, but only a small part of the picture. Given the complexity of ways in which movies may affect values, there is no reason for any kind of single-issue monomania. If, as Bernard Shaw said, war is too important to be left to generals, then values are too important to be left to puritans or to be reduced to any one narrow values agenda.

My goal emphatically does *not* involve a general review of the quality of American movies in (roughly) the last decade. Many of the movies analyzed in this book are not "good" in an artistic sense. My aim is not to review them, or name a ten "best" or "worst" list, but to trace the ways in which they may have reflected or fostered social trends and encouraged social values. Movies do not have to be good to do this; indeed, as noted below, they don't have to have any other purpose besides making money.

My premise is that most movies, even bad ones, have some social content. They reveal and affect the way we think about school, history, sports, work, home life, love, men and women, cities, our legal and political institutions, the nation, and the world. They often embody powerful social myths. By "myths," I do *not* mean lies, but complex modes of cultural or historical self-understanding that are often, at least, half true. Indeed, the precise problem with many film images is not their misrepresentation of American life; the problem is that even half-truths are half-*true* and always have some credibility and persuasive power.

Intentionally or not, in blockbusters or flops, in message films or sexploitation, in *Wall Street*, or one of Freddy's nightmares—myths, half-truths and value judgments often emerge from all kinds of films, whatever their artistic quality. As screenwriter *(Raging Bull, The Last Temptation of Christ)* and director *(Mishima, Patty)* Paul Schrader says, "Movies are about things—even bad movies are about things. *Rambo III* is about something. It has a theme, even if it doesn't want to have a theme."

The theme of *Rambo* movies is easy to spot: resurgent American nationalism. You need not like this to spot it or understand its significance in the 1980s. Indeed, a critic writing a social history of movies who dislikes *Rambo's* message, style, or both, has a *special* responsibility to treat the film as fairly as possible. Otherwise you'll miss why it was important, why it caught on, how it may have altered the shape of the country. Paul Schrader is a smart man and good writer; I envy his talents and power. I also wish he had some of Stallone's mythmaking ability.

This book aims to trace some of the ways in which recent films of all kinds and quality treat nationalism and other political or cultural themes. Domestic movies are the major focus, supplemented by imports (such as *Chariots of Fire* or *The Last Emperor*) that did well here and may have had some influence on American values. The emphasis is (roughly) on the last dozen years or so of movies, with some wider detours to establish context if necessary or if fruitful. Since the book was completed in December 1989 it cannot cover releases after that date, but I have made an effort at the end of most chapters to anticipate future developments.

Movies are taken both too seriously (in the worshipful tones of the art-religion dominant in the cineast and "film studies" world), or not seriously enough, by folks who see them as "just" entertainment. Movies *are* entertainment to be sure—and some of the best of them good entertainment. But they also involve something more—social myths and half-truths about what I refer to throughout as "values." But what do I mean when I use the term?

Values, Old and New

To me, values are abstract terms for realities we hold dear. We value them even if we do not or cannot always live up to them, even if we can't *prove* their existence. We value them even if we sometimes clash with each other—in those most bitter of American debates—about how to implement them in our society.

In a broad sense of the term "values," everyone has them: everyone, even everyone in pain, feels the value of being alive, of *being* itself. In this large, neutral sense of the term, "values" can range from material to moral and include both. In the broad sense of the term, recent movies have placed a high value on sex and power. Judging by the abundant number of sequels and vulgar jokes lately, they also value adventure, sarcasm, foul language and flatulence. In recent years, repetition is also in: many viewers apparently want a new movie (complete with numeral) to provide roughly the same experience as they found before. This book touches on these "values" (distorted ones if you wish, or at best trends in taste). But its main focus lies elsewhere.

The word "values" has, of course, a more restricted connotation. "Values"—as in the common phrase, "a sense of values"—has come to connote something more precise: moral or ethical realities that we hold dear. Indeed, the phrase "values" is often linked to the idea of an "old-fashioned" "sense of values." Some chapters below focus on how movies of roughly the last decade treat some of the key "old-fashioned" values: home, school, patriotism, hard work, justice, and a sense of tradition or delight in history. These chapters are not intended as sermons, but rather trend pieces deciphering, as neutrally as possible, how these values may be mirrored or promulgated in recent films.

But there are two complications. First, why should we limit—or (as is normal in usage) immediately link—the term "values" to "old-fashioned"? This is a valid, and frequent conversational association, as Cher's comments in the epigram illustrate. But perhaps it limits us too much and leaves some other, equally important values out. There are some values that have not been in fashion for too long in history—to choose a few: racial tolerance, international peace, social equity, and harmony with the environment. A full discussion of values in recent movies has to include them as well. Accordingly, peace is discussed in "Nation," tolerance in "Justice," love of nature in "Environment."

Still, a question nags: why don't people discuss "new-fashioned" values as "values"? Just consider how strange "new-fashioned values" sounds, like a contradiction in terms. Perhaps we haven't thought about "peace" as a "value" because people of a progressive and skeptical cast of mind are uncomfortable with the term "values" itself and as a result have been reluctant to invoke it. Right away, they hear the echo in their mind—"old-fashioned"—and run like mad in the other direction. If values come, they fear, can Mom, Dad, and apple pie be far behind? There is no fate to some people—including some movie critics— worse than family. "Values" sounds antique, like an old relative you have to listen to or care for. They may be embarrassing to have around. This is obvious in the way some progressives talk about their values: they rarely identify them clearly *as* "values."

In doing so, progressives implicitly sustain the association of values and "old-fashioned," as if there can be no other kind. To put it another way, they surrender values language to those who would limit values to "old-fashioned"; it's almost as if they are desperate to lose the moral high ground to conservatives by ceding half the argument—the terms themselves—to begin with. What their shyness about values reveals of course is an absurd confusion between moral concern and priggish moralism; they act as if talking about values invariably leads to the latter.

But there is a large difference between expressing moral concern and indulging in moralism; one can discuss the values embodied by movies, or the arts in general, and observe the distinction (see "Notes," p. 199, bottom). In my view, the fact that some people and politicians indulge in moralistic, intolerant discussion of the relation of the arts and social values is the last reason to stop discussing this relation intelligently. Indeed, the opposite would seem to be the case; silence about the relation of art and values may only be counterproductive. As America faces the nineties, it may be that the main reason that we have to fear the imposition of a narrow, intolerant, moralistic values agenda is the absence, or silence, of a morally concerned, pluralist one.

The Color of Money

So far, I have been dodging an issue. What can movies have to do with values if their primary purpose is to make money?

Money is paramount in the movie industry. The last phrase is key, but it gets too cozy from frequent usage, and people forget its meaning. The movie business is just that, an industry, with products meant to be no more memorable than last year's toys on a department-store shelf. Sequels remind us of this: to make a new toy, add new attachments, as in *Star Trek V, Karate Kid III, Ghostbusters II.* Between 1986 and 1987, and again between 1987 and 1988, heavy pre-"crash" Wall Street investments fostered a 20 percent increase in film releases; despite a slight decline after, the boom itself attests to an eighties' zest for entrepreneurship. The first way in which films reflect American values is that the main business of the film industry is business.

But some people stress this as if it ends all discussion of the matter. But in what other industry would that *not* be so? Money is paramount in the nuclear industry, in construction, in banking. This doesn't exclude talking about the possible positive or negative effects of ways of conducting each business. We all work for profit—or else starve. I write and teach for profit—not always enough. All businesses aim at profits; some serve their customers too. No film is made to lose money; a great many are expressly designed to make a bundle. So what else is new? Or rather, what else may be true?

The issue with money and movies isn't profit making, which is central to almost any profession in the country today. One issue may be profit margins, and how much profit filmmakers, like professionals in any other industry, are willing to risk for larger purposes. In 1939, the movie industry made enormous profits with *Ninotchka, Mr. Smith Goes to Washington, The Hunchback of Notre Dame, Beau Geste, Young Mr. Lincoln, Drums Along the Mohawk, Wuthering Heights, Gone with the Wind, Stagecoach,* and *Goodbye, Mr. Chips. The Wizard of Oz* was the only money loser in this bumper crop. There are perhaps several lessons in the tale.

One is simple: the color of money in filmmaking is the *least* convincing reason to claim that movies don't reflect or affect our values. Movies are meant to entertain; entertaining films make enormous profits. But films that make enormous profits can also be analyzed for their possible derivative and secondary effects, especially the effect of their content in fostering or checking the kinds of social myths so evident in the films of 1939. No conflict exists between conceding the commercial nature of the film enterprise and studying the possible impact on values of a movie by Frank Capra or John Ford.

This remains true today. Forget that some films—*A Dry White Season* or *Mississippi Burning,* for example—are made not just for profit but also for topical political or moral purposes. Other films made with an eye *only* for profit don't simply make their producers, directors, and actors rich: they also give the audience new images, perhaps shaping a new cultural ideal—of beauty, heroism, or home life. Sometimes films aimed at big money audiences include, deliberately, some topical touch—as with *Lethal Weapon 2,* whose makers went out of their way to identify its villains as proponents of apartheid. Even purely exploitational movies—made only with an eye for a big box office from sex and violence—can affect our values, if only to demean them.

That is, no matter what the cause or origin of a film, its effect on values— especially a schlock film created only to make money—can be profound. Indeed, schlock films above all may have affected our values in recent times. Ten, twenty, fifty slasher films expressing similar levels of barbarism and vulgarity may not have the same origins; they can have—especially in bulk—the same effect. We may never be a "kinder, gentler nation" in part because of these films and their effects on our values. In short, the profit motive doesn't exclude other factors, some conscious, some unconscious, in the making of films. It doesn't exclude the obvious possibility that a film made with no other purpose than profit might shape or distort (or even, with luck, improve) the values of the audiences that pay money to see it. The intention of the film-makers is often irrelevant to impact.

One final absurdity about movies and money must be cleared away from the start: just because someone seeks profit does not mean he or she can't also aim at moral or artistic value in a film. The idea is dear to two rival but complementary gangs of American film "mafia": the So-Cal vulgarians who reduce movies to a mere "industry" and the aesthetes (in snob neighborhoods and colleges across America) who talk as if nothing popular could be beautiful or significant. Both gangs serve the same end, divorcing high art and a mass public; as Camus so accurately said in his Nobel Prize speech of this kind of unholy alliance, "The more art specializes, the further proceeds public vulgarization."

Seeking profit and serving higher ends is rare, yes—but real; some of our finest authors did both. Theirs was an old dream: great art for a mass public. By some accounts—at least by the rare literary scholars craven enough to take a look at the account books of English literature—the dream has occurred to a few of our greatest writers: Dickens and Shakespeare, for example, didn't exactly defy the popular taste in their day. The same dream moved Chaplin, D. W. Griffith, and the other rare grand masters of modern film. It animates directors today such as Francis Coppola, Martin Scorsese, Oliver Stone, John Sayles, Spike Lee, and (at least in aspiration) Steven Spielberg. It survives in the hopes of many filmmakers who serve Hollywood *in order to* acquire power to make something beautiful. Sure, they want to get rich. What is so bad about that—or so exclusive of enriching others, the viewers they enrich by refusing to accept an either/or distinction between art and money? They simply assume enlightened industrialism is possible. As Judy Tenuta says, "It could happen." Indeed, despite the dumb tone of many recent movies, it still does.

Blame It on the Movies?

What, aside from making money, motivates filmmakers to make movies? By filmmakers, I don't mean directors only, but actors, producers, writers, editors, a whole assemblage of collaborative "authors." Why do they do it, and what are the social results? Are they agents of social change, or passive mirrors? To drag an old chestnut out of the fire, do artists and filmmakers simply reflect, or transform their age? And who will ever prove in which order?

Such questions are worse than rhetorical; they are unanswerable—the ultimate paraphrases of "which comes first, the chicken or the egg?" Philosophers, psychologists, aestheticians, sociologists, and critics have debated it for years, and, to my knowledge, experts have always disagreed. Indeed, increasingly, doesn't this seem to be what experts are for?

We are left with what common sense tells us: any art form or medium both reflects and shapes the culture around it. This is true even considering the full impact of money on movies. Filmmakers are always guided by market pressures; but they are not aliens from other planets. Invariably, even with marketing and genre constraints—even in far-out fields of fantasy and science fiction—their movies must mirror some of their life experiences in the world around them, or at least the dream world within.

Even if we can't always identify a single "author" of a film, the same holds true: directors, writers, producers, stars, editors, cinematographers may all have a hand in shaping a movie; they all shape it, at least in part, because of their ideas, values, or unconscious desires. They all have spouses, kids, dogs, fireplaces, parents, personal backgrounds, and life experiences—all of which mix with the profit motive to provoke and inspire them to create. Their audiences respond, assimilate a created image, and sometimes act according to its message. There's the rub—and critical puzzle. Whatever the artistic, creative, or profit-making intent behind a film, any movie can affect its viewers. But this is rarely as easy to trace as many claim.

Take for example Scorsese's *Taxi Driver*. John Hinckley claimed, of course, that the movie "inspired" him with the idea of shooting Ronald Reagan to earn the love of Jodie Foster. The tale certainly has an "only in America" air about it, but raises interesting questions. Was *Taxi Driver* the only violent film Hinckley had ever seen? Had he idolized gun-toting heroes long before? What other life events—or other movies—may have contributed to his dementia? If you want to blame *Taxi Driver* for John Hinckley, you have to indict other assassination movies such as *The Manchurian Candidate*, *Suddenly*, or even, for all its comedy, *Bananas*, in which Howard Cosell recites campy play-by-play of a Latin American bump-off. The list gets long, the blame diffuse—and unfair. John Wilkes Booth was partly "inspired" in his assassination of Lincoln by Shakespeare's *Julius Caesar*; he even used a theatrical setting for the shooting. But Booth was guilty, not theater and not Shakespeare. At least not of Lincoln's death.

There is no reason to search for simple "monkey see—monkey do" effects from movies. Narrow-minded moralists have cluttered debate about the effects of movies by looking for just these connections—a Hinckley, a Jason or Rambo killer, a serial Freddy freak. A good analysis of the possible effects of films *least of all* requires proving one-to-one correspondence between behavior on screen and behavior in real life. Cause-and-effect just isn't that simple. You can measure the influence of movies when it comes to Farrah Fawcett hairdos and Annie Hall costumes. Much harder to measure is their deeper psychological impact on a single Hinckley or on millions of Freddy, Rambo, or Jason fans.

The truth about the effects of movies is that we can never get a perfect "risk assessment": we will probably never know for sure how media images affect people. Every work or study on the subject can and *will* be attacked by authors of another work or study who have either discovered different findings or (more importantly) *want* to discover different findings in order to poke holes in someone else's position (see "Notes," p. 199, bottom to 200, middle).

To base laws, and possible censorship, on anecdotes is unjust. To base concern on a commonsense perception that movies do influence viewers is judicious. Everyone worried about censorship of movies in part agrees with anyone who is morally concerned with the content of films: it is precisely because of our common sense of the power of the arts and media over their audiences that we so want to keep them free. The flip side of accepting such freedom is, once in a while, discussing its risks. Indeed, it is censoriously close-minded to stop such discussion. But some liberals are very good at this.

In my view, some cause-and-effect relation between movies and society seems to occur; some filmmakers even make this their central theme. Consider Woody Allen's allegory, *The Purple Rose of Cairo*, in which Mia Farrow plays a depressed woman who spends a great deal of time in a movie theater looking for escape. She watches one film so frequently that its hero (Jeff Daniels) finally looks out from the screen at her and demands to know why she keeps coming. He's attracted to her, "leaves" the movie (the other players must sit around whiling away the time until he returns from reality), finds her in the audience, and becomes (briefly) her lover. The fairy tale is both funny and touching.

Woody Allen loves *Madame Bovary* this side of idolatry. Flaubert's title character, like Mia Farrow's, similarly seeks escape through art: in novels she finds a model "hero" by which to measure the next man she meets. As Allen and Flaubert record, images from art or the media do seem to captivate people and affect their behavior. According to Allen, our minds are movies—spliced, reedited versions of all the films we've seen, all the lovers we wish we had, all the heroes we wish we'd been. In his view, it takes a dose of self-awareness to liberate oneself from slavish imitation of what we see. Allen comically portrays such liberation in his *Play It Again, Sam,* where his hero-worshiping character learns finally *not* to act like Humphrey Bogart.

Allen simplifies his tales of media influence for the sake of dramatic focus; with society as a whole, such influence is rarely so direct. Still, it seems safe to assume some of the relation of cause and effect. Films, in general, are not only fun, but a vital part of the education and psychological adjustment of many Americans to reality. They give us models to imitate and images to love; sometimes, they even give us standards by which we unconsciously measure our real-life relations. Still, since there seems no way to prove exactly how this occurs, the chapters following are meant to be suggestions only, not attempts at sociological proof.

The Outer Limits

Besides the difficulty of tracing the influence of films and life, there are important limits in discussing the relation of movies and values, chiefly the temptation to moral reductionism.

Let me be clear: to examine the evolution of a culture's values through films does not mean to reduce the significance of films to their treatment of values. Some critics will do this (and Catholic critics too often have): movies can be too highly praised simply for "good content" or dismissed as "immoral." There are plenty of high-minded movies (e.g., Richard Attenborough operas such as *Gandhi* and *Cry Freedom,* or the baseball movie, *The Natural*) that are "good" on one level, but nauseating on another. In my view, a movie that confirms some widely accepted social value is not automatically a good movie; a movie that assaults such values is not automatically bad. Lately, of course, we've seen the opposite kind of judgment: the hip, critical avant-garde often overpraises films *precisely* for their insensitivity to old-fashioned values. Indeed, among the intelligentsia, an "amoral sermon" is a major art form of our time (see chapter 11, "Irony").

I believe that one must separate moral and aesthetic judgments. For example, one of the most provocative American moviemakers concerned with value issues, John Sayles, can't quite solve the aesthetic problems his depth of vision entails; as a result, despite the beauties of his *Matewan* and *Eight Men Out,* his thinking is still ahead of his image making. From a moral point of view, Sayles is rich and provocative; from an aesthetic, he is talented but still growing. He sets himself intellectual tasks his images—or skills at story telling through images—haven't caught up with. No critic, even one reviewing the moral values in a movie, can ignore the distinction between aspiration and image. This cuts two ways: whatever one's ideals, it is only honest to admit that some filmmakers interested in moral issues lack perfect artistic command while others with great technical and imaginative gifts tend to nihilism (e.g., Werner Fassbinder).

It would probably help film criticism a great deal if these issues were more openly discussed. But as noted earlier, fear of moralism has often led many critics (including many of the best) to avoid discussing moral issues at all. This is understandable, but leads to the de facto censorship of any expression of moral concern. Moralism is to be avoided: it uses no yardstick to measure the worth of movies except a narrow set of values and narrow definitions of morality as (mostly) either prudishness or do-goodism. But moral concern with movies allows for appreciating movies on purely aesthetic grounds; it merely complements such aesthetic appreciation with some consideration of moral values—hopefully, values that are widely inclusive and pluralistically defined.

In this respect, someone with moral concern about movies in general may esteem a particular film with intense sex, violence, or vulgarity; to have moral concern about films doesn't mean to demand goody-goody messages. To a morally concerned observer, a strongly moral movie may have obscene passages, but still expand the mind and heart with its compassionate or profound images of human nature and emotion. Regardless of its "lessons," merely in the richness of its portrayal of characters, such a film can inspire viewers with an excited, sympathetic insight into other human beings; it can stimulate a key source for moral action, our ability to imagine, and project into what other people feel. Whatever its overt "moral" content, whatever its doses of sex or violence, a movie can foster moral awareness by introducing alternative points of view—of other nations, sexes, races, or traditions—and by presenting them in a complex, compelling way. A movie can be profoundly moral simply by satirizing narrow definitions of morality. A movie can be moral just by arousing in its viewers an expanded desire to frolic and share in the pleasures of life, even in the therapeutic form of fantasy revels. A moral movie can encourage exuberant renewal of the self, and reawaken the charity that often must *at least* begin at home; some "moral" movies can indeed make you "feel good."

There are other unusual examples of movies that implicitly inculcate values. A movie could be depressingly bleak in its picture of humanity and history and still lead to virtue, if only the resolution not to add to the darkness humans have already endured. Clearly, the relation of movies and moral values is complex, more complex than any fundamentalism—religious or secular—allows. Religious fundamentalists want art (and movies) to serve a rigid morality; secular fundamentalists (including some of our best film critics) react against that, and ritually declare (or flaunt) art's independence from moral concern. Ironically, both groups share the same narrow concept of morality as a kind of prudish do-goodism. Both also effectively interact to prevent an open discussion of the relation of art and virtue.

Of course, aesthetic and moral judgments should be separated; of course, narrow-minded censoriousness toward movies and other forms of art and entertainment is absurd. But neither proposition means that morally concerned evaluations of movies can't be made. In truth, many more are made than are commonly acknowledged, not by just church-based critics, but secular ones, who too easily assume lack of religion equals lack of a system of values. They have such systems, sometimes intolerant ones. It can happen.

Indeed, *criticism often expresses one kind of judgment only to mask another.* On the surface, a critic judges a movie. Beneath the surface, a critic often judges the assumptions behind a film—its political and cultural value judgments—to which the critic brings his or her own. Too often, movie critics don't acknowledge that their problem with a film is, from their point of view, *its* point of view, or its basic choices in aesthetic strategy. Sometimes, they beat up a movie's faults because they just don't like what it says or how in general a director chooses to say it. It is not hard to mug a movie this way, since, being human creations, *no* film (this is heresy) can ever be perfect. You can always find faults and exaggerate them, if you want to. On the other hand, many moviemakers are overpraised for the wrong reasons. Woody Allen is a prime example; he's often praised not just for his gifts (which are real), but because he caters excessively to the witty, urban consciousness of many film critics. They like him in part because he is like them.

It is hard to be fully conscious of making such mistakes. But we all have biases, a set of ideas about both film and society. Indeed, no book of this kind is without a subjective point of view, not just about film but social issues as well. No doubt my own likes and dislikes show through, not just in passing comments but also in the shape and the very selection of the chapters, in the heat of some of their observations (see especially "Irony" and "Religion"), and in the kinds of movies whose production I more or less openly cheer (see "Cultural Literacy" and "Sports"). Many of my judgments of particular movies derive from my background as a Catholic, as a student in college in the 1960s, and as a teacher afterward: hence, quite clearly, chapter 2 ("Teaching"), which I wouldn't have written without some form of special interest. I'm a Democrat about some social issues (see the conclusion of "Justice"); I appreciate an old-fashioned Republican emphasis on incentive (see "Work"). A movie critic is one of the last persons who should claim objectivity; I emphatically do *not* claim it. We all have a point of view, an ideology.

But *all* movie critics have their own backgrounds or biases that they bring to each movie they see. Once in a while, it might be better if they were more explicit about this; it might help them make their judgments sound less like gospel truth. Take *Fatal Attraction, Working Girl, Do the Right Thing, Platoon,* or *Full Metal Jacket.* It's not easy to separate these films from one's views of men and women, race relations, or issues of war and peace. Of course, good critics try; of course, the best often succeed. Still, some of these films got a load of praise or blame not merely because of their merits or demerits but also because they suited or offended various biases. How can you really trust critics about such films if, once in a while, they don't acknowledge their own political or cultural points of view?

Cultural biases—often involving prejudices about genres and styles—can be as strong as political ones; they involve, if not "moral concern," quite righteous judgments by some critics who regard entire styles of filmmaking as childish. In the last dozen years, a major national critic (perhaps our best) has been next to incapable of praising a single film that tries to handle tenderheartedness, even in a dignified manner; the critic's stern antiromantic ideology forbids it: damned (at best, with faint praise) have been *Chariots of Fire, Tender Mercies, Rain Man, Field of Dreams,* and other *at least* half-decent films. Another major critic dislikes epic moviemaking and loves small-scale films; hence, exaggerated praise for the rich but slick *sex, lies, and videotape* and exaggerated blame for *The Last Emperor,* whose faults, though real, were blown out of proportion. The critic's journal wouldn't name *The Last Emperor* to its "recommended" list, even after it won nine Oscars. Of course, critics are entitled both to editorial loyalty and their own ideology; but it would help if they were also aware of how an ideology, political or cultural, can amount to a blind spot.

In view of these problems, it is false to claim that the only source of moral reductionism in film criticism is a religious viewpoint. Yes, that can lead to puritanical moralism; but there are other, equally fierce sources of harsh judgment, often involving secular ideologies and value judgments about art or life. It is hard sometimes to read some of our best secular movie critics without feeling the lash of an old-fashioned sermon, or smelling the odor of the stake. As a part-time critic, I too am capable of this. If I go overboard at times here, I also try to list places (see "Notes") where readers can find other views of the social implications of the films I discuss. These notes are arranged in a progressive order corresponding to the points in each chapter, and are provided both for the sake of further information and/or alternative opinion. After all, I may be wrong.

The Outer Limits, II

Besides the temptation to moralism, a second problem with tracing the relation of movies and values is dating. This book focuses on films released a few years before and mostly during the last decade. Accordingly, for simplicity, I sometimes refer broadly to "eighties' " movies or "movies of the eighties." This is done, in part, as a matter of focus and convenience. It also reflects my belief that there are consistent themes in releases during this time, and that a label has to be used to identify them.

But you have to be careful of putting everything into too neat a bundle. True, the 1980s have a defined shape; unlike the 1970s, at least they had the decency to begin on time—and with a trend-setting presidential inauguration. Still, as a concept, "the eighties" won't *exactly* do. There is just no way to claim "the eighties" exist as a defined, limited cultural entity or that trends in the eighties, both in society and film, don't have deep roots in the years before. The "idea" of a decade is in fact often little more than a conspiracy between chronologists, trend-spotting journalists, and life-style editors, earnest to reduce complicated social and cultural reality into bite- (and now byte-) size headlines. Our entire culture didn't turn into a pumpkin at the stroke of midnight on December 31, 1979, or even January 20, 1981. It is not possible, for example, to discuss the eighties' glut of sports movies without noting their rise to popularity in the later seventies. Indeed, the roots of sports movies and other genres go back even earlier. Many aspects of the movies that I discuss have more to do with traditional American concerns and conventions of cinema than some recently liberated "zeitgeist." No one has ever seen (or even zeen) a zeitgeist, although Siegfried Kracauer claimed to in *From Caligari to Hitler.*

Release dates for films are provided in parentheses throughout the following chapters either when it is important to note the date of an older film or when recent major movies are mentioned for the first time; many of the latter will have eighties' dates. Still, all this means is that they were released during the decade; many were *begun* beforehand, some a good deal of time before. Indeed, so many of the works that suddenly appear at one time and strike journalists as proof of a "trend" have been produced on very different, asynchronous timetables. Even a work written, produced, or directed by someone with an agenda of some kind—a point to make, a political platform to argue, a social image message to spread—is vulnerable to innumerable vagaries in the film-making process, especially long delays between conception and execution, or between shooting and wrapping, or, sometimes, between shooting one half of one film and beginning yet another. Years can go by in any of these cases; between a writer or director's first fantasy of making a film and actual completion of a project may come decades, as Scorsese's over fifteen-year project on *The Last Temptation of Christ* makes clear.

With such uneven chronologies to consider, it's daring to date "trends" or claim that a new set of films reflects a new set of values. There is nothing especially coherent about the timing of one film, much less hundreds. Accordingly, as noted before, this book is not intended as a sociology of film or an exact film history.

Still, there are cautious ways to establish and identify some unique and consistent aspects of movies released in the last dozen years or so. Some genres were more in style, new twists occurred within each of them, and the sum of the changes may reveal something distinctive about the recent past. Indeed, some of this might even tell us about where we might be heading in the future.

The Big Picture

The late seventies and early eighties have seen developments in a range of themes: sports, justice, business, nature, and love. Why so many sports films and movies about business? Why the disappearance of glamorous outlaws and the parade of law-and-order "avengers"? More curiously, until the late eighties, why the relative decline of films about nature, and—despite the strong emphasis on friendship and family—the lack of love stories?

The loss of the love story helps suggest, at least, one consistent aspect of recent times. Almost all recent films have an obligatory "love interest"—sometimes with no connection to plot or probability; it is a rare film that doesn't have at least one scene of lovemaking, just to get the coveted free advertisement, an R rating. But "lovemaking" and "love story" are not the same thing; the latter means a plot where love itself constitutes or dominates the story line. From decades past, one recalls several glowing, or infamous, movies about love. Just think back twenty years or so, to *Love Story, Doctor Zhivago,* and *Romeo and Juliet.* The latter two, of course, were based on older literature—one source about three centuries old. Yet who would contest that the heady, sentimental flavor of Zeffirelli's *Romeo and Juliet* didn't embody some aspects of the youthful rebellion of the sixties?

Look around now. Where are the love films of the 1980s? I do not mean that there *should* be any. But if there are none, or few, that says something. *Out of Africa* eschews the traditional love story; few viewers were swept off their feet, and most preferred the other half of the film—Karen Blixen's love affair with Africa, signaled by the film's first line. *Children of a Lesser God* had some fierce moments; but the love story gave way to the story of someone dealing with her handicap. Love—especially in romantic lyrical form—just doesn't make films go round the way it used to.

The muting of love is connected to some larger changes in the relations of men and women (see chapter 6, "Home"). It also reflects the loss, for better or worse, of counterculture romanticism, not just about love but also politics and economics. An unquestionable conservative trend is evident in movies in the last decade, a trend that unifies many of the themes covered in this book.

But the cause of this trend is not easy to trace. It was not the result of political fiat; no one gave any orders to moviemakers to turn right; there was no inquisition in Hollywood, no terror to conform; movies seemed to become conservative, at most, by osmosis. Indeed, rather than politics setting the pace for movies, sometimes the opposite seems true: films became somewhat conservative *before* the 1980 election, forecasting the tendencies that later become so prevalent at the polls. In early scenes of the first *Rocky* (1977), four separate characters are referred to as being in a "bad mood," a phrase that serves as a kind of all-purpose explanation for collective grumpiness; maybe everyone was just suffering from Jimmy Carter's "malaise." When Ronald Reagan evoked a fifties' view of an innocent, normal, triumphant America he was echoing a mood already evident not only in *Rocky* but also the patriotic close of *The Deer Hunter* (1978), or retrospectives such as *American Graffiti* (1973), where the sixties were dismissed in favor of nostalgia for Ike, Thunderbirds, and the hop. Changed politics is partly a cause of these images, partly an effect.

In some ways, the conservative trend was healthy. As valid as many of the protests of the sixties were, they were often fueled by disordered impulses that, sadly but inevitably, seem to trouble movements for social change. On the other hand, the later eighties have brought a reconsideration of what good there might have been in sixties' values—the positive ones involving a search for a wider community and hope about the possibilities of human nature. Many movies directly or indirectly invoked some positive sixties' values—*The Big Chill* (as early as 1983), *Matewan* (1987), and perhaps even *The Last Temptation of Christ* (1988). At the end of the 1980s, more direct interest in the sixties returned on screen with films such as *Platoon, Mississippi Burning, Running on Empty, Patty, Imagine* (on John Lennon) *1969*, and *Rude Awakening*. And even "fifties' " time-travel fantasies such as *Peggy Sue Got Married* and *Back to the Future* had positive notes on the sixties and changes for women and minorities.

Sixties-something

James Joyce's favorite historian Giambattista Vico claimed history moved in cycles. In the 1980s we went him one better: nostalgia moved in cycles too. The early eighties recalled innocent Eisenhower days; both in movies and other media, the later eighties looked back in both anger and wonder to days of Kennedy, Johnson, and Vietnam.

No doubt this involved the old Hollywood search for new stories, or a simple change of pace and product. Much of it reflected Hollywood demography: suddenly, there were all these "thirtysomething" filmmakers, who had matured in the sixties, paid their industry dues, served their apprenticeships, and finally had the chance to project their memories on screen with full directorial control. Often, tedious narcissism resulted.

Still, such "sixties-something" filmmaking seemed to involve something deeper—a genuine attempt to combine old concerns with what appeared to be some new wisdom. Directors such as Oliver Stone and John Sayles clearly sought to engage debate on issues that movies elided during the traditionalist "feel good" early eighties—issues of war, work, and race. Fortunately, they also sought deeper answers than the sixties provided. Some directors aimed to reconcile the best sixties and eighties values, synthesizing insights about the need for freedom and the need for stability. If there are heroes in this book, they are among the filmmakers who combined profit making with our broadest cultural challenge: to respect "old-fashioned" values such as home and nation and—at the same time—to remain open to the need to add new ones. History at its best is a progressive realization of new values, but they come to nothing without the firm foundations of the old.

It is hard to find such balance—on movies or anywhere else. America sometimes doesn't seem to progress as much as lurch from one extreme to the other, rushing away from core values that hold culture together and then rushing back to them to close off any view of wider horizons. We go from belief in myths to what critics, especially in the academy, call "anti-myths," or ironic revisions that tend to view social values as hollow pretension. Between such extremes, it would be nice to find a middle ground—not a wishy-washy bog of easygoing blandness, but a mountain where the best values, old and new, coexist on the same summit. People often think of the middle as a place reached by compromise; but a peak is also a kind of middle ground between two low points, reached only—as Aristotle might say—by excellence.

Movie history sometimes seems to reflect the broader patterns in cultural history and our failure to find a rich middle ground. By their nature, movies simplify and sensationalize—in part because they reflect the cultural "mood swings" of their makers. But there is an added problem in the medium itself. Movies fit reality into formulas, select its key events, then hype and melodramatize them beyond recognition. Not only fantasy movies and sci-fi films distort reality. In truth, all films do so, even realistic ones—even documentaries, by their selectivity, editing, pacing, and point of view. Even the most realistic-looking film can distort reality by burying the moral complexities of a story beneath tried-and-true movie formulas.

What happens when such distortions of reality intersect with our cultural mood swings? Movies may make the mood swings wider. All melodrama heroizes or vilifies; movies exaggerate these tendencies even more, pinning symbolic black-and-white hats on characters for easy moral identification. Take images of cowboys and Indians. In the past, cowboys were brave, earnest pioneers, the Indians bloodthirsty savages (*The Searchers*, 1955). During the Vietnam War, movie cowboys (and cavalry) became villains, the Indians earth-loving flower children (*Soldier Blue*, 1970). One set of caricatures replaced another. There may have been some truth in both. But movies don't come in gray tones; everything is black and white. We can only perpetuate simplistic thought about value issues by failing to make enough movies in *moral* color.

Still, some movies express more than one side of an issue; hence, the heroism of directors who see issues from as many angles as possible, and who surmount the sensationalism and simplifying elements of movies to say something genuinely complex. Of course, film is a subtle art; but it is a rare director who uses, or is allowed to use, its technical subtleties for emotional and philosophical ones. In today's

Hollywood, innovation is equated with new special effects, not new insights into human nature and history.

Movies that intelligently examine the tensions of values (such as those of the sixties and eighties) are few and far between. There are very few moviemakers, that is, who think in moral color, or who are allowed to do so. But moviemakers can do this, have often done it (even for profit!), and in a visual culture their power for good can be keenly felt. Would there were more of them! For the recent films that provide the pleasure of fine story telling and rich thought (among others, *Bull Durham, The Last Emperor, Wall Street, Amadeus, Raging Bull, Platoon, Hannah and Her Sisters, Do the Right Thing*) I am grateful. In a way, I even "felt good" when I left them. I hope the following chapters explain why.

2

Teaching

Defy authority, destroy property, and make everyone take their clothes off.
—*Sweet Liberty* (1986)

N o year saw such a film harvest as 1939: *Gone with the Wind,*
Wuthering Heights, Mr. Smith Goes to Washington, Stagecoach, The Wizard
of Oz—all premiered that one year, a classic vintage. But a look at that
year's Oscars is surprising. Best Actor went not to Clark Gable, Laurence
Olivier, Jimmy Stewart, or Mickey Rooney (*Babes in Arms*), but to Robert
Donat, lead in the sentimental, affectionate portrait of an English
schoolteacher, *Goodbye, Mr. Chips.*

Until quite recently, movies have said "Goodbye, Mr. Chips" in more
ways than one. The media, we are told by educational experts, provide
a "hidden curriculum" that supersedes the learning process in school,
a sad index of how educational decline had made America "a nation
at risk." Sadder still are the images in this "hidden curriculum" that
have so often caricatured teachers as incompetent nincompoops or rigid
authoritarians. It is bad enough that teachers have been *displaced* by
the media, but worse that their image—in so many eighties' movies—
has been so distorted. Scores of recent national reports on education
now urge an upgrading of the image of the teaching profession, an
uphill struggle given the prevalent media caricatures of educators. Still,
new movies such as *Stand and Deliver* (1988), *Lean on Me,* and *Dead Poets*
Society (both 1989), are enough to stir hope.

The media assault on the image of the teacher has resulted from contemporary movie marketing, where youth conquers all. Our media are
watched by many different demographic groups; but the largest single
element in the film box office is the young male teenager. As a result,

33

moviemakers have often attempted to reach this audience as if *no other* existed. They also assume the worst about its tastes, often, thereby, creating rather than merely reflecting them. Every "product" must be filled with the least common denominators of sex, violence, and (last but not least) vulgarity. As Alan Alda put it in his otherwise flawed satire on moviemaking, *Sweet Liberty* (1985), every successful movie today requires three basic plot elements: "defy authority, destroy property, and make everyone take their clothes off."

Defying authority, in movies aimed at a young male box office, means defying (or at least degrading) authority figures. In many teenpix this means fathers; in those that focus on school, teachers. In recent years— until 1988 at least—films have mostly provided repetitive stereotypes of dull, power-crazed, or idiotic teachers in many comedies such as *Fame* (1980), *The Breakfast Club* (1985), *Fast Times at Ridgemont High* (1982), *Porky's* (1981), *Summer School* (1987), and *Ferris Bueller's Day Off* (1986). Similar caricatures are found in *E.T.* (1982), *War Games* (1983), and other sci-fi fantasies. No group of teachers has been as clichéd as Hollywood in trashing them.

Even *Teachers* (1983), ostensibly a defense of the profession, was filled with negative images, especially "Mr. Ditto," a devotee of copying machines whose in-class death is not even noticed by his bored students. "Adult" films such as the autobiographies of Woody Allen (*Annie Hall* [1977], *Radio Days* [1987]) often manage to include a satiric image of a teacher in his scenes of persecuted youth. In *Reuben, Reuben* (1983) and *Educating Rita* (1983), college professors are seen primarily as alcoholics; in *Terms of Endearment* (1983) Jeff Daniels's college professor can't stay loyal to his wife (Debra Winger) and not pinch coeds. In *Animal House* (1978), Donald Sutherland plays a liberal professor who cynically used his classroom popularity to seduce girls and to introduce male students to the pleasures of dope; when they challenge conservative campus authorities, naturally, he disappears on them. In *Moonstruck* (1987) an NYU communications professor (played by John Mahoney) who seduces his female students sadly describes himself as a "burned-out old gasbag."

Gradgrind and Sons

Of course, some of these movies are simply newer versions of an old film staple, the campus comedy genre that goes back to *Two Chumps at Oxford* and *Horse Feathers*. They also reflect some real problems. Good teaching is getting rarer on the college and university level; at many institutions, it's "publish or perish," not teach and thrive. In high schools, some teachers and administrators are inadequate or excessively authoritarian. Ever since Dickens in *Hard Times,* free spirits in the arts have justly lampooned such abuses, especially the "Gradgrind" teachers keen on mindless recitation of knowledge at the expense of creative power. "Those who can, do; those who can't, teach," Shaw said of such educators—a comment, perhaps, too often taken from context. Such narrow pedagogy was satirized as recently as John Boorman's *Hope and Glory* (1987), where teachers make children chant multiplication tables in shelters during the blitz (the kids get revenge when a bomb hits the empty school one Sunday).

But many treatments of education before the eighties include positive as well as negative images of teachers. One need not go back as far as Mr. Chips: in the fifties, TV had *Our Miss Brooks* and film *Splendor in the Grass,* with its beautiful treatment of reading poetry in English class; indeed, the last scenes emphasize the power of Wordsworth's poem about growth, "Intimations of Immortality," in helping the central characters adjust to their sense of loss in leaving youth behind. In the sixties, teachers were treated sympathetically in *Up the Down Staircase, To Sir with Love, Spare the Rod,* and a musical version of *Goodbye, Mr. Chips;* in the seventies, *Welcome Back, Kotter* even had a "with-it" teacher. Of course, he was also an *ex-student,* and had once *been* cool.

In the late seventies and early eighties, declining idealism about teaching (reflected in a decrease in the number of students' becoming teachers) dovetailed with a general increase in satire throughout our culture (reflected in the fame of *Saturday Night Live* and *The National Lampoon*). Teachers were sitting ducks for this satiric trend, ready victims for the cheap irony that is the intellectual black hole of our age (see chapter 11, "Irony"). Satirizing a teacher during this period was about as hard as igniting a straw man after a drought. Under the influence of such irony, movies treated schools, in adolescent jargon, as "a complete joke." You have to wonder if this helped make them one.

Take the otherwise-slick thriller, 1983's *War Games.* It provides a good example of the pervasiveness of the trend precisely because it does *not* concern school and teaching per se. Matthew Broderick plays a high-school student more interested in computer games (and scams) than anything school has to offer; a whiz at a terminal, he can't get decent marks in biology. The implicit accusation is that his teachers aren't reaching his hyperactive mind—a fair enough possibility given the limits of some teachers' imagination and training. But the presentation becomes unfair when Broderick, typically late to class one day, delivers witty one-liners that make fun of his biology teacher's sex life. Teachers aren't just bad at their jobs, but "out of it," asexual, uncool. As you might expect, the plot leads Broderick directly out of school; as usual in teenage sci-fi, he ends up saving the world—with no thanks to his in-school education by out-of-it teachers. Like so many other youth films, the film's message is simple: You learn nothing of value in a classroom.

In *E.T.*, Steven Spielberg replaces the "out of it" image with "out of touch." In a memorable lab scene, a male teacher is seen only from a child's (or small extraterrestrial's) view, with just the bottom half of his body visible. His (literally) lofty distance from the task he is setting his class—frog dissection—repels the hero, Elliot, who recognizes how much the frogs look like the beloved "E.T." and decides to liberate them from their enclosed glass bottles. The real question that the scene raises, however, is just exactly who is being dissected.

The images of educators are only slightly better in 1983's *Teachers*, a *Mad* magazine version of *A Nation at Risk*. Nick Nolte plays a veteran teacher, who had been first inspired by the idealism of the sixties, but has since lost nearly all his energy in a crime-ridden, resource-poor public high school in the Midwest. In the plot, a student sues the school for consumer fraud because he failed to learn a thing in four years. His lawyer (Jo Beth Williams) is an ex-student. But in contrast to *Welcome Back, Kotter*, the returning alum belongs to a new generation: like many in the real-world post-Vietnam, post-Woodstock generation, Williams has the brains to avoid a low-paying, dead-end profession. That is, smart students never become teachers to begin with.

The film contains some references to the economic realities of modern education, but not enough. The lawsuit, we are told, is especially threatening because of the additional possibility of general bankruptcy of the local school system. But the film refers to this more as another indictment of education, and less as an excuse for its failure. No link is made between no money and the failure of professional educators: not a reference is made to the low-pay, shabby facilities, and inadequate support services that depress teacher morale and discourage effort.

In addition to the lawsuit and impending bankruptcy, the school in *Teachers* is beset by a wild but ironic accident: a mental patient (Richard Mulligan) gets free from his minimum security hospital, takes refuge in the school, and masquerades as a substitute history teacher who neglects to show up. In a blackly ironic twist, Mulligan is a great success, especially because he channels all his zest for fantasy into playing historical roles that bring the past alive for his students. No doubt the satiric point is partly valid: some teachers could use more enthusiasm, especially in fields like history, which too often involves dull review of dead fact. Still, what a sad index of an era that the best teacher in *Teachers* is a mental case! The detail marks the lowest point in the contemporary film image of the educator.

In the mideighties, some exceptions to these trends appear. Ironically, it was Rodney Dangerfield who first gave teachers some respect in his *Back to School* (1986) where negative images are balanced by Sally Kellerman's performance as a college English professor. Aptly outfitted in colorful shawl and soft book-bag, she starts a semester by reading the end of *Ulysses*, catching Molly Bloom's full-throated ecstacy, "yes I will, yes." She communicates real love of learning to her students (even Rodney, though his mind is also on a simpler form of love). Sports movies also provide positive images: in *Chariots of Fire* (1981), *Karate Kid* (1984), and *Bull Durham* (1988), older males, if not exactly teachers, are at least shown passing on athletic wisdom to youth. Most phys-ed teachers conform to type, however, as ogreish coaches in *Animal House* (1978) and *Revenge of the Nerds* (1984).

The main exceptions to these trends involve the odd foreign film and some very recent American movies. From New Zealand in 1984 came *Sylvia*, a biopic on the educational reformer Sylvia Ashton-Warner who found a way of reaching Maori children whom her fellow white teachers constantly looked down upon; the film records her creative classroom methods that became the source of books that gained her worldwide influence. A Canadian film jokingly asked *Why Shoot the Teacher?* (1977). Unfortunately, most American films provide plenty of reasons.

Until recently, films have not imagined many good American teachers. The 1981 TV movie, *The Marva Collins Story*, was based on a factual account of a black educator in Chicago who dedicated herself to helping ghetto children. In *Children of a Lesser God* (1986), William Hurt is shown as a good, creative, inventive teacher of deaf children and young adults. But the film shifts focus at midpoint into a romance between him and a former student (Marlee Matlin); the change made for memorable fireworks and earned her an Oscar, but took the problem of special education out of the classroom and into the bedroom, where Hurt becomes as much student as teacher. Hurt does less teaching than relating, and his image as a model teacher is limited to the opening scenes.

Live Teachers Society

Only in the last several years have movies treated teachers less sketchily and more positively, in minor films such as *Madame Sousatka* (1988) and *The Music Teacher* (1989), in the sleeper hit, *Stand and Deliver* (1988), and in major studio releases such as *Lean on Me* and *Dead Poets Society* (both 1989). The latter two serve as bookends, so to speak, providing contrasting views of the value of order and authority in education; even with their flaws, they share with *Stand and Deliver* strong, credible images of educators as guides, helpers, and inspirations. Nevertheless, they and *Stand and Deliver* also reflect our uncertainty about how best to solve some of the basic problems in American education today.

Some of the flaws of *Dead Poets* derives from its setting, a posh boys' prep school in 1959, *before* the deluge of the sixties. Some also derive from its ideology: it isn't entirely free of the simplistic urge to "defy authority," that sure way of selling movie tickets—Hollywood's blend of young-at-heart romanticism and cagey marketing. The ideology of the film pits an idealistic English teacher (Robin Williams) against a school establishment that is strong only on order and has no sense of the complementary need for freedom. Williams brings in a zesty, contagious love of literature, and inspires his students with a love of real learning unusual in such a stultifying setting and time.

Two scenes are excellent, one before a trophy case, and one during the term's first class, where Williams has his students tear out a foolish, prim-and-proper preface to a poetry textbook. In these scenes, Williams puts his manic, muscle-mouth energy into low gear, placing his verbal acuity at the service of inspiring love for literature. Thoreau, Whitman, Byron—Williams brings them alive for his students (and films again) by underplaying his power. Director Peter Weir also deserves credit for keeping Williams under control—or cutting the scenes whenever he was not.

But there is a curious aspect to Williams's teaching. We see him bring to life the lines of great authors; we see him take his students out of class to disrupt their addiction to schedule and routine; but we do not see them actually learning very much in class. Fine, they tear the preface out of a mechanically dull preface to poetry; why not show them doing more actual poetry *reading*? True, the students quote poetry, when they are outside, kicking footballs. But this only sustains an outside/inside contrast that allows for no fusion, no reconciliation—one even Romantic poets sought—of the opposites symbolized by outside and inside, freedom and order. Just as the school authorities in the film cannot imagine what can be done "outside" their structures with a good dose of freedom, the moviemakers cannot successfully depict what can be taught inside, albeit creatively, amid order.

This conflict reduces the plot to clichés at times. Williams is seen as a kind of proto–flower child; director Peter Weir includes references to jazz, the beat generation, and Thoreau, to suggest that we are just around the corner from the sixties and "the times they are a-changin'."

Of course, Williams's favorite poets are Romantics; the final disaster springs from this. The school headmaster and some parents are hard-hearted realists; when the movie shifts focus from teacher to students, we are dosed with the overdone school–soap opera conventions of teenage rebellion, adult insensitivity, crises, tragedy, bittersweet triumph, etc. For some viewers, the closing teen suicide was dramatically underprepared and, in today's climate, morally dangerous.

Weir meant it as a warning to parents. The subtext of *Dead Poets* is a parallel between the late fifties and eighties, with the suggestion that young people in both periods undergo too much pressure to conform and the implication that—in tune with many films at the end of the eighties—the sixties weren't all that bad after all. Interestingly, the only parents depicted in the movie have no respect for their son's own instinct, and restrict his studies into highly profitable careerist paths—a reflection of the superanxious eighties' parents (comically treated in *Baby Boom* [1987] and *Parenthood* [1989]) who worry that the wrong preschool means no Harvard, unemployment, and sure homelessness. Still, despite this distant relevance, *Dead Poets* felt too light, a *Goodbye, Mr. Chips* displaced to a never-never Ralph Lauren land.

Creativity *and* Order

Lean on Me addressed the freedom-order issue more imaginatively, but suffered from too much specific relevance. Based on the story of the controversial Paterson, New Jersey, school principal Joe Clark, who used extreme tactics to restore classroom order, it was loud, simplistic, overly optimistic, and dramatically repetitive. The movie makes Clark a hero, but points to aspects of character that trouble even those who support his goals and understand the harshness of his methods. Art and life cannot easily be separated in this case. The movie's flaws are tolerable if you can forget Joe Clark and focus instead on the character created by star Morgan Freeman. It also helps to understand the severity of problems in our inner city schools.

Freeman makes Joe Clark unsympathetic to a degree. Much of the film consists of his either shouting at or sharing a shouting match with rebellious students or teachers who object to his Draconian methods. His role is uninflected, with little internal doubt; his main enemies are a caricature corrupt mayor and a cardboard villainess, a parent angry over her thuggish son's expulsion. It takes an assistant principal to make him understand how his ideas affect teachers; the film shows little of their classroom methods. Worse, in an awful scene, Freeman lambastes

teachers as if they alone were responsible for what is wrong with schools
today.

But as the movie shows, a principal in a ghetto school has a tough
battle, literally in a "war zone," filled with drugs, fifth- and sixth-year
nongraduates, near rioting in the cafeterias, assaults on teachers and
students in the hallways—the kind of behavior still routinely accepted,
for example, in New York City. Freeman plays Clark as a drill sergeant;
martial music accompanies his hall patrols. In his tough speeches to
staff, he declares: "This is no god-damned democracy. We are in a state
of emergency, and my word is law." In the context, such management
style is at least understandable; it gives more than lip service to the
idea that national security is at stake in the schools.

Freeman's Joe Clark is redeemed by his concern for students and his
moral passion. His best scenes are in a quiet mode, where he handles
sensitive student issues in caring one-on-one sessions. Some of
Freeman's best speeches are directed at parents (both white and black)
who he says have failed to protect the innocence of children by tolerating
thuggism in the hallways and accepting less than the best from their
schools. He's had enough; for too long, "we've been crucified by a
process that is turning our black children into a permanent underclass."
This was about the only time in a 1980s movie that this issue was even
mentioned: the main reason for an educator to be tough with thugs
in and around schools is to *defend* students.

The "process" that Freeman alludes to is ruled, in his view, by clichés
that encourage laziness or even anarchy. In his best speech, he points
out the false choice involved in opposing order and freedom.
"Discipline," he says, "is not the enemy of enthusiasm." You could
search screenplays from the 1960s to 1980s and not find another such
line; it is Hollywood heresy to suggest that structure and guidance can
be nurturing. One wishes, indeed, for more of this in Michael Shif-
fer's screenplay—more digging at one of the reasons for our educational
malaise, the extreme pendulum swings between ideologies such as
"spare the rod and spoil the child" to "do your own thing" (or, alternatively, "defy authority, destroy property, and make everyone take their
clothes off"). *Lean on Me* has serious defects, but at least it undercuts
the false antagonism between order and enthusiasm that is shared by
both Gradgrinds and educational anarchists and that stifles an attempt
to shape both coherent *and* creative education.

Stand and Deliver shares some important values with *Lean on Me*: care
for impoverished youth, and courage to see past the false antagonisms
derived from abrupt shifts in educational philosophy. It also addresses
two current issues in today's educational debate: how to combine

excellent standards and equality of opportunity. As its tale of pursuit of excellence from the barrio makes clear, these are not *necessarily* exclusive options.

The film concerns the inspirational real-life story of efforts by a Hispanic math teacher, Jaime Escalante, to get his students to care enough to learn to escape cycles of poverty and degradation. He taught (and still teaches) at Garfield High School in the East Los Angeles barrio, which, as a result of his math teaching, generally increased test scores in the last decade.

Interestingly, Escalante's real story is relevant to the twists and turns of media images of teachers in recent times. Escalante became a teacher only after a successful career in a computer company; that is, he teaches not because of career drift, or desperation, or madness, but *reborn idealism*. His story documents a return of the successful professional to an educational institution—as if the Jo Beth Williams character in *Teachers* decided to chuck law and do something (as often is said) "meaningful." The film presents teaching as a *worthy* vocation.

Best of all, the film actually depicts the process of teaching—no easy thing for a screenplay to record. This film originated in a project of the American Playhouse Theater, and, despite being Hollywoodized, it has a real-life feel about it, the texture of chalk beneath the fingernails, a gritty integrity. *Stand and Deliver* is also good on a number of practical subjects, humor and stress. Presented in his first year of teaching, Escalante (played by Edward James Olmos, formerly of *Hill Street Blues* and *Miami Vice)* uses huge reserves of wit to conquer all. He combats students who resist learning as sissy (Olmos: "Tough guys do fried chicken for a living"). Some want to make ready money at odd jobs rather than graduating (Olmos: "Wouldn't you rather be designing cars than repairing them?"). Many of the girls are just interested in their own sexual power ("Is it true intelligent people make better lovers?" he asks them, mock flirtatiously). Olmos combines deep passion for education with a hip knowledge of pop culture. But his intensity leads to "burn-in" as one young Ms. Malaprop accidentally but aptly calls it. The "burn-in" is a heart attack.

Stand and Deliver is one of a crop of new Hispanic films (with *La Bamba, The Milagro Beanfield War,* and others), which are products of a moderately liberated and marketing-savvy Hollywood that is eyeing our huge Spanish-speaking population. But its story is over a decade old, and recalls a time when things were even less equal. "You have two strikes against you," Olmos tells his charges, "your name and your complexion. But math is the great equalizer."

Alas, not entirely true. The film's crisis involves calculus Advanced

Placement Tests, in which Olmos's students do so well that the Educational Testing Service charges cheating. The students despair; as Olmos says, "they've lost their confidence in the system they're finally qualified to enter." He had tried to inspire them with racial pride, claiming the mathematical genius of the Mayans is "in your blood." He is all the more angry at the implicit racism of ETS, pointing out that it wouldn't be so quick to charge cheating if the same scores came from Beverly Hills.

There are two major flaws in the movie. The first is its implicit support of "test mania"—how educators describe the trend toward letting preparation for standardized (and especially short answer) tests determine scholastic programs. A second flaw is the inference that schools can revive through impassioned teaching alone. As in *Teachers*, money remains a neglected issue.

To a degree, *Lean on Me* shared the defect. It does not deny the money issue; and it notes in passing wider social problems, especially cycles of poverty that hinder so much effort at self-improvement by young people trapped in a ghetto. The movie simply has no solution for these wider problems, except preserving schools to "keep hope alive." Like *Stand and Deliver*, *Lean on Me* focuses on topics that local educators can control: creating effective teaching strategies, reviving will, winning hearts and minds.

The values of these movies are vital. Without moral and intellectual renewal in the schools no amount of money can make any difference. In the old days, too many people (mostly Democrats) looked at money as the main answer to problems in schools; Republicans (George Bush, aptly, offered Joe Clark a job in his administration) emphasize hard work. What if both funds *and* hard work are needed to revive our schools? Why can't a film focus on both morale *and* money? Joe Clark makes the point in his book at least (see "Notes," p. 201, bottom): backbone is stronger when bodies don't starve. Films don't often say this; but neither do many American political leaders.

Clearly, the more recent movies about teachers reflect renewed public concern about education in the later 1980s; they are Hollywood's version of the many government and foundation reports that have lamented the low status of the profession. The movies represent what filmmakers sometimes do well: make money, entertain, and educate too. Did they help teachers? No much, not directly. Still, a little glamour—and understanding of what skillful teaching involves— never hurts. Olmos was nominated for an Oscar; Robin Williams earned a nomination as well. But when will there be Pulitzers or Nobels for their kind of teaching?

Teaching deserves such honors, but not on the basis of creating false expectations of how heroic teachers can be. As *Dead Poets* suggests, movies tend toward either caricature or canonization. But good teaching isn't only a matter of inspirational energy or passion for a subject, as indispensable as these are in the classroom. It also involves down-to-earth craftsmanship, creative alertness to ways of combining educational strategies, and a full understanding of how education affects individual students. Still, as long as Hollywood is given to sensational extremes, the new heroic model is at least preferable to the old.

The best teacher on screen in recent years was even older. In 1986, PBS broadcast the BBC's *Goodbye, Mr. Chips*. Despite the tea and tweediness, enthusiastic American teachers would recognize themselves in Roy Marsden's caring scholar. The best scene involved a quiet salute to good teaching. "I'm only a schoolmaster," the middle-aged Mr. Chipping says to his young bride-to-be. She smiles and says, "But that's the best thing in the world!"

3

Cultural Literacy

You're history.
—*Forever Lulu* (1985)

Gentlemen, we're history.
—*Bill and Ted's Excellent Adventure* (1989)

For Voltaire, history was a pack of lies we play on the dead. For Henry Ford, history was bunk. Judging from films today, one must go one step further: despite *Glory* (1989), history, alas, seems almost dead.

The last twenty years have not been good to history films. Once a staple of Hollywood studios—amply supplemented by imports from overseas—they have now declined in number, some years almost disappearing. Movies like *Reds* (1982), *Empire of the Sun* or *The Last Emperor* (both 1987) were made only because of exceptional individual persistence—by Warren Beatty, Steven Spielberg, and Bernardo Bertolucci. His *Emperor* was distributed, but not financed, by an American studio. All three films also are limited to concern with only the earlier twentieth century, about as far back as most moviemakers will go; most historical attention, if it can be called historical at all, is focused now on Vietnam and the 1960s. But history films for periods before that have mostly gone with the wind. What does their loss imply about the way Americans now value the past? How does their loss both reflect and further "cultural illiteracy" in young movie audiences?

Movies per se are agents of modernism: they foster visual appetite, limit attention span, and decrease the lure of books. Yet the impact of the medium could be softened by a message—once so lovingly depicted by so many directors—that the past was in some way valuable. Just consider D. W. Griffith's *America, Intolerance,* and *The Birth of a Nation,* which

45

one-time professor Woodrow Wilson called "history written in lightning." Or consider for a moment the most classic vintage in American film history, 1939. Movies such as *Wuthering Heights, Gone with the Wind, Young Mr. Lincoln, Stagecoach,* and *Drums along the Mohawk* all concerned the past; the last two were from the craftsmanly John Ford, who constantly tried to forge myths from the past to serve the American present. In the same year Errol Flynn costarred with Bette Davis in *The Private Lives of Elizabeth and Essex,* about a quarter way through a career of swashbuckling as Robin Hood (*The Adventures of*) Francis Drake (*The Sea Hawk*), General Custer (*They Died with Their Boots On*), and a fictional British cavalry officer in *The Charge of the Light Brigade.*

Indeed, until quite recent times the history genre continued to flourish, with thirties' biopics from Garbo's *Queen Christina* and Muni's *The Life of Emile Zola* to fifties' heavy hitters like *The Vikings* (Tony Curtis and Kirk Douglas), *Spartacus* (Douglas again), *Desiree* (Brando, at his worst perhaps), and the slightly better *War and Peace.* The genre continued in the sixties and early seventies with British imports—all successful releases in America—such as *Becket, Nicholas and Alexandra, A Man for All Seasons, Anne of the Thousand Days,* and *Mary, Queen of Scots.*

Not all these films are easy to typify. Not many of them, of course, were valid as real history; some on the Civil War may have fostered some dangerous myths. Their style was also extremely variable, with later films selling less action than thought—or at least less action than chatty talk in royal soap operas. But whatever their accuracy and their style, such films at least had the power to stimulate historical imagination.

Today, to paraphrase Bob Dylan, we are modern, we got everything we need, we don't look back. In Hollywood, few think anymore that history sells. The word *history* itself has acquired bad karma in our youth-centered, "now" environment—witness such common phrases as "that's history," or "you're history," to connote obsolescence. In the 1985 Israeli-American misfire, *Forever Lulu,* the German actress Hanna Schygulla smiles as she mouths the phrases with wry old-world amusement at what they imply. In America, *history*—once linked to prestige, tradition, authority—now mostly seems to suggest only an obituary. Some claim that the phrase "that's history" itself originated in Hollywood (as a way of describing a dead project); if so, it fits like a glove what recent films have done to our sense of the past.

Take the treatment of "history" in *Bill and Ted's Excellent Adventure* (1989). A man from the future (George Carlin) uses the phrase, "we're history," when he takes two American high-school students on a time-travel journey backward in order to help them give a history report.

Carlin has to help them because scholastic failure would mean a parental crackdown against their rock band, whose music is supposedly going to heal the world's woes at some point in the next century; he's on a mission improbable to make things turn out right. Indeed, he even makes history come alive for a short while on a quick fantasy tour of the past, where Bill and Ted meet historical characters like Freud and Socrates ("So-crates," they call him), and drag them back to the present to get the info they need to pass. This awful, bumptiously enjoyable, frighteningly honest film declares straight out that the real meaning of *history* for many young Americans has become merely the pain of studying it. The movie's best scenes have Bill and Ted taking their captives to a So-Cal mall where Genghis Khan creates mayhem with bats in a sporting goods store, Joan of Arc takes over an aerobics class, and Beethoven goes gaga on electronic keyboards. In short, the focus is mainly the present and future, an apt symbol of Hollywood's youth orientation today. It's a teenpix version of the idea of progress.

As a viable subject for a mass audience, history has been accordingly consigned—like social realism and moral concern—to the tender mercies of TV movies, always cheaper to make than motion pictures and thus involving producers in far less risk. The worst of these are trash; the well-intentioned sometimes preserve the letter of history, but hardly ever the spirit. The best history on the home screen often comes, as one critic joked, from the leading American TV network, the BBC.

If movies are part of a "hidden curriculum" for young people, this death—or at least dearth—of the past on screen has unfortunate consequences. Where can young people now find out about the past, or even be exposed to it? Without the validation that the media confers on subjects, why should they pay attention to history at all, or to teachers who try to make it live for them?

The Death of the Past

Today, the media validate everything—trends, politicians, even life itself: witness the thrill many experience on seeing themselves on television, as if the sight of their own flesh and blood in person weren't convincing. Celluloid functions as the new imprimatur of a sacred relic, a piece of time more valuable than life itself. People photograph (or videotape) an event rather than experience it; to have value, everything must be mediated. The problem is that the past generally is not. Indeed, even films from the past—like so many of the 1939 classics—

have to be colorized to fit marketing concepts of popular taste; an old film cannot even look *old*. Even toy soldiers are now built mainly in modern form, without any historical referents—not even to World War II or Vietnam (see "Notes," p. 202, middle).

For a new generation weak on "cultural literacy," the lack of history on screen can only intensify the decline of respect for history in the classroom. What results may be a *China Syndrome* of intellectual meltdown: the less history in the "hidden curriculum" in the media, the harder to teach history in class; the less history that is taught in class, the fewer history films that can hope to find an audience—or get made at all.

Consider a parallel genre to history, the Western, with its embodiment of myths about the American past. After the fifties, the Western went into decline, a development neatly summed up in the treatment of John Wayne's *Red River* in *The Last Picture Show* (1969) where present day antiheroes are reduced to watching old-time heroism on screen rather than imitating it in life. Revisionist Westerns like *Little Big Man* (1969) flourished during the Vietnam era, with cruelty to Indians seen as foreshadowing America's war in Southeast Asia. But revisionism was short-lived, and only mavericks continued with "spaghetti Westerns." Even Clint Eastwood couldn't revive the purer form of the genre in *Pale Rider* (1985), a blend of *High Noon* and *Shane*. In its first year, it made $20.8 million—a pittance, and hardly reason to try again.

The school movie *Teachers* (1983) (see chapter 2, "Teaching") contains a telling irony about the fate of history in American classrooms. One of the roles a replacement teacher and escaped madman (Richard Mulligan) plays in class is General Custer, a character he also played with wild panache alongside Dustin Hoffman in *Little Big Man* (1969). Mulligan must have regarded his Custer in the classroom as a good inside joke; his buckskin jacket even looked identical to the one he wore in the earlier film. But one key difference marked his two incarnations of General Custer; in the 1980s no filmmaker would dare to mount the original, despite story treatments based on some interesting new versions of the Custer legend, including *Son of the Morning Star*, a National Book Award winner by Evan Connell in 1985. Indeed, anyone who would try to produce an old-fashioned history film would be considered as nuts as Custer and headed toward a financial Little Big Horn.

This "death of the past" is not a new phenomenon in the 1980s; it's a basic tune of modern times, for which the media, misguided teaching, and perhaps intellectually impoverished home life are to blame. Sadly, some sincere classroom attempts at solving the problem—normally by high-school teachers, who haven't sacrificed their students to "publish or perish"—are also to blame. As *Teachers* showed, performance enthusiasm, especially in a field like history, is better than dull review of dead fact. But spirit alone, or the search for relevance, cannot sustain true study of history. Students today lack the data base by which the facts of the past can be sorted out and put in a coherent context. From all fact and memorization, history teaching has gone to no fact and loose identification. Balance is still missing.

In response to the decay of history teaching, a back-to-the-classics movement has taken root in some educational quarters. But what support has come from the media? Concerned history teachers have looked for help, and seize on videos of our few good historical films to encourage classroom interest. Television has helped, once in a great while, when a genuinely strong TV movie emerges, such as *Gore Vidal's Lincoln* (1988), where a substantial attempt was made to reconstruct the real history of a hero, human warts and all, and still find genuine merit. But the normal quality of TV movies on history was represented by *North and South*, with modern starlets tarted up in reheated Scarlett O'Hara hokum. New depths were reached in *Josephine* with its initial statement that many events in the tale were completely fictional. At least here Napoleonic heartthrob and Miniseries Queen Jackie Bisset had historical foundation for low-cut dresses; indeed, they might have been a main reason for the production.

Costumes are important in making history films, and they add greatly to their cost—one of the reasons, insiders say, that so few history films get made anymore. Since production costs are in general skyrocketing, costumes may add a burden that many producers would often do without. But nobody balks at costly special effects to create far-off worlds in sci-fi films, or multiple car, plane, or helicopter crashes. Producers risk these expenses because of their greater confidence about market return. The present and future sell, not the past. As an Emilio Estevez teenpix title put it bluntly, *That Was Then, This Is Now* (1987).

There have of course been a few art-house successes to keep history alive on screen such as *Danton*, or *La Nuit des Varennes* (both 1982). But their impact was minimal. General release films about the past have all floundered terribly: *King David* (1984), *The Bounty* (1985), *Revolution*, and *Lady Jane* (1986), directed by Trevor Nunn, whose magic with the past in music drama (*Nicholas Nickleby, Les Misérables*) failed him on film. *Les Liaisons Dangereuses* took the same path (from literature to West End to Broadway to film) in the late eighties—indeed, to two separate films. Still, the first dropped all references to the class conflicts before the French Revolution in its source; it also was retitled *Dangerous Liaisons*

(1988) because its distributor, Warner Brothers, feared terrifying viewers with too much cultural literacy.

Some recent history films have failed because of their quality; but some failed because of the temper of modern times, which has been hostile to real concern with historical issues. Only a few films about history were genuinely successful; most exceptions only prove the rule. For example, an entire category of film about the past really has very little concern with it, the "white flannel" film—*Heat and Dust* (1983), *White Mischief, A Summer Story* (both 1988), and even the superb *A Room with a View* (1985). As in *Dangerous Liaisons*, the appeal of such films has less to do with history and more with sex and satire on the upper classes, who are nevertheless feverishly envied in their fin de siècle opulence or late colonial languor. Their nostalgia for an elegant, even decadent leisurely time makes them au courant in an age of rediscovered polo, Ralph Lauren, and wishful aristocracy.

Other, more shallow approaches to the past have also been successful. Young audiences want macho images, and periodically accept them in "historical" disguise in "Dark Ages" fantasy genre (*Conan the Barbarian* [1982], *Conan the Destroyer* [1984], *Dragonslayer* [1984], and *Ladyhawke* [1985]) related to the fad of computer games like "Dungeons and Dragons." One sad clue to the temper of our times is that the most popular eras among youth audiences have been barbaric. Perhaps only one film about the "dark ages" yielded real value: John Boorman's version of Arthurian legends, *Excalibur* (1981).

Still, even fantasy about the past fared unevenly. Except for Arnold Schwarzenegger's Conan films, most Dark Ages movies died quickly, and at great cost. The real winner in the history sweepstakes—as in so many areas of pop culture in the 1980s—has been Irony. Among the most popular recent "history" films were *Monty Python and the Holy Grail* (1974) and Mel Brooks's spoofy *History of the World—Part 1* (1981). Both fit a different aspect of the age, foisted on us by the cultish contempt for the heroic: our delight in irony and our apparent need to sling mud at all old icons (see chapter 11, "Irony"). If, according to Voltaire, "history is a pack of lies we play on the dead," then, according to Mel Brooks and the Pythons, history is a pack of pratfalls not properly understood. Of course their jokes were funny. But they also fit a trend of our times: flipness is all.

Past vs Present

Some films have tried to treat history by a double focus on both past and present: *The French Lieutenant's Woman* (1981) and *Sweet Liberty*. Both films were not so much about the past as *making a film about the past*. In both, directors viewed the past at a distance: their historical content was framed by present-day stories about the attempt to *film it*. *The French Lieutenant's Woman* paralleled two love stories: in the film-within-the-film, a Victorian love story paired Meryl Streep and Jeremy Irons; in the film proper, a modern love story involved actors on the set of the film-within-the-film, played again by Meryl Streep and Jeremy Irons. Aptly, only the past love story ended happily. They made love the old-fashioned way back then: commitment.

Sweet Liberty concerned the making of a film about the American Revolution, in which satire was focused on a filmmaking crew and their exploitative attitude toward historical material. Alan Alda both directed and starred in this interesting misfire. In the film proper, Alda plays a history professor who wrote a book on the revolutionary period that is being turned into the film-within-the-film. Alda starts to make some tart comments about the filmmakers' values when he gets the full picture. The crew comes to his little picturesque college town for its colonial look, but Alda quickly discovers that is the only authenticity they are after. He wrote a serious family study; they want a lusty Yankee Doodle Dynasty. Indeed, when Alda begins to see how the director wants to sensationalize aspects of his story, he starts introducing himself around the set as "the author of the book from which the film has not been taken."

Sometimes a little bit of Alda goes a short way; his smarmy style can wear thin as his smirk. Still, Alda's movie yields some good satire. As head of a local regiment of "volunteers" who dress as colonial militia and perform historical pageants, Alda offers his services to the filmmakers, then uses his power to give them more authenticity than they bargained for. The film is uneven, but the parallels between revolt against English tyranny and revolt against Hollywood substandards are slickly done.

Still, Alda's work is a concession to his enemy. He didn't make a history film in *Sweet Liberty*. He made a film about the inability to make a history film. Maybe it failed because of its many defects or its complicated satire. Most probably it failed because not enough people cared about the subject matter to begin with. *Sweet Liberty* made $7.3 million in 1986; *Top Gun* $80 million. Indeed, *Sweet Liberty* came in behind a Whoopi Goldberg flop, *Jumpin' Jack Flash*, at $11.1 million.

Ironically, the film-within-the-film *Sweet Liberty* is the one that should have been made, but never was. Think about it: from the 1976 anniversary of Independence to the 1987 celebration of the Constitution, Americans were deluged with bicentennialism. But, except for the transplanted Broadway musical *1776* (1972) and the bomb *Revolution*, it was everywhere but the movies. The rest of the media, even television, was deluged by bicentennial features, mostly puff pieces that conveyed small sense of the difficulty that Americans struggled with in forming a new nation. But puff is better than zero. The absence of movies about our revolutionary past is notable in view of *minor* works from 1939, all set in the Revolutionary War period: *Drums along the Mohawk*, *Allegheny Uprising* (with a young John Wayne), and Cary Grant in *The Howards of Virginia*. None are great movies; all are craftsmanlike; *Drums* is good. The more we live, it seems, the less we need the dead.

The Culture of Solipsism

One reason history films don't get made anymore is because many contemporary directors—products themselves of American secondary and higher education, and perhaps a few years in film school after that—simply don't know about it: they may not be that different from their historically undereducated audience. The one kind of history they do know is film history, a valid field, but perhaps shallow if exclusive. In such an atmosphere, Brian DePalma can count on part of his audience recognizing his allusions to Hitchcock or Eisenstein, especially his adaption of the baby-carriage property from the Odessa steps sequence of *Potemkin* in *The Untouchables* (1987). Does it matter if the audience can't locate Odessa itself, or recall what happened there?

Consider the relation of a major studio and the history genre. History was once a primary resource for the old Disney company (with movies on such real-life and fictional historical heroes as John Paul Jones, Johnny Tremain, and Davy Crockett). But such movies have not been attempted at all by remodeled, exceptionally successful Disney labels—Touchstone and Buena Vista. Indeed, despite releasing some good movies, the main history that the new Disney seems interested in is movie history—as evidenced by the studio's new theme park in Florida, a re-creation of MGM studios.

In the last decade or so, movies could be made not just about moviemaking (an old time-honored genre); movies could also be reduced to clips from movies—e.g., *Movie Movie* (1978), *Terror in the Aisles* (1984), *National Lampoon Goes to the Movies* (1981), and *It Came from*

Hollywood (1982). Lucas/Spielberg operas (_Indiana Jones, Star Wars_ et al.) derive half their fun from their echo of older serials, and cartoons for adults were increasingly based on memories of comic books and TV shows (e.g., the _Superman_ films and _Batman_). This delight in popular culture is fine. But what if movies, cartoons, and comic books become the only aspects of the past that movies consider worth remembering?

This trend also makes even more tempting the cheap resort to mock-heroic in our age (see chapter 11, "Irony"). All that becomes necessary for immediate, low-brainpower jesting is tossing in a few references to some classic scenes _not_ from past events, but from past _movies_. The assumption of almost all mock-heroic movies, from the Woody Allen _Play It Again, Sam_ (1972) takeoff on _Casablanca_ onward, is pervasive audience knowledge of film history, e.g., _Airplane!_ (1980) presupposes having watched _Airport_ (1975). After a while, it only became necessary to quote a bar of score alone, say, from _Jaws_ or _Chariots of Fire_ (see, for example, _Mr. Mom_ [1983] and _Revenge of the Nerds_ [1984], where tunes from both are employed for comic purposes). One notes, as one approaches the present, references to the Hollywood past reach back only a few years, ten at most; in movie history itself, two decades ago is antiquity. Given everything else, why would you expect otherwise?

The Trap of Relevance

It is a truism that, to get moderns interested in history, they have to be shown something "relevant." But maybe the high regard for relevance is to blame for weaknesses in the few history movies that do get made and released. Maybe curbing relevance, or even trying "strangeness" could help revive the genre.

There is a difference between finding relevance in the past and reducing it _merely_ to what is relevant. The logic of relevance is to make people interested; but the latter, reductionist relevance winds up presenting viewers with what looks like a poor reflection of their own lives. If people in the past are "just like us," why bother checking them out at all? Why bother with history if all history contains is present-day people in historical drag? Viewers, particularly young ones, prefer the real thing. In short, too much relevance might be self-defeating.

Take movie images of the Middle Ages. True, American productions about the period are few and far between: about the only commercially viable one was _The Name of the Rose_ (1985). Whatever the virtues of the book, the movie was loaded with anachronisms, especially in the form of a modern value system superimposed on the Middle Ages. Evil is embodied in an inquisitorial villain (played in high, Gestapo-style by F. Murray Abraham) who is bent on destroying innocent victims; good is embodied in the enlightened William of Baskerville (Sean Connery). The caricature villain is balanced by the caricature hero, whose very name suggests the modern Sherlock, a man of reason lost in an irrational past.

Connery's hero is a (well-acted) cliché: he's "just like us." His triumph of wits over Abraham is one more milestone, the movie says, on the road of progress. The politics of *The Name of the Rose* is simple: the past is just a horror show; indeed, almost all the monks in *The Name of the Rose* look like understudies from *Planet of the Apes*. A few voices cry out in the wilderness of the past, which is seen as worthwhile not for its real texture but only as preface. If this is so, you might as well go see *Planet of the Apes*, or *Star Trek* or *Star Wars*, where many of the contrasts in *The Name of the Rose* (Spock as a Sherlock vs evil meanies torturing innocents) are dealt with more directly.

A Paramount-backed English film almost escapes this solipsism, *Lady Jane* (1986), Trevor Nunn's only movie. He not only used gorgeous costumes and wonderful sets (he had use of half a dozen castles), but also added an accurate depiction of the fierceness of religious controversies in Reformation England. Religion is a rare subject for film to handle well lately (see "Religion," below); but Nunn evoked sincere, complicated pictures of faith from Helena Bonham Carter as puritanical Lady Jane Grey and Jane Lapotaire as Catholic Mary Tudor, who were both sincerely devoted and frighteningly intolerant. Without caricature, history—the sad history of the Reformation—was let be.

But not politics. Nunn has admirable political values perhaps, and the worthy goal of using art to convey them (cf. *Les Misérables*). But in in *Lady Jane*, he imposed on history, providing a subplot in which she and her young husband planned an economic reformation of England, for which not a shred of evidence exists. Nunn backreads here, looking for socialists under Tudor beds not because they are there but because he needs them to satirize Maggie Thatcher. Ads for the film stressed the age of Bonham Carter (before *A Room with a View*) and aimed at the large youth audience. But their main result was not to lure youth in but to turn off older viewers, who saw only the promise of jejune romanticism. The movie—as marketing folks say—fell between the cracks. It might have found a real niche had it not courted modern relevance.

Historians are always concerned with an accurate record of the past: the past, being human, always has something relevant to say to the present. But historians emphasize that history involves an understanding of difference as well as relevance, particularity as well as universality. As the renewed emphasis on "original" musical instruments sometimes shows, researching the past doesn't mean dusty antiquarianism; properly pursued it can be highly refreshing precisely because it shakes off the dust of modern assumptions. Good history and good history moviemaking should provide what Monty Python only promises: something completely different.

Valuing authenticity does not mean rigidity. Some makers of history movies have demonstrated that good movies about the past do not have to stick to literal historical truth. *Amadeus* (1984) certainly toyed with the facts of the life of Mozart; its fiction that Salieri poisoned him is based only on rumor. But the film was close to the spirit of the times it depicted; the French Revolution also was briefly but accurately alluded to, with the Austrian Emperor (the magisterially daffy Jeffrey Jones) bemoaning the anxieties of "my poor sister Antoinette." Authentic eighteenth-century concerns—such as the contrast between Mozart's new operas and heroical opera seria—were presented faithfully; Mozart was also represented as what he sometimes was, a vulgarian. As Aristotle said, changes in the actual letter of history are tolerable given fidelity to its spirit, and, in the case of *Amadeus*, to some larger tragic goals.

Strangeness and Beauty

The best recent history movies have the right kind of authenticity. Take the French film *The Return of Martin Guerre* (1983). It has a touching, appealing love story; it also complements its romance with a full sense of the tremendous value that the Middle Ages placed on truth—truth above all, even if it means the destruction of love. The film—made with assistance from a Princeton historian—is superbly authentic, not just in its external props (village, peasant costumes, nasalized medieval music) but internal spirit. By being so, it proved something not only about the value of history but also the history of values.

The Last Emperor has much in common with *Martin Guerre*. Both films emphasize nonheroic personalities—the kinds stressed in new history textbooks that substitute social history over political. Both movies focus on "normal" men; the whole basis of *The Last Emperor* is that it marks the end of dynastic China, and its central figure doesn't have the old kingly grandeur. The more modest success of *Martin Guerre* also rests on a democratic vision of life and re-creation of the authenticity of sixteenth-century peasant France. In this respect at least, the filmmakers make the past come alive by finding something relevant to our age.

But both films also involve a special kind of authenticity—not just the external authenticity of production design, but the internal authenticity of a re-created worldview far different from our own. Difference is the keynote of *The Last Emperor*. Its appeal rests on more than splendid costumes, Bernardo Bertolucci's flamboyant direction, or even the use of Peking's Forbidden City as a set: its soul was the strangeness of the history and attitudes of Asians toward each other. In contrast to many other films about third-world countries, *The Last Emperor* has the strength of foregoing much familiar Western presence—except for the few scenes with Peter O'Toole as the emperor's tutor, who, fortunately, gives one of his typically diffident demonstrations of *not* being there. The plot covered the last stages of imperial rule, the early civil wars between Nationalist and Communist forces and the early 1930s invasion of China by Japan. This slice of history few Americans know, since most date World War II from Pearl Harbor in 1941. In short, one merit of the film is its refusal to make the story *relevant* to known Western history.

Indeed, *The Last Emperor* was made not only because of Bertolucci, but because of the Chinese government, and for particular propaganda reasons. China had wanted to remind the world of its experience in the 1930s and 1940s and warn about possible remilitarization of Japan; it also wanted to blow its own horn as the great agent of Chinese "purification." The People's Republic of China, as we have been reminded since the movie, is perfectly capable of not telling the truth. Nevertheless, the movie focused Western attention on some real and important points: that not all Asians are alike, that Asia (like Europe) is filled with its own long history of tension and resentments, that much has gone on between other nations that Americans do not even begin to conceive or contemplate when seeing the world (as we too often do) in exclusive "bilateral" terms (e.g., America vs Communism, or vs one of the Communist giants, or lately, America vs Japan). Indeed, liberal Americans could even watch this movie and reflect on what so many seem too guilt-ridden to consider at all, that America has not been uniquely evil or error prone among modern nations.

Director Bertolucci deepened the movie by moving the story beyond politics to the savagery and pathos of world history itself. Even with its propaganda element, *The Last Emperor* provided audiences with an expanded, sad, but humane image of mankind struggling through aeons of suffering; whatever its politics, its tone has the grand humanism of the book Bertolucci originally wanted to film, Malraux's *Man's Fate*. Perhaps much of the success of the movie in America involves (besides luck and cagey marketing) its expanded sense of the human experience, and the odd, non-Western point of view from which it is depicted. "There is strangeness in beauty," wrote John Ruskin; and the exoticism of *The Last Emperor* goes beyond costumes to the heart itself.

Many were puzzled by the awards given to *The Last Emperor* in contrast to Steven Spielberg's *Empire of the Sun*. The former won nine Oscars; the latter, with nine nominations, won none. Some of this can be attributed to the Oscar bandwagon and block-voting effects, and some, perhaps, to bias against Spielberg. But indeed there were good reasons for preferring *Emperor*, if not by such a margin. Despite its strengths, *Empire of the Sun* was not quite as striking a movie. More precisely, it seemed two movies: a strong and weaker one spliced together scene by scene. Focused on a boyhood destroyed by World War II, it moved between childlike and childish; excellent scenes were followed by mawkish bathos.

The early part of the movie has some stirring tableaux—especially the arrival of the Japanese army in Shanghai, with an ad for *Gone with the Wind* on a wall in the background; Spielberg provides here one of the few bits of recent movie self-referentiality with real bite. Affecting scenes in which the young English boy (Christian Gale) looks for his mother (Spielberg's Holy Grail) precede adolescent adventure material where he tags along with a China Seas rogue (John Malkovich). A prisoner-of-war camp is initially shown in dire terms, but then Spielberg goes for false sentiment with a salute to Japanese pilots and nauseatingly swelling John Williams musical climaxes. Later scenes involving friendship between Gale and a young Japanese pilot in training are also weak: the bitterness of history is supplanted by the Boy Scout ideology of youthful good spirits conquering all; it is a given that the "friend" has to suffer a sentimental death near the close of the film. In short, half the film is powerfully strange; half is all too cloyingly familiar.

Back to the Future

At the turn of the nineties, history got a little support from some imaginative sources. Producer Freddie Fields and director Ed Zwick (creator of *thirtysomething*) released *Glory*, concerning a regiment of black infantrymen during the Civil War; the movie not only focused on some lost social history, but the often poorly treated subject of race relations in America (see "Justice"). Other filmmakers were also showing interest in the Civil War. *The French Revolution*, a feature film from abroad, was scheduled as a TV miniseries, giving that rebellion equal bicentennial treatment with our own. In late 1989, Paul Newman also starred in *Fat Man and Little Boy,* a study of the decision to develop and to drop the atomic bomb. Too bad, with over statement, it dropped a big one.

Will the history movie recover, survive, or disappear? It depends on the degree to which moviemakers value the past and remain confident about their audience. Surely *some* audience exists. In 1988, magazine covers with historical themes were among the best-sellers in the industry; from their readers must have come some of the mature audiences that made *Reds, The Last Emperor,* and *Empire of the Sun,* if not blockbusters, real money winners. A youth audience might even be revived through the right kind of "back to basics" movement in the classroom.

With luck the audience for history can be large; more usually, it will be small but substantial. Given the risks involved in reaching out to it, filmmakers might as well go the whole hog, drop easy relevance, and try instead for strangeness.

4

Work

It's about money.
—Paul Newman, *The Color of Money* (1986)

Tucker (1987) was not among the best films of the eighties. But it may have been one of the most significant movies in some time about our culture's confusion over the value of hard work.

Tucker tried to revive an old-fashioned story: the tale of the maverick inventor in the tradition of movies such as *Young Tom Edison* and *Edison the Man* (both 1940) or *Alexander Graham Bell* (1939). As many film critics and historians noted, Hollywood mythmaker Frank Capra (director of *Mr. Deeds Goes to Town*, *Mr. Smith Goes to Washington*, and *It's a Wonderful Life*) would have loved *Tucker*—assuming he could have overlooked its style.

Tucker was directed by Francis Ford Coppola at his expressionist best and brashest. With its bright colors, loud big-band score, cartoonish effects, and a hero whose smile was as big as a myth, it could certainly never be accused of understatement. Still, however much artsy in means, *Tucker*'s theme was American as apple pie: the value of hard work, ingenuity, and what we used to call "know-how." This time—in contrast to old "Capra-corn"—it all ends sadly. "Know-how" is trumped by "know-who," or rather who-you-know. Tucker loses because he lacks friends in high places.

The movie expresses even more about the economics of modern America. It gives life and color to laments about our decline in industrial leadership, our poor balance of payments—our loss, in a phrase, of "know-how." The movie embodies brazen nostalgia for that time of heady hopes after World War II, when Capra-esque myths still seemed to find an echo in real life, and when the nation's businesses were more productively lean and competitive.

Coppola focuses on the late forties, when the real Tucker (played by Jeff Bridges) challenged Detroit with an unusually designed car. The "Tucker" combined advanced engineering (a streamlined look, rear motor, fuel injection system) and advanced safety features (seat belts, pop-out windows, and three headlights—one in the middle—to provide greater surface coverage at night). As presented in the film, Tucker is unusual: he's an entrepreneur with the heart of a consumer advocate. In eighties' terms, he blends the sensibilities of Steve Jobs and Ralph Nader—a major reason why Coppola was attracted to the story to begin with.

Is *Tucker* historically accurate? As always, experts disagreed (see "Notes," p. 202, bottom). Whatever the actual facts, Coppola used them to fashion a myth about the value of inventiveness. His myth is pure populism, based on an all-American alliance of creative businessmen such as Tucker, enthusiastic workers, and grateful consumers—all fighting against Detroit "big boys," lawyers, and government.

When Tucker loses, Coppola gives him the dignity of prophecy. In a closing court scene, beneath high sunlit cathedral-like windows (a typical Coppola effect), Bridges claims his case is symbolic: if small businessmen are stiffed, America is in trouble. "If you let big business block inventors like me," Bridges claims, "in thirty years we'll be buying our radios and cars from our former enemies." True or not of the real Tucker, the line reflects an underlying concern about America in the 1980s, a decade when we stopped making money the old-fashioned way: building things. That was left, increasingly, to "former enemies." *Tucker* was only one of several films in the late 1980s that addressed a value Americans had long taken for granted: material prosperity on the basis of hard work. The film implied that it wasn't just one man who was defeated in *Tucker*; it was America, fooled by temporary success or deflected by selfish lobbies from the inventive cooperativeness vital to creative change.

Other eighties' films second some of *Tucker*'s insights about the decline of the American economy. *Wall Street* (1987), *Working Girl* (1988), and even the schlocky *The Secret of My Success* and *Baby Boom* (both 1987) make up one chorus: America has financial and legal wizardy aplenty; it lacks hands-on diligence, creativity, and cooperation. Swamped by lawyers, MBAs, and discouraged underemployed and unemployed, America, these movies said, is understaffed with competent executives, creative and inspired personnel, loyal workers, and team spirit. Many Americans do not value productive work, these movies implied; those who do often aren't rewarded enough for performing it. "The American century"—which Henry Luce declared around 1950—lasted, as *Time's* critic Richard Corliss observes, a mere three decades. In "thirty years," as *Tucker* retrospectively foretold, it would be Japan and Germany, "our former enemies," who would have the lead.

What do our movies tell us about why?

The House of the Rising Sun

The shadow of one of our former enemies, Japan, was even found in comedy. Take, for example, *Gung-Ho* (1986) with Michael Keaton. The plot concerns Keaton's attempts to restart a bankrupt Midwest factory with the financial and management aid of Japanese executives. The title is, in part, a double reference: first, to a "gung-ho" attitude, confidence in one's ability to do a job, esprit de corps, energetic teamwork. But the title also punned on an old World War II film with Randolph Scott (*Gung Ho!*, 1943).

The original, made in the aftermath of Pearl Harbor, depicted seaborne US Rangers counterattacking by raiding an isolated Pacific island held by the Japanese. The movie was grossly propagandistic, and was filled with anti-Japanese stereotypes then popular (perhaps for understandable reasons) in the United States. But the film was also well directed and acted, with a special emphasis on the Rangers' reliance on intangibles to get the job done: surprise, innovativeness, confidence in each other, cooperation, teamwork, and "know-how." In World War II, it was the American perception that we had this value, not the Japanese.

In the new *Gung-Ho*, the situation is comically reversed. American management bungles an auto factory; its new Japanese owners find that they have to reeducate their American workers in sound "team" practices and pride. Instead of assembly-line work, they are retrained according to the principle, "every man must know how to do every job"—a labor practice that attempts to increase productivity by avoiding monotony and by helping workers to identify with the whole product of their labor. American workers are scolded for lateness or tolerating design flaws. The Japanese want "zero-defect" autos—at which Keaton complains, "we're just making cars, you know; it's not brain surgery." Alas, as the movie shows, that attitude is a source of the problem: lack of respect for craftsmanship breeds poor workmanship, which breeds poorer products, fewer sales, and possible unemployment.

Other recent movies reflect problems with work, especially

Americans' failure to value hard work highly. They show that some workers may have good reason to feel this way: some work is depressing—lack of work even more so. Movies can't change this. Still, to work well, a culture needs images of work that help inspire and motivate. It needs films that honestly depict the difficulty and tensions of working with other people. It needs satires that correct uncaring management and uncaring workmanship, both of which stifle productivity. It needs movies, like *Tucker*, that indict our loss of know-how and instruct us on how to recover it.

We have had such movies in the past, but few that express a balanced view of both virtues and vices in business and corporate life. In the sixties and seventies, old-fashioned affirmation of business gave way to harsh satire (e.g., *The Graduate*, *Putney Swope*, and even Altman's *McCabe and Mrs. Miller*). Until the early eighties, the general treatment of business—and some times, in Aquarian days, the concept of work itself—was mainly negative. Then, suddenly, the media fell in love with business, first on TV with *Dallas*, *Dynasty*, and *Lifestyles of the Rich and Famous*, and later in movies that recycled the old fantasy of marrying rich. As Paul Newman's Fast Eddie Felsen says in *The Color of Money* (1986)—before he rediscovers the joy of competition—playing pool has a simple meaning: "It's about money." In the eighties everything was.

Why have these changes occurred, and what may be the effects of new images of work in movies? How do films reveal shifting—and often trendy—evaluations of work? What do they say about the values one puts on certain jobs or professions? Aside from showing people making money, what films show people making money well? Finally, what connection do movies make between our new ways of making money and problems in American economic productivity?

Hot Jobs

Work isn't the strong point of many movies, for simple reasons. Most people don't go to films to see other people work; they go to escape their own. Moreover, if a movie does focus on one line of work, filmmakers risk offending its professionals who may complain that their images were untruthful. To save time, costs, and research energy, and perhaps avoid complaints, filmmakers don't usually delve much into their character's occupations. Characters are often given jobs to fill out their identities; less frequently are these jobs given real significance in the plot. Even if important to the plot, the *texture* of a character's work, the substantial reality of what he or she does, is rarely felt in the screenplay. Not surprisingly—since films are the work of filmmakers and actors—the most usually presented and best-detailed treatments of work probably are found in films about filmmaking or showmanship (*Cabaret, All That Jazz*), and acting (*Tootsie*).

This underemphasis on work is understandable but unfortunate. Even "quality" films ignore work as an aspect of character depth. In *Hannah and Her Sisters* (1986), for example, Woody Allen expands his usual suspects (actors, actresses, TV producers, writers) by casting Michael Caine as an accountant. Except for one slim scene, he gave no detail to the job description. But jobs can be, and have been depicted on film with success, even gusto. Certain movies focus so intently on jobs that they provide unusual kinds of pleasure—for insiders, the pleasure of a familiar scene rendered faithfully (every abused secretary must have reveled at revenge on the boss in *9 to 5* [1980]) or the pleasure of a behind-the-scenes look at something remote (see, for example, Barry Levinson's inside look at aluminum siding sales in *Tin Men* [1987]). When the brave new world in question is glamorous, the pleasure of a behind-the-scenes peek is even greater.

For example, journalism has always appealed to directors, with genre movies stretching back to the thirties featuring the sharp, wisecracking camaraderie of the newspaper office. In recent times, the genre has thrived because of two factors: the glossy, high-tech production design such films allow and the special prestige of a profession that brought down a President. From *All the President's Men* (1975) to *Absence of Malice* (1981), *The Mean Season* (1985), and *Broadcast News* (1987), reporters and broadcasters seemed among the hardest, and often-happiest, workers on the American screen. Journalism was fun even if it did not pay well, as in the fine, offbeat look at the underground press in *Behind the Lines* (1977); it was so "in" that even getting shot at as a foreign correspondent in *Under Fire* (1982) and *The Year of Living Dangerously* (1983) seemed glamourous. The ultimate liberal profession, journalism got post-Watergate America's highest respect. J-schools became Meccas for the ambitious youth in the midseventies, all ready to be the next Woodward and Bernstein.

The fact that Robert Redford and Dustin Hoffman play the reporters in *All the President's Men* didn't hurt the glamourous image of journalists. But the movie conveys something substantial as well: good journalism is damned hard work. Redford and Hoffman are shown prying information from unlikely or unwilling sources, and by a blend of bluff, bluster, deceit, and detection getting the data they need. Hoffman is especially good in one interview scrawling notes down on any piece of paper he could find—old scrap paper, napkins, you name it. No movie ever better celebrated a writer's know-how. Director Alan Pakula's crisp pacing makes such energy seem even more dynamic.

More recently, films shift from print to electronic media in *Eyewitness* (1981), *Broadcast News* (1987), *Switching Channels* (a bad remake of *His Girl Friday*), and *Talk Radio* (both 1988). The shift reflected how, at J-schools in the eighties, students exchanged idolatry of reporters for TV anchorpersons. Electronic journalism appealed to an era hooked on glamour, when media superstars began to earn enough to adopt life-styles of the rich and famous. Still, trendiness again yielded one excellent portrayal of work. *Broadcast News* handled the style of electronic journalism perfectly, particularly in the story of crackerjack producer (Holly Hunter) and her creative hustling for footage and stories. The film includes brilliant sequences on craft, especially the sequences showing Hunter editing under deadline pressure or feeding information to anchors (especially William Hurt as the anchorman with whom she finds herself reluctantly in love). Even air-head Hurt grows to wonder "what's inside all that energy." Although she longs to add love to her life, Hunter's producer is a complete person simply by being one of the most energetic workers ever on screen.

Discouraged Workers

Sadly, energy and determination don't help much in professions so lacking in glamour and glitz that few serious movies about them can even get made. If the few that were made can be trusted, the worst jobs in the last decade and a half belong to teachers (see chapter 2), farmers, and blue-collar workers.

Three acclaimed late seventies films document labor woes: Paul Schrader's *Blue Collar* (1978), *Harlan County, U.S.A.*, 1977 Academy Award winner for Best Documentary, and *Norma Rae* (1978), Marty Ritt's popularly appealing work on the difficulty of organizing unions in the modern South. In retrospect, the last now resembles a last gasp of liberalism before the conservative deluge. Viewers loved Sally Field as Norma Rae, but, increasingly, many did not like unions, and sided with President Reagan with his tone-setting breaking of the Air Traffic Controllers' strike in 1981.

A few directors bucked these trends. Screenwriter and director John Sayles, for example, sympathetically looked at labor issues through a historical lens in *Matewan* (1987). Of course, Sayles intended some rough parallels to the 1980s by examining another conservative age, post–World War I America. His *Matewan* is a searing view of life in the West Virginia coalfields in 1919, when striking workers were "broken" by gangs of thugs brought in by greedy owners. The miners take no pleasure in their work, but pride themselves on their courage and diligence and want to be paid for it. *Matewan* explores what cheated workers can do, or how far they can go, when they are being deprived of fair wages. Sayles's miners are sorely tempted to fight back unethically, but struggle to find the right thing to do. Tragically, the result of their wrestling with economy and morality is undeserved disaster. As in *Eight Men Out* (1988), Sayles uses history to study the hardships of laborers and to map the pitfalls that victims fall into—a reflection, no doubt, of his own experience with student radicalism in the 1960s. What his spirited but sentimental films show is that in an uneven struggle, the downtrodden have no margin of error to make mistakes. Aptly, *Matewan* ends in a disastrous, Western-style shoot-out.

Some directors and producers searched out the value of manual labor in the present day, however downtrodden it had become. Throughout the eighties, TV movies tried, in their sporadically responsible way, to dramatize contemporary work problems. In films such as *Heart of Steel* (1984), they struck gold with the story of steelworker Peter Strauss whose job is lost when his mill goes under to foreign competition. The union—a source of strength for workers as late as *Norma Rae*—can't help him. Neither can his keen sense of value of hard work: as he explains in despair and confusion to his retired father, suddenly hard work no longer pays. Drinking heavily, Strauss is nearly overwhelmed by his experience, and begins beating his wife (the fine Pamela Reed) and children. Although he survives and they partly reconcile, his newfound resolve only leads him to move on and find work elsewhere; there is no rescue by the Japanese, unlike the new *Gung-Ho*. In the movie's bleakest scenes, one of Strauss's buddies shows up at the closed factory only to kill himself.

Suicide links *Heart of Steel* and the best movie in the farm trio of 1985, which included *The River* (with Sissy Spacek), *Places in the Heart* (with Sally Field again as an indomitable working mother), and *Country*. The last has true grit, the result of the determination of Jessica Lange, and her desire to portray farming earnestly but unsentimentally; *Country* has none of the pretty cinematography and happy ending evident in *Places*. Lange founded her own company, "Pangea" Productions, to make the movie; the name is taken from the designation of the original land mass of earth before geologic plates broke into continents, and reflects some of her concern for the farm environment. Like Sayles's, Lange's work suggests an ongoing if muted life for some of the better, populist ideals of the sixties.

Country concerns the northern central plains where Lange grew up, and where, in the 1980s, farmers were hit by severe depression; she also starred as a farmer's wife and strong participant in the family business that falls prey to bad weather and newly imposed tight-money policies of a federal loan agency. Under the same types of pressures, a friend eventually kills himself; naturally, the suicide, as in *Heart of Steel*, must take place in the key place of work that has been deprived of meaning—not a factory now, but in a barn, beside a milking cow on a lonely morning. This is the last straw for Lange's husband (Sam Shepard) who falls apart emotionally and takes refuge in drink and beating his son. Lange holds on; but, unsentimentally, the movie ends with no sure sign of how the struggle will turn out.

The suicides in both *Country* and *Heart of Steel* are important symbols of changes in American life. Contrast them with *The Deer Hunter* (1978): where suicide resulted from combat in Vietnam, not social injustice in the steel mills of the industrial Northeast. There, *The Deer Hunter* said, work was significant. It even had nobility; helmeted at their furnaces, the steelworkers resembled medieval knights; at their favorite bar, drink doesn't involve alcoholism but ritual. Americans do not drive Americans to suicide, *The Deer Hunter* said; only foreigners do.

The depression on farms and in steel was twofold, economic and psychological. The few movies that focused on the first bitterly caught the second. In 1987 the government even recognized what these movies mirrored about loss of faith in the value of work. The Department of Labor coined a new, official designation of a labor category "discouraged workers" for those who were not just unemployed, but did not seek work of any kind. The label is historically revealing: in contrast with the past, productivity problems no longer existed at the upper end of the scale—a traditional result of laziness by those who have made it. Rather, productivity slowed at the lower end, where economic depression had taken psychological and even suicidal dimensions. Workers in *Country* and *Heart of Steel* no longer dream in America.

Only two happy blue-collar workers light up the screen in the eighties, and one is a small businessman as well, Sal the Pizza Man in *Do the Right Thing* (1989). Debate about the film focused on race (see "Justice," conclusion). No one noticed that its image of a working, white small businessman is among the most sympathetic in film in the whole decade; it took a black director with class consciousness (Spike Lee) to create it. The only other happy working Joe is construction worker, onetime "milkman of the month," and gas station owner, Melvin Dumar (Paul LeMat) in *Melvin and Howard* (1980)—an exuberant, feisty piece of Americana that catches Dumar's indestructible verve. According to the plot, Dumar had the good luck for Howard Hughes (Jason Robards, in a wonderful cameo) to have met him at his liveliest; hence the claim that he willed Melvin his estate. On screen and in life, Dumar never got a buck—the one aspect of the film that fits other images in American movies in the late 1980s. Farm and blue-collar workers see themselves or are seen as losers; Melvin is just a beautiful one.

At the Cutting Edge

Farms and blue-collar work are also seen—at an interesting distance—in movies about the real winners of the 1980s: businesspeople. As the eighties progressed, America moved from a J-school to B-school culture, with students flocking to the new romance of money. On screen, the road to Rolodex started with the high-finance *Rollover* (1981); around then, the media fell in love with business. Consider one pervasive commercial of the time: the ad for computer or phone networks or fax systems, with young hip execs interfacing in an intense, jargony conversation about hardware while being filmed in tense, super close-ups and tight head shots from a nervous "subjective" handheld camera. As Garrison Keillor said about his tough-guy cereal "Raw Bits," you had to apply in triplicate to join such ventures. But this was on *Prairie Home Companion*, sly irony from a losing province.

Executives may have been anxious, but not "discouraged"; no one, no matter how silly or dumb, is depressed in a big business movie. Ensconced in gorgeous skyscrapers, movie businessmen and women realized that their room with a view was a window of opportunity. As *The Secret of My Success* (1987) shows, young men leave the heartland for "cutting edge" cities; if they wind up, as in *Secret*, among blue-collar workers (who resent businessmen as "suits"), they still maintain their upwardly mobile mentality. Among the rich, or those with a reasonable chance to become so, there is no depressed fatigue, only the drive to become richer.

Secret focuses on one such driven youth and asks the question: how you gonna keep him down on the farm after he's seen New York? The movie was adolescent fantasy; my head still reels from its basso phallic score. Star Michael J. Fox has to make it big with the boss's wife in some campy but extremely vulgar scenes. It reveled in degraded images of materialistic success; its cinematography often amounted to a hymn of praise for the new, zigguratlike office blocks whose towering weight overwhelms many urban districts. Still, the movie had some content—and even managed to raise important issues about our romance with money. Even the references to farm life ultimately have half a brain.

At the opening of *Secret* Fox leaves the farm where he grew up in Kansas, armed with a degree from a local college to try to make it in the glass-and-aluminum Oz of New York. What happens? He's forced to become a blue-collar worker, a corporate mailman. Fox's determination to rise is framed by the context of farming and blue-collar work, which in themselves are treated as fates worse than death. Nevertheless, although the film is filled with images of yuppie great expectations, it sometimes lambastes them, using values from farm life and the blue-collar class to do so.

Take, for example, the farm opening. Of course it evokes old movie clichés about a rural kid on a rite of passage to the big city. But the film used this background to suggest that Fox's values were rooted in a past that could be a real business asset, enabling him to become a better manager than some paper-pushing executives. The movie caricatured these as "corpocrats"—managers with inadequate knowledge of the products of business, inordinate love of expense accounts, and little idea of how to cut costs besides letting people go. Fox's "uncle" (CEO of a large corporation) personifies corpocracy; the only vice he lacks is nepotism. Instead of helping his nephew, he puts him in the mailroom.

Determined to succeed, Fox begins a double life, masquerading as an executive no one knows but everyone accepts by clothes and manner. His biggest goal is his own success, but he also wants to stop the company from closing Midwestern factories and putting laborers out of work. Yuppie types, in chorus, claim the firm has to cut costs; Fox counters that they can raise profits by expanding productivity with labor-intensive policies. Key scenes involve Fox poring over maps of the Midwest where factories lined up for closure are sited, explaining to other executives how their current operations could be more profitable if they took advantage of local transit and geography. He's a believer in what theorists at decade's end termed "patient capital" as opposed to panic over negative quarterly stock reports.

Of course, many scenes in *Secret* are simply farcical—with some good slapstick sequences of Fox racing back and forth from mailroom to boardroom. Still, the film uses the comedy to stress the value of knowhow: hands-on knowledge yields productive power. Despite its worship of money and upscale life, *Secret* touches on a key theme of the better satires about business in the later eighties, the revolt of productivity against finance.

Women's Work

Perhaps the most unusual study of labor in the last decade is *Working Girls* (1987), a sardonic look at prostitution (see "Notes"). But with ever-increasing numbers of businesswomen, the more upbeat *Baby Boom* (1987) and *Working Girl* (1988) were bound to happen. Besides wise marketing, what did they actually reveal about the problems facing women at work or other business issues?

Except for Diane Keaton's comedic gifts, *Baby Boom* was nearly worthless; more formula filled its prefab plot than an infant's bottle. About its only other decent feature was its end, when Keaton earns a bundle an old-fashioned way, farming. First in her class at Yale, a Harvard MBA, and "Tiger Lady" at a top firm, Keaton *inherits* a baby from a dead relative—an investment banker's immaculate conception. When she can't handle the pressures of business and family (few women can even in today's Hollywood), she flees to Vermont; there, lacking money and rolling in apples, she cooks a ton of applesauce, bottles it, sticks her baby's picture on a label, and markets it at country stores where chichi tourists grab it up, giving Keaton new success from the grass roots. Intentionally or not, *Baby Boom* endorses the value of getting your hands dirty.

Working Girl was a female version of *The Secret of My Success*, and, despite its fluffiness, it was a better movie. Some critics (see "Notes," p. 203, bottom) called it antifeminist, but this requires ignoring key aspects of its treatment of business, which it shares with *Secret, Baby Boom, Wall Street*, and *Tucker*. The film isn't antifeminist, but anti-MBA; its values aren't chauvinist, but populist. The movie focuses on a secretary (Melanie Griffith) with great expectations of rising in the brokerage business. Griffith plays Tess McGill, whose female boss (Sigourney Weaver) an Ivy League MBA, encourages her in coming up with ideas for business deals. "We're a team, aren't we?" Weaver asks Griffith, then steals her best idea.

True, there is some antifeminism: Weaver plays a caricature yuppie shrew. True, Griffith's revenge is only effective because she is able to steal her boss's wardrobe: smart clothes make the modern businesswoman. Still, the film placed strong precise emphasis on particular values of diligence, hard work, and profiting from one's own ideas, not stealing those of others—values that remain vital to many in the business community. Griffith's methods fuse research, math, and an openness to ideas from all sources. Her Tess is a model of alertness: she puts together her deal by enriching her command of finance with an energetic knowledge of pop and business culture. As in *Secret*, the non-MBA wins not because of dumb luck, but a blend of intuition and informed knowledge of the industries her deal involves. *Working Girl* simply reflects the claim of many *in* business that it wouldn't hurt if young MBAs knew more about the actual merchandise produced by the companies that they buy and sell. Like *Secret*, *Working Girl* champions productivity over short-term finance.

Some critics accused *Working Girl* not of sexism but capitalism. What they wanted was not a different movie but a different system. *Working Girl* at least implied a way of improving things as they are. It traces split loyalties between classes—the yuppies whom Griffith wants to join and the secretaries with whom she grew up. The movie stresses this with shots of secretary pools filled with gum-chewing women with excessive makeup and bouffant hairdos. The screenplay makes Tess the kind of person who can bridge the gap but remember her roots. Its final scenes, between her and *her* new secretary, suggests that she understands the need for managers to respect labor. She is a serious version of Fox in *Secret*: she must link two worlds in mutual respect.

Is hope for solutions based on caring management delusive? Perhaps. But in peddling its myth about ethics and upward mobility, *Working Girl* stands in a line of works that extends back a long way. Not only Frank Capra, but also Charles Dickens is alive and well in the fable of Tess McGill. Radical critics prefer ruthless attack on all business values. Still, the history of populist mythmaking makes you wonder: are tales about good business values deceptive if they actually wind up encouraging them?

How to Succeed at Satire by Really Trying

Working Girl was directed by Mike Nichols, who had also made the antibusiness *The Graduate* almost two decades before. *The Graduate* represents its age nearly as well as *Working Girl*; just recall Dustin Hoffman's classic sixties-style reaction to the idea of a future in "plastics." Many critics said the two movies reflect a change of heart about business; perhaps a better description is a change of approach. *Working Girl* still makes its satiric points. Despite its flaws, it might even make them better. American values didn't change because of movies like *The Graduate*, which rejected business out of hand. All we got was backlash, as the gurus of the counterculture delivered the economy, and economic image making, over to our new robber barons.

Working Girl satirizes business, but intelligently. It seeks a middle ground between "selling out" on ideals and quixotic, superidealistic dissent. It indulges in mythic, healing allusions both to the American past and fairy tales as old as Cinderella. Still, it is more hardheaded than many credit; it reflects the acquired wisdom of some bright film-makers about how to change the world, if, indeed, it can be changed at all. Destructive satire that rejects all capitalist and business values can't do it; constructive satire might. Accordingly, *The Graduate* and *Working Girl* represent less a change in values than a shift in strategy.

A similar if sadder attempt at constructive satire is found in *Wall Street*, an especially important film because of its broad, comprehensive look at American business values. Its conclusion expresses a populist faith in the American system, but along the way it provides a darker look at the prospects of reform than any other movie of our time. Perhaps its darkest aspect is its view of the current value of know-how. *Wall Street* illustrates the literal "triumph of the market" in the 1980s—the stock market. The movie's hero-villain investors and speculators make money the new way: liquidating. No film better depicted the contrast between financial wizardy and real productivity—the contrast that has many leading economists worried about the future. According to some theories, the wealth of nations must finally mean more than mergers and acquisitions; somebody, somewhere, sometime has to labor to *make* something. *Wall Street*'s focus is on the value of making things—and making money—as opposed to the danger of a whole country trying to make money only by moving money around.

Despite its considerable flaws, *Wall Street* takes us inside high finance realistically enough to make this morality fable credible. Its director, Oliver Stone, has some defects in style, but also an incisive and inclusive vision of social issues. In *Wall Street*, Stone presents business fairly, pro-viding satire without caricature. He satirizes simplistic emphasis on "toughness" in business ads and the yuppie pursuit of pleasure, but avoids trite stereotypes of bad businessman, as found in *The Graduate* and other old satires. Stone dedicated the film to his father, a stockbroker who had frequently complained to him about monotonous media caricatures of greedy tycoons. Indeed, Stone uses *Wall Street* to undercut simplistic attitudes to business, either from the left or right. As in *Platoon* (see "Patriotism"), he depicts social institutions as com-plex mixtures of good and evil. His evenhandedness results from real knowledge of the market, evident in scenes where its jargon is put into everyday terms, or in scenes of rushed, hectic buying and selling. Stone also respects business energy, evident in the minor character Marv, dedicated to making his mark even if it means years of "cold calling." Stone's typical "Michael J. Fox" yuppie is played by Charlie Sheen, everybody's friend, aptly named "Bud." A friend of Marv, "Bud" doesn't want to work his way to the top: he wants to leap. He works with ethical men (e.g., Hal Holbrook as a senior broker), and is close to his father (Martin Sheen) a machinist for a New York–based airline, who is proud of his $47,000 salary. Young ambitious Bud dismisses him; "Dad, there's no nobility in poverty anymore," he says. Bud wants to be a "player," one of the few that really matter on the street. When his father inadvertently provides inside information on the airline business, Bud grabs his chance.

In pursuing his dreams, Bud becomes not just a worshiper of Big Money Fast, but of Gordon Gekko (Michael Douglas). The Gekko character is modeled on financier Ivan Boesky; indeed, his movie speech, "greed is good" is taken from one of Boesky's speeches in real life. Gekko ("I create nothing, I own nothing") increases his riches through paper manipulations (liquidations, takeovers, takeover threats, megamergers) rather than creating real wealth (products for use). Like many of the big-time financial "players" indicted for insider trading in 1987, Gekko too winds up in jail.

Stone began shooting the film before this wave of Wall Street arrests; his shrewdness in anticipating them is remarkable. He also points a strong moral about the consequences of greed, both in Bud and Gekko's cases. Still, the value of honesty does not come across so well in *Wall Street* because of some weak acting and because Stone divides his "good father" figure in two (Holbrook and Sheen). He did better in *Platoon*, where a "good father" (Willem Dafoe) has the personal power and magnetism to match a "bad" (Tom Berenger).

In *Wall Street*, Stone also gives Gekko some wickedly fine lines. Consider, besides the "greed is good" speech, one later exchange between Bud and Gekko. "Why did you wreck this company?" Bud asks when shocked by his mentor's tactics. Instantly Douglas shouts back, "Because—it was wreckable!" His total aplomb catches the early eighties atmosphere, if not actuality, all too well.

In *Wall Street* Stone laid on his own shoulders an old albatross: how to make good interesting—or at least as vital as evil. Milton faced the problem in *Paradise Lost*, as other artists and filmmakers have innumerable times since. But the problem has a specific contemporary side. We have not been long lately on charismatic spokesmen for the common good—either in art or life. Gekko's "greed is good" speech begs a question: when was the last time that anyone spoke equally commandingly about ethics and public life? President Reagan's rhetorical gifts lay elsewhere. The recent cast of "good guys" who stress communal responsibility have been, for the most part, short on charisma: John Gardner, Jimmy Carter, Michael Dukakis—it's Snoresville Central. By contrast, the flamboyant, headline-grabbing egos in the eighties (Boesky, Trump, Icahn, the Helmsleys, Steinbrenner) may have given loads to charity, but they didn't exactly use their charisma to spread social enlightenment. For a dozen years, the mayor of New York's favorite question was "How'm *I* doin'?" Despite his personal honesty, the emphasis is apt for our age. That is, both *Wall Street* and the world it mirrored lacked a figure whose ego was not just big but *grand*—big enough to join the world's and his own interest in one. Gordon Gekko put it bluntly: "If you want a friend, man, get a dog." 10 to 1, his would have been a pit bull.

A Model Modern Businessman

Wall Street lacks the mythic element that *Tucker* revels in: an image of a businessman with an inclusive set of values. As noted, *Tucker's* hero is after profit, fame, better safety and engineering, and combines public responsibility with creative ambition. Care for consumers, he believes, can *enhance* profit—if competitors play fair. Real competition (without government favoritism to the Big Boys) benefits individuals and society. Often it seems that Coppola had just read the popular study *In Search of Excellence*, with its high valuation of entrepreneurship, care for employees, and concern for consumers. Excellence—in this populist/capitalist vision—does not mean exploitation, but shared productivity by all for all. To rebut Gekko, Coppola even surrounds Tucker with dogs, a crew of nuzzling dalmatians.

Consider also how Coppola presents Tucker's business leadership. Despite post–World War II anti-Japanese feeling, he employs a Nisei engineer; he involves his family (in an inspirational way) in his work; he mock-threatens an innovative employee, "If you ever do that again, I'll—give you a raise!" Scenes with Tucker's crew, wife, and daughter depict a teamlike camaraderie, an extended family feeling, which, the film implies, is essential to productivity. Even if viewers get their noses rubbed in these values too often, the values presented are real. Indeed, there is plenty of evidence to show that openness and caring for workers cost money *only* in the short run. In the long, it inspires all with a sense of sharing in enterprise. Or team spirit.

Wall Street implicitly shares with *Tucker* a hope for reform. Like *Tucker*, it pushes media treatment of technology and business past both blind worship of greed (cf. *Dallas* or *Dynasty*) and simplistic antibusiness satire. Both imagine (*Wall Street* less successfully) that there can be such a thing as an honest and self-interested businessman. On a higher level than *Secret* or *Working Girl*, they resurrect the old populist-capitalist

dream that social and personal interests can sometimes work as one.
It doesn't help if movies can't provide such images or foster such
hopes. If they cannot, young, ambitious people are left only with the
choice of making money *or* being "true" to themselves and others.
Guess which option they will choose? People need ways of imagining
that they can fulfill ambition *and* cooperate at the same time. Divorce
the two—as the counterculture did—and blind ambition always wins.
Uniting the two means indulging in mythmaking; it also involves a
hard-nosed faith that sensible myths can be reconstructive of social
reality.

Futures Markets

Because of the prestige of high finance, films are likely to keep focus
on the American economy: expect more movies such as *The Bonfire of
the Vanities* to play off our fixation with megabucks. Films with working-
class settings (e.g., Fonda and De Niro in *Stanley and Iris*) are likely to
be fewer and farther between. *Roger and Me* (1989) is merely the exception that proves the rule.

The best images of work on American screens are likely to come from
another source. Beyond doubt, the hardest worker in films in the 1980s
was the terrierlike Miyamoto Nabuki, star of successful recent Japanese
imports such as *Tampopo, The Taxing Woman,* and *The Taxing Woman
Returns*. It was perhaps no accident that Japanese films provided our
best images of someone who knew the value of hard work and who
trusted her culture to reward her for it. It fit: in late 1989, Sony climaxed
long years of industry rumor by buying Columbia Pictures. Nabuki
represents the Japanese who make money *our* old-fashioned way: know-
how. Gung-ho.

5

Sports

I know God made me for a purpose, but He also made me fast, and when I run, I feel His pleasure.

—Chariots of Fire (1981)

W as there ever a better baseball movie than *Bull Durham*? Was there a better-written film in the later 1980s? The feeling of being there, the texture of life in the minor leagues, the gritty fatalism of a veteran catcher staring at the end of his career—all this spiced the screenplay: here was hotdogging with plenty of mustard, but not an ounce of false sentiment; here was energy, realism, slapstick, hope, and disillusion in total equipoise; here was the best thing a sports movie can convey— love of a game and knowledge a game is never as big as life. And here was baseball, real baseball, "ground balls with eyes, flares, dying quails"; here was a story around which myth grew as naturally as out- field grass. The movie was so inclusive it even featured cultural literacy—quotes from Thomas Gray, William Blake, and Walt Whitman, perfectly positioned in a plot in which romanticism about athletics duk- ed it out with realism for first place honors. Winning wasn't everything in *Bull Durham*: but it was sure fun.

Bull Durham was written and directed by Ron Shelton, who had spent time in the Oriole farm system, gone to writing school, and found the perfect way to harvest both experiences. His range of experience shows in the plot, which focuses on maturely recognizing the limits of talent. Indeed, *Bull Durham* is a comedy about maturity. It has, to be sure, seedy language—the jargon of the locker room of the "Durham Bulls" (the real name of a minor-league team in North Carolina). But values emerge from the seediness, mostly an adult attitude to winning rare in a sports film.

Winning is also rare for the Bulls until the aging catcher Crash Davis (Kevin Costner) arrives and puts spunk into the team. Crash is near the end of his career, and he is charged with tutoring "Nuke Laloosh" (Tim Robbins)—a fireballing young right-hander who can't hit the broad side of a barn. Nuke is a dunderhead; Crash has to get him to think a bit, or even just *suspect*. In the process, Crash becomes one of the best teachers on screen in the 1980s.

His enemy? Another teacher, Annie Savoy (Susan Sarandon), part-time English instructor, ad hoc mystic, and full-time devotee of "the church of baseball." Savoy ritually likes to bed one of the Bulls each year, naturally chooses Nuke, setting off a fine, furious battle of the sexes with Crash. The basis of their clash is the conflict of romanticism and realism. To win arguments, Annie quotes romantic poetry; she believes in reincarnation and claims to have been Francis of Assisi. Crash asks her why it is that no one who claims to be reincarnated was ever anyone insignificant before. I wish he had been around in the sixties.

Larger value issues are also at stake, despite the movie's slapstick tone. Crash struggles to wean Nuke away from Annie and into greater maturity. All Nuke values is force; Crash teaches him finesse and "control"— both on and off the field; he struggles to make the young fireballer less egocentric and use brains, not only raw power. In portraying this process, Shelton makes *Bull Durham* the truest, most authentic baseball film ever. Its emphasis is not on sensational plays by lone heroes; baseball is not seen as momentarily glorious but consistently intense; home runs have their role but also fielding and contact hitting. Good pitching involves control as well as power; force alone is self-defeating. Crash wants Nuke to throw a smarter, if not a gentler fast ball. The writing is so acute that, while more truthful about the game, it is also more, not less, truthful about life.

Best of all, *Bull Durham* spares us the clichés of final apocalyptic, bottom-of-the-ninth-inning rallies, with two-strike counts and a formulaic affirmation of heroism. Its heroism is not by recipe, but real, and involves adjustment and going on when the game is over. Crash's Nirvana is "the Show," the major leagues; he was there once "for twenty-one days," where "the ballparks are as big as cathedrals." Such mythmaking is believable in *Bull Durham* because of its roots in the real character of the game, in the edgy realism of Crash Davis, and in his final recognition that his career is nearly over. It's Nuke who gets to go on to stardom in "the Show"; Crash must adjust to failure to make the majors and a new career as a minor-league manager. Playing, and playing to win, was important to Crash. But it wasn't the only thing. There was, in addition, how he loved, and how he taught the game—

and how he gets Annie, in one of the better and more credible on-screen romances of the decade. It fits: Crash really knew about finesse and when to throw a curve.

The Superboom

Not all sports movies have *Bull Durham's* vivacity or spine. But there were certainly a load of them in the last decade or so. The last dozen years include the entire *Rocky* sequence, *Breaking Away* and *North Dallas Forty* (1979), *Raging Bull* (1980), *The Karate Kid* (1984) and its sequels (1986 and 1989), *The Natural* (1984), *American Flyers* (1985), *The Best of Times* (1987), *Streets of Gold, Eight Men Out,* and *Bull Durham* (all 1988), and *Major League* (1989). Not all were widely seen: at least two (*The Slugger's Wife* [1985] and *Stealing Home* [1985]) struck out with no one looking. But the list also includes two Oscar winners for Best Picture (the original *Rocky* and *Chariots*), other Oscar winners and numerous nominees, and some of the most profitable movies of recent times. A number of films focused on women in sports: *Personal Best* (1982), *Heart like a Wheel* (1983), the Canadian *Hockey Night* (1984), the dumb Goldie Hawn vehicle *Wildcats,* and TV movies like *A Love Affair: The Eleanor and Lou Gehrig Story* (1978), a *Pride of the Yankees* from the widow's view. As *New York* film critic David Denby wrote in 1986, "Lately it seems that the only theme of any American movie is winning."

Of course such movies (about male athletes) have been around before, from *Knute Rockne, All-American* (with Ronald Reagan as George Gipp) to *The Winning Team* (with Ronald Reagan as Grover Cleveland Alexander) to John Garfield boxing melodramas and television serials such as *Joe Palooka*. The basic conventions of the sports genre, established early, have changed only slightly with time: an athlete's struggle to make a name, an initial victory, a near-crushing defeat, and an inevitable comeback (via surprise knockout, miracle touchdown, or game-winning home run).

These conventions aren't new: their pervasiveness is. As Gene Siskel noted on one *Sneak Previews*, sports imagery has become so widespread that the debating movie *Listen to Me* (1989) tries to get by by treating debating contests with standard sports movie conventions. The genre dominates the 1980s. Why? What values do sports movies teach? How do they treat "winning"?

Sports movies are normally fun: many of us participate vicariously in their heroics, comic or serious. They reflect the enormously high value Americans now seem to place on sports itself. They derive from it; in classic chicken-and-egg fashion, they probably foster it further. At least, in the eighties, they seemed part of a general fusion of sports and media in one grand entertainment enterprise. We live not just in an age of business and baby boom, but a sports franchise population explosion. Baseball, football, and—even more so—hockey and basketball teams multiplied rapidly; the only real expansion failure was the USFL. For some high-school and college students, sports (always a vital element in the curriculum) became the main emphasis. At some colleges, at some cost, "athlete-students" replaced "student-athletes."

The media have supported the sports boom in many ways, some not so obvious. As Billy Crystal's comic character "Fernando" used to say on the mideighties' edition of *Saturday Night Live*, "It's more important to look good than to feel good, and you look marvelous." Advertising, always a preacher of beauty, made it essential for a "me generation" to "look marvelous." Women were subject to a fashion industry that equated looking marvelous with shedding weight, sometimes at the expense of health. Fortunately, through improved coverage in women's magazines, many found health and sports regimens that served their real interests.

Sports pervaded TV, from *Monday Night Football* to the explosion of sports on cable. It ruined holidays, broke up marriages, or in one film, at least forestalled them: in *Diner* (1982) director Barry Levinson—nostalgic for the Baltimore in which he grew up in the late fifties—imagines one of his young heroes insisting that his fiancée pass a Colts' trivia test before he marries her. In a fitting climax to this kind of conservative, early eighties' romance with the fifties, wrestling experienced a revival and returned to TV; ESPN even televised cheerleading competitions.

In *Sport and Society*, Jay Coakley calls the relation of sports and television a "symbiosis," with both parties fueling each other's revenues. How have sports movies contributed to this, or intensified sports/media collaboration? How have they shaped attitudes toward sports and their relation to the rest of life? What do they teach about the value of athletics, or other values that can be achieved in competition? What especially do the many formula movies teach young audiences—the bulk of the contemporary box office—about the value of winning? According to the most dominant football coach of recent times, Vince Lombardi, "Winning isn't everything; winning is the only thing." As coach Al Davis of the Oakland/LA Raiders says, "Just win, Baby." What do movies say about winning? Or which movies enrich such messages?

Rocky and Beyond

The first *Rocky* (1977) had true grit, and in several fine scenes, real emotional power (Stallone's outburst against Burgess Meredith, "Adrienne's" against "Pauley"). Despite the racial undercurrents in its focus on the white lower class (see below), its surface was a quiet, oddly dignified pathos. The movie even had the courage to end in a split-decision loss and a call to love; it was going the distance and "Adrienne" that mattered.

But in *The Natural*, *The Karate Kid*, or *Rocky* sequels and imitations (including Stallone's arm-wrestling epic, *Over the Top* [1987]), winning comes to dominate the simplified plotting. The heroes of such movies are all engaged in simple struggles of good against evil. Their basic natures, their devotion to sports, their relations with friends and family are relatively unconflicted. Conflict comes from the need to beat the competition—often bad guys in one disguise or another. Of course, other values are implied in these films: family, friends, hard work. Indeed, sometimes these values are earnestly presented. Still, the simple flattening out of plot and character means that formulas take over, and feeling is drained. Family and other loyalties exist as supports, as stage properties, maneuvered only to sustain, support, or inspire success. Winning may not, technically, be the only thing; but it sure beats out the competition.

In symbiosis with the sports superboom of the last decade, such formula movies might have had unintended consequences. Even the better of these sports movies—the Indiana basketball film, *Hoosiers*, for example—are shaped around the winning shot, goal, touchdown, or home run: in plot terms, winning is what mainly matters; formulaic repetition and conventional triumphant conclusions tend to push other values into the background. Viewers of such movies already spend a large part of their time at play; the movies tend to suggest that only *one* result in play is acceptable. They also misrepresent sports themselves, leading many viewers to think that they all come down to one play, one sensational hit, one catch. Few are the games that come down to one single moment of crisis; but rare is the movie that doesn't.

One traditional justification for sports is that they teach values of fair play and camaraderie that are important for the rest of life. Sports also sharpen competitive impulses and aid a nation's economy. Certainly the heightened economic competitiveness in eighties' America mirrors the sports boom and fascination with "winning." And when good coaches talk about "winning"—indeed, when Vince Lombardi and Knute Rockne did—they often say a good word for other values too. But some movies present winning so powerfully that these other values can easily recede into the background. As a result, the symbiosis of sports, media, and sports movies may have weakened, not strengthened us as a nation. Formula movies especially (if unintentionally) dovetail with the other messages young people receive to "just win, Baby"—whatever the impact of preparation for winning on the rest of life or, for example, the rest of school. But what nation can be Number One if its citizens can't run and read at the same time?

Grace under Pressure

Some critics try to get at something deeper in a sports movie by reading it for its "metaphors" and "deeper meanings." Of course these exist; in *Field of Dreams* (1989 [see below]) they abound. But not everything exists as a "metaphor" for something else. Critics should first focus on what sports movies have to say about the playing fields themselves, where much of the movie audience spends much of its free time. Almost all sports movies tell them winning is good for you. Some sports movies, however, enrich the picture in *literal, nonmetaphorical* ways. They view the value of winning comprehensively, test it, and often reaffirm it beyond cliché. Winning is valued, but family or other values are equal, competing points of loyalty, which—as often in the real world—complicate the pursuit of athletic excellence.

Take the British film, *Chariots of Fire* (1981), one of the first surprise hits of the 1980s. In the film's best scenes, one of its heroes, a Scots Presbyterian evangelical missionary who has developed Olympic-level running skills (Ian Charleton), is reprimanded by his zealous sister (Cheryl Campbell) for neglecting church work by pursuing medals for track. Scolding him, she says in her broad Scots accent, "You're head's so fu' a' runnin' that you've got no time fo' standin' still." But her brother likes to run; he likes especially to win, so he takes her to a promontory overlooking Edinburgh and explains his sense of values. "I know that God made me for a purpose," he tells her. "But He also made me fast, and when I run, I feel His pleasure."

The line is a powerful synthesis of the values that the film presents, equally emphasizing winning at races *and* moral integrity. In the plot, his dual value system helps explain how he can try to keep two commitments at once; he can run to win because he believes in a God who pleasures in human excellence. Ideally, his response to his sister even implies a kinship between joy and duty. The movie's appeal, and, for some, inspirational magic, involves exactly this synthesis of personal, even pleasurable, and religious values.

The movie makes clear that this synthesis isn't always easy, and that personal and moral values don't always coincide. Eventually the runner has to choose between running in a race for an Olympic medal he is sure to win or observing the Sabbath; the first heat for the gold is scheduled for a Sunday. Faced with an unavoidable choice between running or keeping his moral code, he chooses to keep to it despite his lyrical, youthful ardor about running before. As a result, the runner becomes a *believable* moral example because he's not a moral automaton. He has old-fashioned values, but he also knows the thrill of victory.

By presenting both aspects of his character so forcefully, *Chariots* successfully depicts an athlete who understood two truths at once: winning is valuable, but not winning *at any cost*. It is difficult to contemplate two related, apposite truths at one time, an irksome fact as our lives become ever more complex. Given the sensationalism and simplification normal in the film medium, for a movie (especially a sports movie) to do so is impressive.

Chariots of Fire was a typical eighties film in many ways, combining two popular genres—sports and nostalgia. But it also enriched both genres by adding something to the value of winning. In *Chariots of Fire* and other movies, the value of winning isn't denied or derided, but put in a larger context. These films are important because they can reach mass audiences with images that they can understand; on the other hand, they don't treat the images simplistically, and place them inside a pattern of life that often involves painful choices. By trying to reconcile the demands of body and spirit, these movies provide deeper views of grace under pressure. In any age and in any competition, being able to deal gracefully with value conflicts is important for everyone. But in an age of intensified competition, sports boom, semi-professionalized college athletics, recruiting violations, lowered academic standards, steroids, cocaine, and bribes, sports movies that help their viewers to deal intelligently with such conflicts are vital.

The Year of Playing Baseball Dangerously

In transcending formulas, not all sports movies are created equal. Not even all baseball movies are. Forget if you can about *Bull Durham*. Consider *The Natural* and *Eight Men Out*. Both had superb production designs and reveled in their backgrounds of bygone Americana. Both had good baseball sequences: few stars have ever looked better at the plate than Robert Redford swinging Wonderboy; for *Eight Men Out*, actors were made to go through strenuous preproduction workouts to see if they were like the quick, lithe ballplayers of pre-Ruthian days, before home runs took the suspense out of fielding, hitting, and running. Both films also touched on the sore spot in the American sports memory, the gambling scandal in the 1919 World Series. In *The Natural* a fictional hero rejects a bribe; in *Eight Men Out*, the Black Sox (including the famous "Say it ain't so, Joe" Jackson) take it.

But there are key differences between the two movies. *The Natural* epitomizes some of our gravest cultural problems with the value of winning. It was a popular favorite for some obvious reasons: the increased popularity of baseball, the force of nostalgia, its poetic cinematography, and the heroic lead by Robert Redford. But its intense overstatement caused problems, and the film endorsed some questionable values. Many critics noted, and some complained, about the way director Barry Levinson altered the ending of the source, Bernard Malamud's novel of the same title. The change was made for obvious Hollywood reasons; in Malamud, Roy Hobbs (Redford's golden boy) takes a bribe and throws a game; as in so much modernist literature, losing is de rigueur. In the movie, Roy Hobbs rejects the bribe, gets up off a sickbed, and knocks a winning homer that crashes against a light tower and sets off a spectacular display of special effects.

What Levinson was after—indispensable in this crowd-pleaser—was a happy ending no matter what, and the special effects didn't hurt. The "natural" has to endure the last temptation of a great slugger, but he evades it quickly, relatively unscathed, and then rebounds quickly and spectacularly into glory. Great Scott, the screenplay is so clichéd that, at one point, with Hobbs in the hospital, all he can mutter is, "Baseball has been good to me." But notice the result: the value of Roy Hobbs's honesty is never keenly felt; because character depth is so lacking, character choice seems foreordained. Indeed, some early shots of Redford's amber waves of hair seen against Midwest wheatfields removed the need of a halo. His purity is paralleled by his girl friend (Glenn Close), always shot in a broad white hat (another halo) and clean white dress high in the grandstand. *The Natural* doesn't put as much energy in the issue of choice between good and evil as it does in "winning" via the big home run.

Simplification of sports values in *The Natural* is evident in other ways, especially in gross simplification of the real texture of the game itself, which teaches the values of teamwork, strategy, and alertness. Malamud invented and Levinson preserved a set of unrealistic "cut-'em-out" allegorical elements basic to the plot: Roy Hobbs plays for the New York

Knights, a woesome team managed by the weary "Pop" Fisher, and saves them using his lightning-honed bat, Wonderboy. So: the Round Table, the Fisher king, and Excalibur. It's a neat bundle: you can see the whole scenario diagrammed on a blackboard. In *Bull Durham*, by contrast, you feel the texture of idiosyncratic, felt-and-lived experience.

The film *The Natural* also misrepresents baseball. Despite resemblances between Roy Hobbs's and Kirk Gibson's World Series home run in 1988—or Redford's smoothly powerful swing and Ted Williams's—*The Natural* consistently reveals its shallow roots in the subject matter. Redford said he liked baseball—it was a heroic sport of "one against nine." The truth is that baseball is more often nine against nine—a game in which fielding, the rest of the lineup, the players on the bench, are all part of a shifting series of consecutive calibrations. As underdog teams without great stars have shown, baseball is one of the ultimate team games. No slugger's home run wins a game unless the rest of the team scraps to keep the game close.

The Natural presented an untrue image of heroic individualism. It's not just "winning only"; it's *one* man "winning" "only." In real baseball, the opposition would have always walked him—a possibility never represented, a kind of guerrilla warfare strategy that (as has been seen in several recent real wars) underarmed competitors sometimes used to beat heavy hitters. The point isn't idle. If young people watching such films are fed a steady diet of hyped-up heroism, their sense of teamwork and cooperation isn't helped. In some ways, *The Natural* was as American as apple pie. But it also overdid emphasis on the "I." There is nothing wrong with a movie enriching truth with fiction once in awhile (see "Cultural Literacy"). But *The Natural* impoverishes it.

Better baseball realism and deeper soulfulness are found in *Eight Men Out*, even though it presents the story of ballplayers who took money to throw a championship. This movie is flawed in its pacing; ironically, the flaw results from a great strength. The fine baseball writer Roger Angell once wondered (see "Notes," p. 204, top) why the movie did not present what academic critics now call an "anti-myth"—a set of images that emphasize the feet of clay of the heroes we are used to worship, or are made to worship in the repetitive formulas of the sports genre. *Eight Men Out* focuses on a baseball fix, but does not make its players into villains or failures; they occupy an uneasy middle ground between *Natural*-type formula and anti-myth. Why? What was the director, John Sayles, up to in making a film that does not fit such categories?

The film's focus is simply the World Series of 1919 whose "fix" cost eight Chicago White Sox players (the so-called "Black Sox") their careers. The "Black Sox" place a high value on winning: but they also place a higher value on getting real pay for their work, and thus fall prey to a temptation to take a gambler's bribes to throw some games. To them, winning has become less than everything, not because of moral values, but economic ones. Accordingly, Sayles initially focuses on how athletic integrity can be compromised by financial need.

Sayles is one of the most interesting (if never completely satisfying) independent filmmakers of our time—not just a baseball fan, but a history buff, with a deep interest in America just after World War I. Ballplayers didn't make much money then; none were free agents; some (like the White Sox) were close to poor. In a daring, rapid-fire opening to *Eight Men Out*, Sayles shows how the anger of the talented White Sox against their skinflint owner, Charlie Comiskey, moved them to throw the championship. No one more embodies the conflict of honesty on the field and anger over economic injustice than pitcher Eddie Cicotte (David Straithern). Although he makes the wrong choice, his wrestling with moral values has far more weight than Roy Hobbs's in *The Natural*.

Sayles's movies always address values; his other film set in 1919, *Matewan*, addresses similar issues as they evolved in a coal miners' strike in West Virginia. These value-laden films also have a serious weakness: Sayles sympathizes with so many of his characters, and tries to pack so many stories in the screenplay, that his films seem to flatten after half an hour. Sayles can't seem to evade the problem: his appreciation of many different human types and a broad view of social complexity mean, invariably, that he spreads himself too thin and his pacing collapses. It would be easier for him if he had a simple ironic point of view: making fun, or making hash, of everyone is much easier than trying to understand how basically good people can make awful mistakes.

Eight Men Out illustrates "no good deed goes unpunished"; it is precisely because Sayles is thinking beyond the basic categories of both formula films and ironic anti-myths that he gets into trouble. Sayles can't indulge in myth or anti-myth because he sees too deeply. His main characters are always complex mixtures of good and evil; he can't give us *The Natural* or an anti-myth because he doesn't believe "heroes" come only in supermen or anti-hero sizes. The film loses its way, that is, because it's too subtle for saccharine hero worship or the bitter ironies of a simplistic deconstruction of heroism. In short, its weakness derives directly from Sayles's strength, his insight into character and the capacity of average people to fail. Too bad he has yet to find a way to express the fullness of his personal vision.

The flip side of this weakness is Sayles's skill in evoking good performances from an ensemble of actors; in *Eight Men Out*, his "team" style finds its perfect subject, a team game in which no single individual dominates. Indeed, Sayles labored hard to restore the team nature of baseball in the days before Ruth. Check out the high number of triples in *Eight Men Out*. They are not only historically accurate, but exemplify a game where more than one person is needed to score a run. Sayles presents a team game and team acting because he wants to emphasize a value beyond self. To win, *Eight Men Out* teaches, you have to cooperate.

Has-Beens

The saddest, most vivid recent film about a sports figure is *Raging Bull*, Martín Scorsese's study of middleweight champ Jake LaMotta's inability to handle athletic success. The film is much more sophisticated and affecting than any other sports portrait; indeed, despite its excellently re-created ring scenes, *Raging Bull* passes far beyond the sports genre to near tragedy. In many ways, it's almost too rich in detail and gorgeously eccentric in style to reach the audience other sports movies have; the use of opera tunes to back up boxing's lyrical mayhem indicates both how fine, and how specialized, the director's taste is. The movie's production design provides a wonderful evocation of the 1940s and 1950s; Scorsese brilliantly uses a small, old TV set as a prop in one scene of a terrible *out of ring* fight between LaMotta (played perfectly by Oscar winner Robert De Niro) and brother-manager (in a great supporting role, Joe Pesci). Visually, the film is a black-and-white stunner—with such contrasts emphasized in character, costume, hair color, you name it. Using such devices, Scorsese deepens the tale of a fighter who can't manage his talent or contain paranoia over his marriage. *Raging Bull* richly contrasts sports championship and real-life bungling.

Everybody's All-American (1988) also tackles real-life bungling, with less force but perhaps with wider range. Its hero (Dennis Quaid) is one Gavin Grey, "the gray ghost," an LSU tailback in the late 1950s who knows something has to follow All-American status and a career in the pros. As played astutely by Quaid, Gray never plans it well enough, and winds up in a boozy, self-pitying middle age. He can't figure out what to do to live when the touchdowns are over, and bumbles into alcoholism and reliving the past at alumni confabs. *Raging Bull* negates *Rocky*; *Everybody's All-American* teasingly evokes it when Quaid tries the inevitable formulaic comeback and falls flat on his face. The film was widely regarded as a throwback to an earlier period because of its aura (spread especially by previews) of nostalgia for a golden age of college football, macho halfbacks, homecoming queens, and torchlight rallies. In truth, it also recalled movies about aging athletes who don't find a new life after sports: *Easy Living* (1949) with Victor Mature as a retired pro halfback; or *Requiem for a Heavyweight* (1962), with its strong Rod Serling script and a brooding Anthony Quinn at sea outside the ring.

Like *Bull Durham* and *Eight Men Out*, *Everybody's All-American* both celebrates and satirizes sports mania. It declares winning is good, but adds that it's not everything; you have to prepare for life as well. It covered plenty besides football, with a double-edge nostalgia that might help student athletes consider the perils of making sports everything. As the figure of "the ghost" falls, for example, others rise, especially his Magnolia Queen girlfriend (Jessica Lange; see "Heroines"). A second twist is the contrast of the ghost's downward career and the upward mobility of a black ex-athlete (Carl Lumbly, from television's *Cagney and Lacey*). Denied a shot at college, Lumbly turns cook, joins in the civil rights movement, and becomes a successful restaurateur. Directed by Taylor Hackford and based on a book by *Sports Illustrated*'s Frank Deford, *Everybody's All-American* avoids "anti-myth" for something more complicated: a satire—albeit an affectionate, understanding one—on sports machismo.

Sports, Films, Race

Carl Lumbly's role in the plot of *Everybody's All-American* raises some important value issues. Lumbly plays a black businessman, who, pushed out of sports, does well for himself. The screenplay explains at one point that he had no alternative: discrimination was so strong in the Southern football world (even after Jackie Robinson and other black athletes had opened up baseball) that he couldn't hope to get into a leading Southern university. Implicitly the film teaches the value of racial tolerance for black efforts in sports and beyond them.

But the racial subplot begs a key value question. Why is there so little realism about sports and race on screen? Where are movies about minorities who feel that they have no other outlet but sports? Where are films that depict the dilemma of the young black athlete who doubts society will ever reward him for what he does with his mind? Where is a *Bull Durham* for the minority player who never gets that shot at managing when his career is over? Yes, there was *The Jackie Robinson Story*—almost forty years ago. But what about a *Frank* Robinson story?

In recent sports films, greater realism about both the texture of a sport, the value of winning, and the problem of retirement is valuable. But one wishes the realism could go farther—into the volatile mix of drugs and sports, into the clash of study and sports for any college athlete, and into the racial problems that American sports illustrate. In general, Hollywood was uneasy in eighties about tackling racial subjects, especially if they involve black-white tensions of any kind (see "Justice"). As a result, filmmaking about sports has become particularly unreal. The only recent films about blacks in sports are minor works, *The World's Greatest Athlete* (1973) and *The Bingo Long Traveling All-Star and Motor Kings* (1976)—both made under the sign of Aquarius. Before that, one goes back to the Jackie Robinson movie and *Jim Thorpe, All-American* (1951), for representation of the problems of minority athletes.

This is not to say that black or other minority issues should be ghetto-ized in sports movies; neither should minority professionals. Movies involving lawyers, doctors, or nearly any profession should have minority presence. All movies about the problems of racial minorities need not involve sports. But surely more sports movies ought to depict the successes of and challenges facing black and minority athletes. *Bull Durham* managed a Dominican first baseman stranded in North Carolina; the Durham Bulls, however, included no blacks. Basketball, track, and football movies have the same problem. Many sports are dominated by black athletes, yet few sports films include them on their rosters. Such movies don't need affirmative action, just a little realism.

Consider the most extreme cases of black underrepresentation: box-ing films. In the last half century, there has been only one white heavyweight champion of real note, Rocky Marciano. Yet, as far as films are concerned, *Rocky* is the supreme heavyweight champion; he dethrones a black man, Apollo Creed. *Rocky* is a film version of "the great white hope," a boxing persona periodically embodied in any palooka with a white skin (indeed, Stallone was inspired by Chuck Wepner, Ali's "chump of the month" in 1976). Creed is such a nice guy that, in *Rocky III* and *IV*, the dethroned black champ becomes his friend—a fantasy that implies interracial harmony only blossoms as soon as the white man wins. At least *Raging Bull* had a basis in fact. As good as that movie is, however, no producer has rushed to make *The Sugar Ray Robinson Story*.

Field of Dreams also flubs the racial issue. The plot, of course, involves magical transformation of a cornfield in Iowa to a baseball field where old stars magically reappear. One night, while he is working his corn-field, a voice whispers to a farmer (and ex-sixties radical, Kevin Costner) "if you build it, he will come." Costner imagines the voice means for

him to build a ball field over part of his corn; to the dismay of his
neighbors—but not his supportive spunky wife (Amy Madigan)—he
goes ahead. Lo and behold, Joe Jackson (Roy Liotta) literally
materializes. Soon other older ballplayers show up too, all to realize
some long-frustrated dreams of their own.

Again, at the weird instruction of the voice, Costner also brings a black
man to his "field of dreams," Boston recluse Terence Mann (James Earl
Jones). In the novel, this apparently was supposed to be J. D. Salinger.
But changing the character's skin color is important, and the filmmakers
could have been more sensitive to what it meant. At one point, Jones
mouths off an embarrassing ode about how good baseball has always
been, kind of odd given the lack of any black players from Joe Jackson's
time on the "field of dreams." Baseball only recently became color-blind;
in Jackson's day, black stars had to compete in the Negro Leagues.

Sociology isn't required of movies, just honesty; moral truth is not
the enemy of hope, or even of healing fantasy. Indeed, with a little
thought, facing the race issue frankly could have fit perfectly in with
one theme of *Field of Dreams*, fulfilling frustrated hopes. Satchel Paige
could have shown up in that cornfield, or another Negro League
veteran. Then we might have really been able to test the movie's subtext:
this "field of dreams" isn't Iowa, but just this side of Paradise.

Metaphor, Myth, Anti-Myth

Field of Dreams was not about race, of course, or even baseball exactly.
It could have used more edge, and not just on race: given many recent
sports scandals, some reference to "Black Sox" Joe Jackson's errors (at
least in judgment) in 1919 would have been advisable. Like *The Natural*
and *Eight Men Out*, *Field of Dreams* rubs that old World Series wound—a
wound recent movies clearly see as a kind of national fall from grace.
Too bad that *Field of Dreams* avoids any mention of what Jackson and
his colleagues may have done. Treating it would have fit the movie's
theme: after all, everyone should be able to find forgiveness on a field
of dreams. Or, as Browning wrote, "What's a Heaven for?"

Field of Dreams was originally titled *Shoeless Joe*, from the novel by
W. P. Kinsella. It is faithful in tone to its source, an exercise in magical
realism; Costner even plays a "Ray Kinsella." No plot summary can do
real justice to its strange texture. No amount of argument is likely to
persuade those who dislike its tone, or ostensible subject, baseball. It's
the kind of movie that either nauseates or works perfectly on its own
terms.

Despite its weaknesses, the great strength of *Field of Dreams* is its lack of embarrassment over big things. More than any recent sports movie, it uses baseball as a cover for talking about much more: bright sunny days, a bright white farmhouse, a gracious front porch, the memory of loved ones, and the myth of lost innocence rediscoverable somewhere out there just beyond the prairie's horizon. The movie is unabashedly—literally—*corny*. Indeed, from the first scenes onward, like a hundred sentimental movies about the American heartland, it tries to persuade us that corniness is next to godliness. In its imagery of amber waves of grain it rivals *The Natural*. Its real subject isn't baseball, or even America, but fulfilling dreams, happy endings—"winning" in the broadest sense of the term, maybe even making Heaven.

To some, the film's sentimentality is offensive; they hate not just the corn, but the related emphasis on sports and winning. It is a crutch of the intelligentsia to link sports with a complex of traditional and conservative values; winning at sports is often seen as guilt by association. It seems too all-American, old-fashioned, reeking of the locker room and recalling the obsessions of a gym teacher or overzealous coach; it conjures up tacky floats, cheerleaders, and junior chambers of commerce. If winning comes, they anguish, can Mom, Dad, and winning one for the Gipper be far behind? Accordingly, despite its preaching against book banning (and despite corny old Iowa's strong progressive tradition), *Field of Dreams* was treated by some (see "Notes," p. 204, bottom) as a neo-Wagnerian call to arms, a last good-bye from the Reagan era.

There is no doubt of a link between attitudes to winning in sports and life. Stallone as the veteran Rambo merely politicizes the attitude of Stallone as Rocky when he asks a former commanding officer who wants him to return to Vietnam, "This time, do we get to *win?*" Rocky/Rambo is the kind of guy who takes a straightforward approach to effort: he believes in a triumphant return on his investments of time and energy. He wants to win.

But who doesn't? Granted, some sports movies such as *Field of Dreams* often treat "winning" sentimentally. But is the value of "winning" itself simplistic? Because some movies misrepresent it, does that make "winning" invalid? Does "winning" mean conquest and dominance, or fulfilling an urge to excellence? It depends on one's definition of winning, doesn't it? Or how society defines it. Or, rather, *who* defines it for society, and whether or not one does so in ways that appeal to fellow citizens.

Sports movies will be with us for years to come; the real issue is how intelligently they will present the urge to win. Intellectual critics who dismiss all sports movies and their mythmaking out of hand fail to understand how vital the best of these movies are in redefining and reintegrating winning and other values in life. One reason we have lost our sense of balance about the place of sports in schools and national life is the fact that too much of the country wants baseball without brains, and too much wants brains without baseball (hence the more general loss in the death of Bart Giamatti). Without such voices, we are doomed to a dialog of the deaf between blind faith and knee-jerk disbelief, conservative credulity and hip irony about winning, formulaic reassertions of old myths and cynical "anti-myth."

In truth, the opposite of a myth is *not* an anti-myth. Anti-myth complements myth; it turns heads tails, it merely inverts heroic formulas. Myths are about winning; anti-myths losing; they're both on the same simplistic valence. Anti-myths are simply an ironist's way of dissenting from convention with a new (and equally imprisoning) set of conventions (see chapter 11, "Irony"). To be sure, "anti-mythic" sports films are rare; even the pessimistic *Raging Bull* has deep sympathy for its central character and respect for his athletic efforts. But consider the source of *The Natural* in Malamud: the main reason for the allusions to the old heroic myth was to show—as in any doctrinaire piece of modernism—that the old myths were dead. The film was recipe heroism, the book recipe irony. And both recipes poison.

Central to both was simplification about sports heroism. The movie equates it with winning and wearing halos. The book defines it as recognition of how great we *no* longer are; modern heroes are losers. Name one in modern literature who isn't. Malamud's Hobbs must take the bribe because there is no god but Irony (see chapter 11). But as *Chariots of Fire* and some other movies show, the answer to one orthodoxy is not another dogmatism.

Closer to reality, more strenuously wrought, is the down-to-earth remythologizing in *Eight Men Out*, *Bull Durham*, and *Everybody's All-American*: games are wonderful, winning is fun, but it is not everything, and life goes on beyond the world of sporting myth once games are over. Our best filmmakers are too realistic to swallow the old myths; still, they do not play intellectually trendy anti-mythic games. They provide something as old-fashioned as Aristotle's golden mean: compete, for goodness' sake, but remember other goods besides winning. If you want to get our Rockys and Rambos to read and think, this is the way. The ancient Greeks knew this; why is it so many of us seem to have forgotten?

6

Home

E.T., phone home.

—*E.T.: The Extraterrestrial* (1982)

Y ou know the face: sour, old, fleshy, mustached, mounted on top of a massive, muscular body. He's been in the outdoors, you'd reckon, by the ruddy cheeks, weathered skin, and—when you hear his voice—broad Western drawl. "Quaker Oats," he says as he eats breakfast cereal. "It's the right thing to do."

No face more represents the renewed value American culture placed on home in the 1980s. It's Wilford Brimley, one of the best-known supporting actors of the decade, a grandfather in *Cocoon*, other films, and TV's *Our House*—where he is almost a father in a family that has lost its own. Brimley's is the sage face of moral authority. He knows a thing or two, you see, he's been around a while. He knows not just the right things to eat, but *do*. He's not mad, just emphatic: he wants you to *do* Quaker oatmeal. *Do* —not as in "let's do lunch" (one of them new-fangled, city-slicker phrases), but as in *"do* it," a (whatchamacallit) moral imperative. Thou shalt *do* Quaker oatmeal. You better, by golly.

In nearly every movie role, Brimley embodies a solid down-home, "goshdarn" honesty. "Old-fashioned sincerity," screenplays would scream, and directors would respond, "Get Brimley!" Gradually, by design or accident, Brimley became an icon of all-American authenticity. He wasn't no hero, mind you; hell, no; he'd just never steer you wrong. In *The China Syndrome* (1979), he plays a friend of whistle-blower Jack Lemmon, and can't mouth power company lies after his murder. In *Absence of Malice* (1981), he steals the show as a senior Justice Department lawyer who straightens out its unethical Miami office. In

Tender Mercies (1983) he is a road agent whom all musicians trust; in
The Stone Boy (1984) and *Country* (1985), a grandfather who helps
younger generations cope with tragedy. In *End of the Line* (1987) he's
a grandfather again; he works as the last Ozark railroad engineer until
rendered obsolete by new technologies run by distant corporate
smoothies.

It's no accident that Brimley's star rose during the grandfatherly
Reagan presidency. One of our emphases is youth, to be sure: we live
in an age of baby boom, of stroller gridlock, where Jennifer, Jessica,
Jason, and Joshua inherit the mall. But it wasn't only Russia that worked
by gerontocracy in the early eighties. The old slogans of dissent—"Don't
trust anyone over thirty," "the generation gap"—had gone with the
wind. In politics the result was an elderly president *most* popular,
perhaps, among the *very* young; in movies, the result was a new generational harmony around the hearth. Brimley was one of its most visible
symbols.

If anyone was born to play such a role, it is Brimley. No actor more
embodies the myth of a lost continent of America, a place in our myths
called Lost Integrity. His whole manner defines sharp but homey rectitude. "I may not look smart," his grumpy landmass of a face says.
"But just try to slip one past me!" "Quaker Oats," you hear in your
mind again, "It's the right thing to do." Suddenly you wonder: *right*,
as in *not* left?

Neo-Traditionalism

Brimley won *Advertising Age*'s Presenter of the Year award in 1989 for
his Quaker Oats and other homey commercials. It was apt. Domestic
images dominated the decade in ads, on TV, and in movies from *Terms
of Endearment* (1983) to *Cry in the Dark* (1988), *Ordinary People* (1980) to
Baby Boom (1987). The media luxuriated in recovering all sorts of "basic"
values after their loss in the 1970s: family, stability, roots, heritage,
oatmeal, individual retirement accounts—in a word, "home."

Anxiety about "home" saturated the 1980s. Some of our homes were
revealed as savage hells of spouse and child abuse. Some of our deepest
anxieties were embodied in the vast numbers of homeless. Contrary
to Robert Frost, home became a place where, when you had to go there,
they didn't have to take you in. Despite—or because of—these horrific
images, the value of home seemed to be stressed as rarely before. "Come
home, America," the Democratic party pleaded during the last stages
of the war in Vietnam; the slogan didn't win national elections,

but still articulated a need for finding peace and quiet after an era of social and political turmoil. Home meant good-bye to the antihome 1960s. Some Americans even preferred travel only as accidental tourists.

Domesticity broke out all over. In the early eighties, the *New York Times* started its *Home* section, and other major newspapers expanded home coverage. Big marriages came back, and even Hugh Hefner got hitched. Besides fancy domed stadiums and theme-park sports complexes, baseball parks in Baltimore and Chicago were planned along "neo-traditionalist" lines; Wrigley Field's comfy texture even survived lights. One of the best art books of the decade (Witold Rybcinski's *Home: The Short History of an Idea* [1985]) explored the long evolution of desire for and decorating of a pleasant home of one's own. Indeed, Rybcinski noted that architects, especially when armed with modernist assault designs, had slighted a basic element in homes: an owner's comfort. He actually liked Victorian houses, and later built one for himself. On PBS, Bob Vila made a TV career repairing half of New England's homes.

New words were invented to cover related trends: people didn't just *go home* after work; they *cocooned* as *couch potatoes*. The whole culture seemed intent on designing *a new cocoon* —echoing, not by accident perhaps, Brimley movies about young and older earthlings joining with benign E.T.s to make a home together (*Cocoon* [1985 and its sequel, 1988]). It was the right thing to do.

What did this all signify? Some critics in film journals (see "Notes," p. 205, middle) write as if images of happy home life on screen were "right"—as in a dangerous, even "reactionary" way—and as if media emphasis on home cloaks a conservative agenda to get people (particularly women) back in line. They have a field day spotting the ways in which even the best movies about home skirt some central, difficult issues; such superficiality, they claim, is necessary to avoid looking at the ways that homes can go bad.

Granted, recent movies ain't Eugene O'Neill; if you use our best drama as a standard of measure, such films are sitting ducks for potshots. But does this mean any positive image of home life on screen must be superficial or "right" as in "reactionary"? An alternative term from advertising is *neo-traditional*—implying a return to home, but with more flexible arrangements in careers, child care, and housework. Which is more accurate? Were movies and other media encouraging a return to the home in order to imprison people, or to reflect their search for new ways of keeping home?

Home Movies

Television, always a mirror to the audience watching it, had been stuffed silly with homey images ever since *Ozzie and Harriet* and *Leave It to Beaver.* In the eighties, it continued to be dominated by images of home. But new sitcoms have been more spicy. On some, women have become equal breadwinners with men; roles are more flexible and races more represented. *Cagney and Lacey, Roseanne, The Cosby Show, Family Ties, Kate and Allie,* or *thirtysomething* all provide images of home life that are less formulaic than in the past—in a word, more hip. A classic late eighties' commercial for United Airlines featured a businesswoman flying to a power lunch in a big city, then flying back home in time to meet her young daughter just getting out of school. Sometimes, being homey did not mean being a domestic slave; in some media, at least, women could have it all. Homes may have been the right thing to make, but there seemed more right ways of making them.

Movies about home—or rather our new set of "home" movies—present a more complicated set of images than television. At first glance, at least, their sheer number impresses—with works on children (from *Kramer vs Kramer* [1979] to *Parenthood* [1989]); parents and grandparents (from *Trip to Bountiful* [1985], to *Cocoon*); friends (from *Stand by Me* [1986] to "brat pack" opera like *St. Elmo's Fire* [1985]); and fathers and sons (from *Missing* [1982] to *Misunderstood* [1984]). Indeed, from Hoffman to Lemmon to Hackman to Gleason, hardly a major actor did not play Daddy during the decade.

Of course, many father-son films are often made with money in mind: if both actors are mature, such movies provide a way, like the buddy film, for pairing two stars in lead roles and appealing to audiences *across* generations (e.g., Sean Connery and Harrison Ford in *Indiana Jones and the Last Crusade* [1989]). Even Eddie Murphy used a "father figure" (Richard Pryor) in *Harlem Nights* (1989).

Still, too many of the movies about home were too earnest to be dismissed as mere commercial ventures. Even "hip" maverick filmmakers joined the trend: witness John Huston (*The Dead* [1987]) and Woody Allen, whose *September* (1987) replayed the mother-daughter conflict in *'Night Mother* (1986). Allen also focused on family in *Another Woman* (1988), *Radio Days* (1989), and the much better *Hannah and Her Sisters* (1986).

Sisterhood was powerful in *Big Business* (1988) and *Crimes of the Heart* (1986) but brothers remained top draws. In newspapers at Christmas, 1988, Schwarzenegger and De Vito (*Twins*) stared across pages at Hoffman and Cruise (*Rain Man*), a marketing version of tag-team wrestling for most appealing long-lost brothers title. Earlier that fall *Dominick and Eugene* had appeared, and in 1987 the brother-sister *Light of Day*. The formula for every film set of twins (brothers or sisters) is as old as ancient comedy; reunited families have been a staple of drama since. But even Polonius might be impressed by the degree to which we have been "harping on" daughters, brothers, and even *Cousins* (1989).

Consider eighties' Oscars, where "home movies" dominated, with three Best Pictures (*On Golden Pond* [1981], *Terms of Endearment*, and *Rain Man*); two fathers as Best Actors (Henry Fonda in *Pond*, Robert Duvall in *Tender Mercies* [1983]); and six daughters, wives and/or mothers as Best Actresses (Sissy Spacek in *Coal Miner's Daughter* [1980], Katharine Hepburn in *Pond*, Shirley MacLaine in *Terms*, Meryl Streep in *Sophie's Choice* [1982], Sally Field in *Places in the Heart* [1985], Geraldine Page in *Trip to Bountiful* [1986], and Cher in *Moonstruck* [1987]). In addition, numerous Best Supporting Actor and Actress awards went to performers in a variety of family roles. Of course, players in such roles had won Oscars before, but rarely so frequently—a testament not only to trendiness but also to the emotional power of the "home" theme, at least for audiences. In 1989, with awards mostly going to *Rain Man* and *Accidental Tourist* (see below), the Oscar broadcast shamelessly reveled in homeyness, with presentations from Hollywood couples (Goldie Hawn and Kurt Russell), spouses (Demi Moore and Bruce Willis), and expecting parents (Melanie Griffith and Don Johnson).

Such displays were manipulative but also revealing of how widespread the need for reaffirming home had become. Indeed, anxiety about family life was so pervasive you can even find it in science fiction. In two eighties' time-machine films, *Back to the Future* (1985) and *Peggy Sue Got Married* (1986), family relations provide the central theme, and plots hinge around the possibility, dread or desired, of undoing them. Even in a horror variant like *Aliens* (1986), the family theme is present when Sigourney Weaver becomes a mother symbol, a feminine and feminist Rambo-like protector of young children against space monsters.

Home and the need for a good mother saturate the work of the sci-fi master, Steven Spielberg, whose treatment of home goes far beyond the pathetic yearning he put into the mouth of E.T. Spielberg's human homes start broken; the plot of many of his films involves, in some way, the reconstruction of the hearth. E.T., for example, is a healing force for Elliot because he compensates for an absent father, who has separated from the mother (Dee Wallace). In Spielberg's *Close Encounters of the Third Kind* (1977), two homes are broken up, but mothers or mother symbols work to reunite all: a baby stolen by extraterrestrials is reunited with his mother (Melinda Dillon) at the end; meanwhile, a father from a second home (Richard Dreyfuss) enters into the maternal womb of the gigantic, extraterrestrial "mother ship." Spielberg's earth homes are always detailed with loving affection: they are cluttered with games, pizzas, sodas, and "cool" appliances teenagers love to play with; you can almost read the movies as self-portraits of the director as a young tinkerer. No filmmaker today is more nostalgic about home (even in *Empire of the Sun* [1987]); no director knows better that home is the right place to *do*.

Or consider again the pathetic, "E.T., phone home." It was a lost little creature's agrammatical explanation of what he had to do to survive. Perhaps on a larger scale, it was a reflection of American culture's sense of being lost and needing home. But the phrase sounds—read another way—like a moral imperative too.

"Git Me a Toddler"

Consider another moral imperative about home: this, appropriately, from a film by two brothers, Joel and Ethan Coen, the directing/producing team of the camp comedy *Raising Arizona*. An infertile couple played by Holly Hunter and Nicolas Cage plot to kidnap a baby from a group of recent quintuplets. After approaching their home, Cage cannot quite go through with it and retreats to Hunter who is ready to escape in the getaway car. The babies are too cute to steal, he pleads. "Hi," she seethes with mad maternal passion, "Go on in there and git me a toddler!"

"Git me a toddler": few moral imperatives seemed stronger in the 1980s. *Baby Boom* (1987) was the title not of one film but a nursery full: *Adventures in Babysitting, Three Men and a Baby* (both 1987), *She's Having a Baby, The Good Mother, A Cry in the Dark* (all 1988), and *Parenthood* (1989). The first danger sign actually came in *Micki and Maude* (1983), where Dudley Moore has babies by *two* women at once. Of multiple pregnancy and bigamy there are other examples—indeed, one is the most surprising of all (see *The Last Temptation of Christ* in chapter 12, Religion).

Why all this harping on childbearing? One cause is naked marketing by demography: like TV, films ached to hold a mirror up to the audience. When *Ghostbusters II* (1989) used the "baby prop" (and Bill Murray pretended to like one), you knew the trend had plenty *not* serious about it. The audience that watched was undergoing two epidemics of fertility: one among folks in their twenties, having children more or less according to schedule; another by the large number of people in their thirties who had delayed settling down, the original Baby Boomers (born between 1946 and 1955), procreating Baby Boom II. For them, having a baby was a big thing—something not taken as the course of nature, but an option deliberately chosen (and therefore worth talking about) after a careerism or sixties-style soul-searching. So, many dawdled over their infants; so, films and TV aped them and reaped the profits.

But money is only one explanation. Babies were valuable on screen because babies had become so valuable to many Americans, including many filmmakers. Teenpix director John Hughes made *She's Having a Baby* (1988) as a semiautobiography on his first experience as a father. Movies may concern extraterrestrials, but they aren't made by them, and once in a while simply reflect slices of real American lives. As production notes for *Parenthood* (1989) said, the plot was "familiar territory for all concerned" in making the film; the director, producer, and screenwriter "are raising fourteen children between them." Half of Hollywood seemed pregnant in 1989. One reason for *thirtysomething* was mimesis.

Commercially intended, autobiographical, or both, the new home movies also touched on values both ancient and modern. Their first lesson echoed the moral imperative in Genesis: replenish the earth. Indeed, in this context, "git me a toddler" is a suspicious-sounding phrase: did the makers of *Raising Arizona* mean "git" to pun on "grab" or "get" as the "beget" of the Bible? The film played with religious reasons for having children, and closed with an ironic, ambivalent fantasy of Cage and Hunter as grandparents of a Mormon clan in Utah. As the Coens imply, religion is one of our primary reasons to value such "getting." Movies about babies may have indirectly reflected and furthered a return to religious values in the 1980s, or at least a religious emphasis on childbearing (and related suspicion of feminism).

But baby films also gave power to new secular slogans about motherhood. The seventies anguished over population growth, the eighties forgot environmental concerns and checked the "biological clock." Films frequently alluded to the pressure young career women feel to have babies—in or outside of wedlock—while time allowed: *The Big Chill* (1983) made this a key plot element.

Sadly, most films about having babies, or raising children, have been distressingly shallow. The big hits involve cheap humor through role reversal, as in *Three Men and a Baby* (1987). Films showed fathers learning to play a stronger role in child raising (*Kramer vs Kramer*) but at the expense of mother. The babies were viewed with cutesy sentimentality; diapering became a comic-adventure—for the men or ex-single women who get to do it; real mothers were hardly ever seen. In *Baby*

Boom, the little one never ages. As Molly Haskell writes, "Movies haven't created the baby craze, but they've helped to fixate it at its most appealing and photogenic moment, when babies are babies, not children, not people, not human beings with a full array of needs."

One of the few movies that skirted honesty about the difficulties of having children was *Parenthood*—an uneven work crowded with too many stories, too much slapstick, and still a bit more attention on men (Steve Martin, Jason Robards, and Tom Hulce) than women (Dianne Wiest and Mary Steenbergen). A tougher one was *Mask* (1984) where emphasis falls equally on a teenage son's disfigurement and a mother's loving, strong-minded determination to help him handle it. *Mask* could have been a sentimental handicap film, a TV movie of the weak. Its strength—and the sterling acting by Cher as one tough but needy momma—was all too rare.

The Death of Romance

There is an even darker side to the baby and children movies: what they say about the present state of relations between adults. Central to all new home movies is the value placed on family, but not sexual love. Family love does not include much romance, and its dominance in the eighties reflected a change from the romanticism of the immediate past. In the sixties, a popular song told us, "What the world needs now is love, sweet love"; in the eighties, films instead sang, "Home, sweet home."

Love *interest* of course continues to dominate films, but not romance in the grand old manner. No decade was more dry of love stories than the 1980s. Gone were the sublime if often brief encounters of the sixties—*Doctor Zhivago, Romeo and Juliet,* even *Love Story.* Their closest parallel is *Out of Africa,* in which a great white lion hunter (Robert Redford) cannot give up the joys of being single. On TV's *Beauty and the Beast,* a woman found it easier to love a lion than a man. In *Splash* (1984), Tom Hanks had one of the decade's better loves—with a mermaid; in *Making Mr. Right* (1988), Ann Magnuson loves an android.

One-to-one relations between the sexes saturate many recent films; but they don't bring anyone to any heights; they aren't seen as all that *valuable.* In *Peggy Sue Got Married* or *Everybody's All-American,* women consider undoing marriages; in *Just between Friends* (1986), *Fatal Attraction* (1987), and *Falling in Love* (1984), marriages are ruined (or almost ruined) by adulteries, which lead to no real, lasting satisfaction, or involve mortal danger. Unusual loves blossom: in *Tootsie* (1983), in drag; in *Personal Best* (1980), *Making Love* (1982), and *Lianna* (1984), in homosexuality. Sometimes singles make it, as in *Murphy's Romance* (1985); but nobody (especially in the audience) was "swept away." Two good love stories involve handicaps *(Children of a Lesser God* [1986]) or comic disfigurement *(Roxanne* [1987]); in both, emphasis is only partly on the love relationship. As noted, the best "handicapped" love story involved mother and son in *Mask* (1985). Family values are so strong that they literally kill the romance between Kathleen Turner and Jack Nicholson in *Prizzi's Honor* (1985).

In the homey eighties, romanticism is out, family stability in. Audiences were so starved for a happy story between sexual equals they flocked to light fare such as *When Harry Met Sally* . . . (1989), which traces the rocky road of romance (between Meg Ryan and Billy Crystal), and only manages a happy ending after the heroine proclaims her hatred of the hero. As Billy Crystal says, "The sex thing gets in the way" of friendship; in *Dangerous Liaisons* (1989), it means war. Eighties' films emphasize the value of affection across generations, not love within them.

Some films depicted the dark side of emphasis on home and affection across generations: incest, abuse, or at least sexual manipulation. *Private Lessons* (1987) merely exploited this; some recent films took it seriously as in the prototype import *Get out Your Handkerchief* (1978), *Shoot the Moon* (1981), *Blue Velvet* (1986), and *Smooth Talk* (1985). These films suggest that one result of our apparent despair over equal heterosexual relationships may be the increasing number of incidents of sexual abuse of children. If films mirror society, one price for our loss of romanticism about love within generations may be perversity between them.

Even a sweet fantasy like *Big* (1988) played lightly with an oedipal subtext, the erotic attraction between a young man and older woman. The opening of *Kramer vs Kramer* also contains strong, romantic oedipal imagery, with Meryl Streep in pietàlike fashion bidding good-bye to her sleeping son before she leaves her home and marriage with Dustin Hoffman. In Spielberg, as noted, the strongest love is always *across* generations.

Cross-generational love is obvious in films about mothers and sons *(Mask, Eleni)* and fathers and daughters *(On Golden Pond, Cookie* [1989], the superbly begun *Coal Miner's Daughter,* and the thoroughly superb *Tender Mercies).* The opening minutes of *Daughter,* focusing on Sissy Spacek and her father (Levon Helm), are pure magic and about as good as any American film gets in the 1980s. In the latter movie, Robert Duvall faces down the irony and pain of losing his only daughter (Ellen Barkin) just after he has begun again to get his life in order. Every ounce of sentiment in the film is earned; every feeling it evokes has backbone.

But the big winner—no accident in a male-dominated industry—is the love (often after years of fighting) between fathers and sons. *Kramer vs Kramer* begot *The Great Santini* (with Robert Duvall [1979]), which begot *Ordinary People* (with Donald Sutherland [1980]), which begot *Missing* (with Jack Lemmon [1981]), *Misunderstood* (with Gene Hackman), *Harry and Son* (with Paul Newman [1984]), *Nothing in Common* (with Jackie Gleason [1986]), and comedies such as *Back to the Future* or the clones, *Vice Versa* and *Like Father, Like Son* (both 1988). Although without direct political reference, many of these films show fathers and sons making peace, not war, and may reflect a reaction to specific generational stresses of the Vietnam War years.

But they may also have deeper roots. As scholars have shown, the rapprochement between father and son figures is an old theme in American culture; in our great novels, it often occurs at the expense of women, especially mother figures (see "Notes," p. 205, top). Recent father-son films update the tradition of backlash against women, perhaps spurred by the growth of feminism. Consider *Kramer vs Kramer* again: the whole film is shaped as a redemption of Hoffman as he responds to Streep's departure by becoming a caring father. In *Ordinary People*, Donald Sutherland undergoes a similar rapprochement with son Timothy Hutton—and the wicked-witch mother played by Mary Tyler Moore is expelled. Both films don't seem to be able to affirm fatherhood (a good thing) without attacking mothers too (see "Heroines"). As in so many male "buddy films," sadly, increased sensitivity between fathers and sons doesn't translate into affection for women.

Male Bonding

One of the best father-son movies at least included affection for a woman, perhaps because it derived from one, *The Accidental Tourist* (1988). Based on Anne Tyler's novel, it combines the prevalent father-son theme with a need for home that almost takes the extreme form of agoraphobia—fear of the outside world. The fear was almost palpable in the cautious, careful screenplay. Indeed, the basic aesthetic problem of the movie was its lame pacing: after a while, it was hard to watch star William Hurt emote on remote. The film was directed by Lawrence Kasdan, who also made *The Big Chill* (plus *Body Heat* [1980] and *The Right Stuff* [1983]—no masterpieces, but good blends of language and character on screen). Kasdan co-wrote the screenplay, which suffered, ironically, from being too faithful to Tyler's book.

Kasdan works in different genres, but likes the home theme (see *The*

Big Chill, below). His hero, Macon Leary (Hurt), is a paradox: he writes books on travel, but hates going abroad at all. He is "leery" of life: cool, distant, watchful. He writes "accidental tourist" series, tailored for business travelers who wish they had never left home and want minimal contact with places they visit, especially overseas; on Champs Élysées, they search out a McDonald's. The film's initial scenes artfully catch the comedy of Tyler's send-up of a certain kind of American abroad. But beneath the comedy there's the deep anxiety of the 1980s: between Vietnam and terrorism, the urge to "come home, America."

For Leary, retreat into the home follows loss of its center, his only son who was murdered while away at camp (an episode dealt with both in novel and film only in flashback). Leary becomes absorbed in the loss, so affectless and morbid that he drives his wife (Kathleen Turner) away from him. Alone and depressed, he retreats back to his original family (two eccentric brothers and sweetly daffy sister, played by Amy Wright), one of those groups of ever wacky siblings from below the Mason Dixon line that show up in eighties' home movies such as Horton Foote's *1918* (1984), *On Valentine's Day* (1986), or Beth Henley's *Crimes of the Heart* (1986) and *Miss Firecracker* (1989). Like them, *Accidental Tourist* serves up Southern fried fear of the universe.

Even Macon's recovery is tied to home. He only comes alive again after meeting and (to the degree he is capable) courting a second woman, the flamboyant animal "hotel" owner and dog trainer, Muriel Pritchett (Geena Davis). Muriel is vulgar, abrupt, unpredictable, demanding—everything Macon and his wife are not. But she finally hooks him with an eighties' gesture, warning him that he better not make promises to her kid (about taking him places and teaching him things) that he doesn't intend to keep. Such is the eighties' rebetrothal: vows to the children count most. The real love story that follows is between Macon and the boy, not Macon and Muriel. For Macon, the whole plot of the movie is not quite "git me a toddler," but it's close. Trust a woman of Anne Tyler's gifts to say, gently, men hear biological clocks too.

Rain Man sums up the antiromantic drive toward home. Like *Accidental Tourist*, it's another bit of asexual male bonding; it fuses several genres, turning its two brothers both into best buddies and mutual father and son. One of the brothers is Raymond, an autistic savant—a single-note performance played so well by Dustin Hoffman that one loses awareness he is *acting*. Hoffman had autism down cold, adding one of its rarer traits, sweet innocence and a singular cerebral gift. In *Rain Man* it is math, with which Hoffman impresses brother Tom Cruise, a West Coast foreign car salesman fast with deals, women, and life in general. At first Cruise is frustrated by Raymond after he takes him from an institutional home in Cincinnati and starts a cross-country trek; but Cruise learns to be less tough, less conventionally masculine, and more open and sensitive in his brother's company; Raymond the Rain Man softens his steely surface. The film loses gas somewhere out West. Still, in Nevada, it provided one of the best images of emotional fulfillment in any eighties film: two brothers, dancing in a hotel above the chintzy lights of Las Vegas. The scene was echoed, albeit with significant variations, in *The Fabulous Baker Boys* (1989). Dancing with your siblings in the 1980s: it's the right thing to do.

Sixties-something, II

Emphasis on family in part represents a "right" turn or reaction against the turbulence of recent American history. But the new home movies also reflect something deeper. At their best they creatively attempt to make sense out of the past and to reconcile the diverse heritage left us by the fifties and sixties.

Consider the clash of fifties' and sixties' home images. Problems at home are minimal if *Father Knows Best;* if disasters occur when you *Leave It to Beaver,* Ward and June will straighten things out. Housewives are homebodies, until Mary Tyler Moore escapes from the home confines in *The Dick Van Dyke Show* and gets one with a career of her own. "She's Leaving Home," the Beatles declared in the late sixties; Dustin Hoffman follows suit in *The Graduate,* and Jack Nicholson in *Five Easy Pieces.* In *Alice Doesn't Live Here Anymore* (1974), Scorsese concurred. By 1978, you had to be ready to live up to your potential as *An Unmarried Woman,* even if it meant *Looking for Mr. Goodbar.* Romance was good for you—with the proper stranger. Marriage suffered; but not affairs. In *Divorce American Style* (1967), *Loving* (1970), *A Touch of Class* (1973), men left women and women left men: one had to focus on *Starting Over* (1979).

The most intriguing couples of the sixties and early seventies are not husband and wife at home, but the cult heroes and cultural outlaws *Bonnie and Clyde* or *Harold and Maude.* A trio bedhopped in *Shampoo;* a quartet bedshared in *Bob and Carol and Ted and Alice.* From fifties' homes where everyone found fulfillment, everyone went out "on the road again." To the counterculture, home was a dirty four-letter word—a convention maintained only in some terminally Bohemian English films today. In America, even divorced couples won't leave home anymore (as in *War of the Roses* [1989]); they should call Bob Vila and subdivide.

Recent films have reemphasized the value of home partly in reaction to the conventions of sixties' dissent. Of course, this has "conservative" elements, and is allied to broader movements in American culture and politics—or perhaps even health problems, such as AIDS. Still, it is a mistake to reduce—as progressives often do—the values of "home" mythology to mere reaction (see "Notes," p. 205, middle). The best of today's home movies attempt to get beyond the stale debate between the conservative fifties myths of an unbelievably happy home and the radical sixties and early seventies with their anti-myths of home as a prison.

The images and formulaic rhetoric of the "traditional home" and "nuclear family" do have conservative implications; their tried and true nature attests to how long they've been around. But just because the value of home has been presented in a clichéd fashion doesn't mean every home is a bad place to be. Because homes have been tenanted by a set of conservative myths doesn't mean that home can't be redefined more openly. To find a home seems a human instinct, having no political valence. In the best of the new home movies, filmmakers attempt to provide newer, more liberal images of home and the stability it provides. They reflect a larger, unconscious desire by Americans to synthesize the two mutually complementary half-truths of the fifties and sixties and an attempt to shape a whole truth: we need homes; we need freedom. How, these films ask, do we find the right balance?

Take that perfect transition piece between sixties' radicalism and eighties' conservatism, The Big Chill. The movie ostensibly concerns a reunion of mildly radical sixties' students; it also is a burial of their extremism, personified by the dead friend whose suicide brings the group together. In effect, he is *their past*. The film doesn't bid it a total good-bye; its message is that some sixties values can be preserved among small pockets of friends, especially when they convene in the home of the strongest couple, surrogate mom/dad Glenn Close and Kevin Kline.

In The Big Chill, a hip sense of homeyness conquers all. Kline provides one of the friends (William Hurt) insider stock tips—the kind of behavior later satirized in Wall Street. But in The Big Chill the value of the tip isn't in outlandish profit but camaraderie; it's done to help someone searching for a new start. Closer to the hearth, Close decides to help one of her friends (Mary Kay Place, playing a single lawyer who hears that old "biological clock" ticking away) in an unusual way as well. Close encourages Place to bed her husband Kline in order to get pregnant. Close's role here is opposite from Fatal Attraction, where she plays a career woman aiming at a hostile takeover of another's marriage. Nevertheless, the value systems of both movies are consistent. In The Big Chill, looseness with marriage vows is presented as acceptable for the same reason it is condemned later; in *The Big Chill* extramarital sex is okay if it promotes domestic tranquility and means bringing up baby. *The Big Chill* values sex and money, but also friends and toddlers.

The Big Chill displayed "hip" freedom with morals (perhaps too much for some tastes); still, its values centered around the hearth. Indeed, slick as it may have been, its synthesis of unconventional methods for attaining conventional ends foreshadows what the best recent meditations on home have been all about. These better screen treatments of home match broader rhythms in American society between the consolidation and self-confidence of the fifties and dissent and rejections of the sixties. But as *The Big Chill* indicates, the better movies about home in the eighties tried to find a middle ground. To a degree, this reflects a "right" or neoconservative mood in the country. It also reflects a desire to do more than *react* to the past; it may even represent something like learning from it.

Two Hip Homes

Consider *Moonstruck* (1987), a lighthearted but well-written example of growing recognition that a home is a hard but vital place to be. Cher is engaged to Danny Aiello, who leaves for Italy to see his dying mother; meanwhile, she falls in love with his brother (Nicolas Cage). She goes to the opera with him where she meets her father, out with his secret mistress, while her mother (Olympia Dukakis, Best Supporting Actress for her Mama Mia routine) is flirting, slightly, with a single professor. But at the end, of course, order is restored, father and mother are reconciled, home is preserved, and a new home, with Cher and Cage, is begun. Even Aiello is included: when he comes back, all are apprehensive, but he says he doesn't want to marry Cher anymore because his mother *didn't* die. "You're part of the family," he is told; indeed, the only reason he didn't join it more directly is because of *his* family. Family conquers all.

These patterns are hoary with age, and sexual infidelity has been the stuff of comedy since ancient times; mismatched partners, chaos from disrupted commitment, and final restoration of order spice Plautus, Shakespeare, Beaumarchais. *Moonstruck* has no exact contemporary reference to the clash of sixties' and eighties' values. Still, there is a night at *La Boheme*—an apt opera to suggest problems caused by romanticism. Other elements also position the film in the search of a hip home. "Do you love him?" Dukakis twice asks Cher. For Aiello, she answers "No, but he's a good man," and her mother rejoices, "Good, love them and they drive you crazy!" But when her mother asks whether she loves Cage, Cher answers, "Yes," and Dukakis despairs. The film implies she is half right, and so too is Cher for making a different decision than her conservative mother wants. Homes without romantic love might look safe, but defy nature by their squareness. The issue becomes—as many women's magazines attest—how to combine fun and fidelity. As Cage tells Cher, "Playing it safe is just about the most dangerous thing a woman like you could do." In the long run, moderate romanticism is the right thing to feel.

Cher also embodies hip and homey impulses in *Mask*, where counter-culture references give the search for a stable loving home more resonance. Her son (Eric Stoltz) needs her love and backing: with his disfigured face, he needs her support to negotiate school, adolescence, and possible rejection. But she too needs him: she indulges in drugs, she works "free-lance," she hangs out with Hell's Angels-type bikers. The movie celebrates the home mother and son make for each other—and the love they give—without sentimentalizing, and even without trying to make them resemble a "nuclear" family (despite the presence of Sam Elliot as Cher's biker boyfriend). Being together seems the "right" thing to do—not in a political but in a human, humane sense.

No actress of our time is better than Cher at mediating hipness and cocooning; she's all tough bluster, then suddenly, without going weak at the knees, believably tender. In real life, she likes to think of herself as a rebel; squareness bores her and provokes her into performing what she thinks of as antiauthoritarian gestures—e.g., the shock-effect getups, the wild, half-naked music videos. But she bakes a cake in *Mask*; it does not seem to lessen her free-spirited independence. I just wish it had been apple pie. That indeed would have been delicious.

Woody Allen Relaxes

A related movie also searches for the hip home: Woody Allen's *Hannah and Her Sisters* (1986), the best "home movie" of the 1980s because it addresses so many of the tensions in half-truths about home in an inclusive manner. Of all Woody Allen films, it also may be the easiest to take; the story is crisply told, with some of the best film editing of our time; the score, ranging from Bach to Bobby Short (in person) on jazz piano, is a delight; the screenplay is nicely lightened by Allen's restraint in making his own role, anxieties, and self-concern only half the story. The other half is women, often Allen's best subject.

The story of the sisters and the men who love them could be called "up from romanticism." One sister, Holly (Dianne Wiest, a Supporting Actress Oscar winner) is a sixties' survivor. Holly's a perennial would-be artist, part-time actress and (for cash) part-time caterer (with a fellow actress who steals parts and men from her). Eventually Holly realizes that she's a full-time "loser." In desperation, she tries writing, having to borrow money from her settled, married (yet successful) actress sister Hannah (Mia Farrow). Allen's character (a TV producer) had been married to Hannah, but, alas, he was sterile, unable to "git" her a toddler, and they got divorced. After the divorce, he dated Holly, a disaster due to their different tastes and her drug habit. Allen writes in a parallel plot: a third sister (Barbara Hershey)—living with an older artist contemptuous of the "bourgeois"—is being pursued by Hannah's current husband (Michael Caine, in a weak story line), who is looking for something more than his wife's "giving" nature.

The film questions the need for home and the ease of making one. It derives added depth from Hannah's parents (Maureen O'Hara and Lloyd Nolan) who are not always amiable or sweetly clichéd, and whose personalities raise the theme of caring for older people to a richer, more human level. Home is affirmed in *Hannah*—more persuasively because it shows that the course of a good one never did run smooth. The film is sentimental in a good sense: it shows that feelings for home and for freedom are hard to reconcile, but that maturity requires the effort to do so.

The film is framed by two Thanksgiving dinners a year apart, both warmly and affectionately portrayed, and shot in rich, earthy gold and brown colors; one signals the start of sexual chaos, the other the close. The year between allows for exploring the chance for romantic fulfillment. Peace around the hearth is won only by allowing for search; real fidelity, the film implies, is not easy, but can exist when happiness is sought, and fought for, on a level deeper than most clichés about the subject.

At the same time, Allen implies that romanticism must learn to look beyond the whim of the moment, and to reroot itself in understanding. The movie endorses the value of being hip *and* the importance of being earnest. The concluding scenes, when Allen and Wiest meet again and work through their prejudices about each other, provide a short case study in how two people can overcome the worst in their own makeup and see the best in one another. It does help that Allen and Wiest were in a movie, where second chances happen, even second chances with "getting" babies—as at the movie's end. But even endorsing the value of second chances implies one of Woody Allen's prime values in this film: patience. Obviously a reactionary; take him away.

Future Home Movies

Since Oedipus, home has been a staple of all drama, and family melodramas and comedies are not likely to stop coming now. At the turn of the nineties, with *She Devil, Immediate Family, Dad,* and *War of the Roses,* America's recent, especially intense preoccupation with the theme showed no sign of declining. Unfortunately, all four films conformed to predictable patterns, with two doses sweet and two sour. Even *War of the Roses* conformed to a simple formula, albeit ironic, in its elaborate and literal deconstruction of home.

From somewhere, one hoped for what we needed most: images of domesticity that provide new, more realistic, more truthful myths about home life. Movies don't have to be profound to do this; they do have to avoid the simplistically heartwarming clichés that make home life out to be a bowl of cherries. Dumb myths only provoke smarmy disbelief. But it seems at least that some moviemakers may be learning how to create sensible myths that do not lie about a darker side.

7

Environment

Who you gonna call?
—*Ghostbusters* (1984)

A rabbit hunches on a snowy hill over a frozen lake. A man walks over its rigid surface, snowshoed, backpacked, armed with a rifle. Only three colors exist: white, blue sky, and mute brown in the bare trees, rabbit, and obscure human figure. The only sound is the crunch of his snowshoes on the drifts. We focus in on the man; a furred hood masks his face, but he hears a slight sound: a distant "boom" like soft thunder miles away. We cut to the rabbit—he is motionless, as if hiding—then cut back again.

The man stops, puzzled, takes a few steps, then halts once more when the "boom" recurs. He can't make it out. But with his next step, *BOOM!* He plummets through the ice—all that time thawing underneath—and sinks to the lake bottom. Shedding backpack and rifle, he rises, then panics as he can't find the hole he fell through. The rabbit watches, silent, still, indifferent.

The scene is from Carroll Ballard's *Never Cry Wolf* (1983); despite its uneven plot, no movie in decades has caught wildness as freshly. It tells of a greenhorn biologist (Charles Martin Smith) who comes to the Yukon to study wolves to see what can be done about their attacks on caribou. The lake scene is crucial in his learning to understand the wilderness better: immersion underwater is a baptism in beauty and terror, and rebirth into a new identity.

Like all true environmentalists, Ballard and Canadian author Farley Mowat (whose book provided the source for the film) know that nature kills; only sentimentalists ignore the indifference in its beauty. But

Ballard and Mowat also know and stress the burden on the human species to do no *needless* killing. It's a fair burden, *Never Cry Wolf* implies. Just behold the man: he's armed, dangerous as no animal elsewhere in creation. And then, suddenly, he's struggling just to keep his head above water.

The scene gives bone-chilling renewal to some old clichés, literalizing how pride goes before a fall, dramatizing a new deck chair arrangement on the *Titanic*. No doubt director Ballard also meant it as a prophecy. After the *Exxon Valdez* oil spill in 1989, one wondered whether or not he wasn't at least partly on target.

Benign Neglect, I

The reception of *Never Cry Wolf*—far better than its makers expected—attests to the continuing value Americans placed on the environment in the 1980s. But early in the decade, nature seemed to be devalued, not just in politics, but even perhaps on screen.

Take *Ghostbusters*. It was not, of course, about pollution, but its best line seems to have reference to our consciousness of pollution problems: "He slimed me," Bill Murray complains, after being gloppily run over by an astral presence. But if the line co-opts environmental language, the movie itself *derides* environmental concern. The nominal villains are demons haunting the metropolis—from ancient Persia, we are told, for which you may want to substitute modern Iran. But worse than these spectral forces is the local villain—an administrator from, of all places, the Federal Environmental Protection Administration.

Ghostbusters Bill Murray, Dan Ackroyd, Harold Ramis are young, daring entrepreneurs who have a healthy, if eccentric, line of work. The EPA man is one of those darned pointy-headed, busybody governmental regulators who gets in the way of business enterprise. A classic nervous Nellie, he wants to knot up enterprise with environmental rules and regulations. Indeed, go deeper: he is more worried about their ghostbusting *lasers* (the high technology that President Reagan proposed for Star Wars) than the real enemy, an external one, terrorizing our citizens from an Evil Empire in the East. He's ready to sacrifice both profit and national security to red tape. Thank goodness that supercool Bill Murray used his one-liners to ridicule such a bureaucratic zealot into insignificance.

Ghostbusters was made for (and made enormous) profit. It was outrageously funny, not just with zingy jests but a well-crafted screenplay that made the most of arch nonsense about ancient Persian gods invading New York. Still, the movie also reflects one aspect of its times in a more substantial way. Like Bill Cosby's failed *Leonard Part VI* (1987), which relied on animal rights activists/terrorists as villains, *Ghostbusters* aims half of its wit at environmentalists, whose political power, if not numbers, declined in the early and mid-1980s. *Ghostbusters* is a wacky reflection of the triumph of deregulation.

The EPA plot line in *Ghostbusters* also reflects what appears to be a relative decline of environmental values in American politics in the Reagan era. True, the 1980s yielded the best films ever about interaction between man and animals—not only the vibrant *Never Cry Wolf* (1983) but also the sporadically moving *Gorillas in the Mist* (1988). One small, successful "art" documentary—the oddly titled but beautifully shot *Koyaanisqatsi* (1983)—expressed the most forceful discontent with civilization since Chaplin's *Modern Times*. In the eighties, movies about the environment are sincere, but infrequent. Their heroes are embattled cranks, their outcomes pessimistic; environmental assassination becomes one of the key plot lines (cf. *Silkwood* and *Gorillas in the Mist*). In the seventies, movies with environmental values were more pervasive, and had crowd-pleasing endings with sentimental easy-to-identify-with heroes, as in *Jeremiah Johnson* (1973), *Wilderness Family* (1975), *Further Adventures of the Wilderness Family* (1978), *Mountain Family Robinson* (1979), *Watership Down* (1978), *The Black Stallion* (1979), and *The Life and Times of Grizzly Adams* (1976).

The best recent films about man's relation to nature were begun long before the eighties (*Quest for Fire, Greystoke*), or are based on books (like Mowat's and Jean Auel's *Clan of the Cave Bear*) or projects (Dian Fossey's field studies depicted in *Gorillas in the Mist*) begun in the previous decades. The animal rights film *Roar* was released in 1982, but made almost ten years earlier. Eighties movies with strong environmental values, that is, seem to reflect the continuing half life of an earlier consciousness. They are strong *minority* reports in the Reagan era.

Other contrasts with seventies filmmaking are also striking. The noble savage pervaded seventies films, with *Little Big Man* (1969), *A Man Called Horse* (1970), its sequel (1974); TV films such as *Ishi: The Last of His Tribe* (1978) or *I Will Fight No More Forever* and imports such as Academy Award winner *Dersu Uzala* (both 1975). In the 1980s the South African cult-hit *The Gods Must Be Crazy* (1984) alone strongly embodied the theme. In the early 1970s, "natural" was popular; ads for every beer, cereal, and hair coloring claimed its aura. But there was no "Earth Day" in the eighties, only a belated "Planet of the Year" *Time* cover in 1988. Of course, throughout the decade, environmental activism survived, or picked up when James Watt proposed expanding roads and concessions at national parks. But in general environmentalism was in retreat. Fuel efficiency was out; stretch limos in. Energies in conservation were directed less to nature than culture; fine-looking woodwork replaced wood stoves. Movies reflected these concerns, from townhouse-renovation comedies like *The Money Pit* (1986) to the frequent use of Laura Ashley patterns in production design. Nature was popular—at least on a wall.

Perhaps these changes in emphasis or the relative decline in environmental values on film made little difference. But movies can educate, and loss of one subject narrows their hidden curriculum. In this case, the loss of visibility is more dangerous than usual. As environmentalists warn, even small decreases in vigilance can be dangerous: ecological problems have a way of festering slowly, unnoticed, until their full danger emerges and preventive action is impossible. Not thinking about ecological threats is another mode of arranging deck chairs on the *Titanic*.

Movies alone weren't guilty of failing to think about the environment: the subject declined in general throughout the media. Neither reporters nor filmmakers put their fingers in the air to check which way the wind is blowing. But they did breathe in the new national political atmosphere. The political victors of the 1980s favored freedom for business, which meant getting rid of federal red tape, which meant deregulation, which—intentionally or not—meant fewer restraints on practices that could be polluting and dangerous to consumers. President Reagan governed nature according to his old sounding off on GE Theater: "Remember, at General Electric, progress is our most important product." Appointees such as Watt at Interior or Anne Burford at EPA stressed the need for development and deregulation. Not by complete coincidence, movies such as *Airport* were out and *Airplane!* in.

Of course, filmmaking cycles have something to do with this: certainly by 1980 it would have been hard to make another *Airport* bomb. But changed attitudes toward the environment and technology on screen parallel trends outside film. The "disaster movie" genre, while exploitively sensational, in part reflected the seventies anxiety about runaway progress, as in *The Poseidon Adventure* or *The Towering Inferno*; at the end of the decade came Steve McQueen's *An Enemy of the People* (1977) and—in time for Three Mile Island—the much finer *The China Syndrome* (1979). In the eighties, only *Silkwood* (1983) successfully picks up their themes, and, despite its power and sass, pursues them only halfheartedly.

By osmosis, movies picked up and furthered the benign neglect of nature that characterized our politics and culture in the 1980s. For almost a decade, little was done to deal with environmental problems; decreased media and movie attention to the issues certainly did not help. By late summer, 1988, inattention to ongoing problems resulted in a kind of new man-made environmental layer—a compound of drought, global heating, syringes on beaches, excess ozone in our cities, and (in apt contrast) too little ozone at the poles. When the real slime hits the fan, "Who you gonna call?" Not Ghostbusters. Not Bill Murray.

Splendid Gizmos

Other shifts in values also reflect benign neglect of nature. In early and mideighties movies, the man-made environment was often the right place to be—acceptable enough; the real issue is *how much* to value *what* about it. Environmental extremists too often dismiss the value of cities and technology with a shrill know-nothing primitivism. Still, in the eighties, things often went to an opposite extreme: machines were beatified, or, as in R2D2 and C3PO, petted to death: cities were lovingly photographed (even their shabby down-and-out districts). Technology and urban areas can be beautiful; but their worship can also encourage dangerous complacency. When a culture high fives high tech and high rise, check out the safety exits.

Consider images of technology in 1980s movies. In the 1970s, machines often betray humans and cause disasters; in the 1980s, technology is supportive and pleasant to use and inhabit. Offices in eighties films are always equipped with a set of bright, inviting computers—with no questions asked about drain on the electrical supply, or effects on the eyes. If computers or robots malfunction, they do so innocently, even playfully (see *Short Circuit* and its sequel [1986 and 1988]) and end up finding out something wise that humans have missed. The computer in *War Games*, charmingly named after the child (Joshua) of its inventor, goes through multiple war-game scenarios and comes to see what is beyond the vision of its war-room programmers: nuclear war is unwinnable. In sci-fi, machines are always reliable, with spaceships routinely zipping across galaxies; the only danger is other spaceships. Sci-fi focuses less on environmental problems, as in the fine *Silent Running* (a 1971 yarn about attempts to keep earth's vegetation samples alive in outer space) than on the danger of evil meanies or an extra- or subterrestrial version of our old nemesis, the animal (*Aliens, The Deep, The Abyss,* etc.).

Besides machines, buildings also do well in films of the eighties. No one dies because of their defects; in *The Secret of My Success,* the roof is fine for jogging; in *Working Girl*, skyscrapers symbolize a secular grail; in *Hannah and Her Sisters*, urban architecture is treated as a kind of lyric poetry. The only danger that big buildings pose in eighties films is that terrorists might catch you there (*Die Hard* [1988]) and start an inferno by discharging weapons; the buildings themselves are basically safe.

Indeed, the early eighties spoofed anxiety about technology. *Airport* (1970) and its spin-offs in 1975 and 1979 or TV films such as *Crisis in Mid-Air* (1979), *Crash*, and *I Alone Escaped to Tell Thee* (both 1978) gave way to spoofs such as *Airplane!* (1980) and its sequel (1983). The disaster genre had precedents, fifties' airplane melodramas like *Zero Hour* or *The High and the Mighty*. Seventies' disaster movies extended such anxiety beyond air travel to more general anxiety about technology and progress. Spoofs on such anxiety may signify no more than a good laugh; in this case, they also seem to reflect an age in which, for a while, we thought all was—as President Reagan so often Freudian-slipped— "well."

The only eighties' movie about an airplane disaster was on television, where "serious" (if not moralistic) treatment of social issues found its home in the early 1980s. The film was *Flight #90: Disaster on the Potomac* (1984), which documented the Air Florida crash in Washington in 1983. The National Transportation Safety Board later determined that the crash, which killed almost ninety, was caused by failure to deice the wings after the plane had sat out on the runway in a raging snowstorm. On the black-box tapes of the doomed airplane, the captain and co-pilot were heard laughingly discussing whether or not they ought to deice the wings again before takeoff. Flippantly, the captain chuckled and joked that they should do it just to quiet the feds. As Bill Murray might say, those darn pointy-headed federal safety regulators—what killjoys!

The Very Big Apple

Cities were often seen as the right place to be in the eighties, in part because of their *real* environmental values: civilized cities often combine the best of man and nature. Woody Allen, for example, clearly loves New York's energy and pizzazz; he also finds ways of capturing its preserves of beauty. At his best—the little symphony of shots of urban architecture in *Hannah and Her Sisters*—he photographs odes to some of the best things ever built in the civilized world.

New York got a lion's share of screen attention in the early eighties, partly because of its place in national culture and long-standing role as a base of the entertainment industry. New York also naturally starred in movies about the financial business (*The Secret of My Success, Working Girl, Wall Street*). But most important was the astounding promotionalism of New York under showman/salesman/celebrity Ed Koch. Movies became a giant *"I LOVE NY"* poster as the city aggressively lured filmmakers inside its bounds by providing generous financial breaks and other incentives. No one ever accused Ed Koch of neglecting publicity: his "Mayor's Office for Film and Television" generated both income and good PR from a list of movies produced in New York scores of pages long. Even *The Verdict,* supposedly set in Boston, used New York interiors. Often you couldn't walk New York streets without fear of being mugged by movie crews. Too bad if you happened to live there.

There were greater dangers in this, especially in a romanticization of the city that made it look as if it were the only place to be. Central Park never looked so pastoral as in *Tootsie* (1983), *When Harry Met Sally . . .* (1989), or *Hannah and Her Sisters.* Indeed, *Manhattan* isn't just the title of one of Woody Allen's films; it's the center of his universe, exile from which is a fate worse than death. In *Annie Hall* (1977), the provinces are anti-Semitic; California is a vast wasteland; New Jersey is an area of garbage surrounded by weeds (*Broadway Danny Rose* [1984]); Brooklyn is a place to escape *from* (*Radio Days* [1987]), not to. At his worst, Allen is parochial, not cosmopolitan. What does he say to calm himself in *Hannah* after taking some tests for cancer? "Nothing is going to happen to you. You're in the middle of New York, surrounded by people and restaurants and traffic." Yikes.

It almost sounds like the plot of the ultimate New York movie, *My Dinner with Andre* (1983) a film whose sets included a subway and a restaurant. Oh, I know, that was the point; it was (theory had it) interesting to watch scenes sustained merely by lively conversation (especially from Andre, who had toured Tibet and the forests of Poland). We didn't get Tibet or Poland; we got Andre and the waiter (so much for scenic relief). Cineasts fluttered about how the film's static style defied action conventions. Maybe. Or maybe it was all the Emperor's new clothes.

The pervasiveness of such urban images is understandable; the problem was how they reinforced the slick glamour that the rich-and-famous and culturally pretentious eighties overdosed on. If New York solipsism wasn't bad enough, Hollywood has made things worse, with scores of movies that took daring looks at Southern California (the Blake Edwards opera, *Troop Beverly Hills, Beverly Hills Cop, Down and Out in Beverly Hills,* and several TV offerings; check out any film index for the dates of films with "Beverly Hills" in the title). Paul Mazursky, who made *Down and Out*, likes other places: an island in the Mediterranean (*The Tempest*) say, or Manhattan island in *Moscow on the Hudson* (where you see none of the Hudson but much of that eighties' in spot, Bloomingdale's). Some of these films have excellent comedic moments; geographically they amount to a screen version of the obnoxious *New Yorker* cartoon of America as a desert between Broadway and Malibu. They provide a celluloid version of the little columns about the comings and goings of filmmakers in *Variety:* "New York to LA, LA to New York."

The air gets even more constricted in other films set in cities, the large number of movies that glorified down-and-out urban neighborhoods. Soho and LA directors especially delighted in the trash of their petty bohemias. Consider *After Hours, Desperately Seeking Susan, Choose Me, To Live and Die in LA, Slaves of New York, Forever Lulu,* or the first part of *New York Stories*. With the unconventional conventionality of the avant-garde, these films tediously celebrate only one value, the joy of wrecks. Blight, their hip audiences are told, is beautiful.

There are, to be sure, some good reasons for focusing on downtown. The energy of the "scene" has always attracted directors; bohemian districts have often been the source of creative artistic energy; and many contemporary directors know of this firsthand as graduates of NYU's film school in Greenwich Village. Much of the work of NYU graduate Martin Scorsese (*Taxi Driver, After Hours,* for example), involves descent into the underside of urban life, but for a precise artistic reason: his obsession with themes of sin, guilt, redemption. All Scorsese sets stand in for purgatory; the nether world of garbage-strewn streets, abandoned factory lofts, and all-night bars does quite nicely.

But other moviemakers often reduce his trend-setting concerns to a worship of "downtown" values such as avant-garde aestheticism, hip nonconformity, and a "Just say yes" life-style. Actors in such films—with their punk haircuts, leather jackets, and torn jeans—should really have been costumed with a sign, "I'm a nonconformist too." Despite its strength as a woman's film, one of the most annoying of such movies was *Desperately Seeking Susan:* in the trading-places plot, we must ignore the fact that there were pleasant aspects of New Jersey, and that the "wild and crazy" scene in Soho was *uniformly* "wild and crazy."

Even the cast of wiseguys and girls at *Saturday Night Live* affirmed these trends with their constant emphasis on hip urban values. The show's opening montage was a perverse hymn to New York—with rapid-fire shots of cast members fleeing under neon lights, down darkened streets, out of subway tunnels. But terror ran second place to excitement: the big city is the place to be—and the bigger, the more blighted, the better.

Such images suggest that beneath the strenuous urbanism of the eighties lay the cynicism of the post-Vietnam era. With hope for social reform dormant, hip folks took to ironic scowls, bitter narcissism, and celebrations of the grotesque. The appeal of irony in art circles in general, in film schools, in "lampoon" circles, and among the disillusioned avant-garde left little room for openhearted feelings of any kind, least of all for nature (see chapter 11, "Irony"). It wasn't just the right that treated nature with benign neglect in the 1980s, but the hip urban left. For them, what remained of nature? As contemporary urban satirist Fran Liebowitz wrote, "Nature is the distance between your doorman and a taxi." Isn't that special? James Watt would surely smile.

Places in the Heart

Not every urban image, or praise of cities, is offensive, just the relentless snobbism of some directors. Not every place outside a city is benign. A few movies, for example, questioned the pace of suburban growth: in *Poltergeist* (1982), a real-estate developer is exposed for building over an Indian burial ground; in *E.T.*, Spielberg makes California developments look ample, but desperately in need of something to break their rigid development patterns. They get idiosyncrasy in spades, a little green thing, a lost bit of nature that eeks in the night.

Idiosyncrasy had other allies. Many local government film offices copied New York and sought film productions for business and publicity purposes. Many filmmakers devoted themselves to smaller cities and bypassed regions where everything had not been compressed into megaurban and suburban conformity. Some neglected regions were lyricized by directors such as Robert Benton and Barry Levinson, one a maker of Texas films (*Places in the Heart, Nadine*) and the other primarily of Baltimore (*Diner, Tin Men*). Other localities were also successful in luring moviemakers—e.g., Seattle (*War Games, House of Games, An Officer and a Gentleman*), Indiana (*Breaking Away, Hoosiers*), Chicago (*Windy City, About Last Night . . .*), and North Carolina (*The Big Chill, Crimes of the Heart*). In some of these films, directors showed a genuine feel for neglected land- and cityscapes. British Columbia lured away a few productions (e.g., *Cousins, Roxanne*) with the promise of fine views and low costs. Canadian crews make films the old-fashioned way: they work at them, even on the set.

Some of these movies were even able to use their landscapes as more than passive backdrops, especially *Breaking Away, Places in the Heart,* and the female teenpix *Mystic Pizza,* (1988), with its views of eastern Connecticut marshland. Landscapes especially came alive in the lush, poetic cinematography of transplanted Australian Peter Weir (*The Year of Living Dangerously, Witness, Dead Poets Society*); indeed, the last recaptures some of the haunting power of his down-under masterpiece, *Picnic at Hanging Rock* (1975). Bruce Beresford used the flat prairies of Texas to complement the understatement of *Tender Mercies* (1983). Australians are still in touch with the wilderness; it shows in films ranging from *A Cry in the Dark* to the blander but pleasant *Crocodile Dundee* (1986), which no American studio at first rushed to pick up. No one thought that the eighties' audience wanted to see a "man in the wilderness" fable.

Still, no landscapes are more beautifully photographed in any 1980s' film than in *Never Cry Wolf*. Given the tenor of the times, even the modest success of this wilderness movie was a big surprise. When it was released by the just-reconstructed (and not yet profitable) Disney company, Touchstone, marketing executives also had little faith in its success. Even Carroll Ballard, its director, was apprehensive: such a film, he said, was out of synch with the times. Young urban audiences, Ballard said, looked for stories with modern settings—or alternatively with high-tech, sci-fi futuristic textures.

Ballard had tried to market the film by making its central character, a young biologist, something of the "nerd" figure so popular in adolescent comedies. But he worried that such compromises and courting of contemporary genres would still not guarantee success. Who would want, he wondered, to see a movie about a lone man and animals— especially with long passages of it practically silent? Despite studio anxieties and lukewarm reviews enough people did want to see it, suggesting that the public at least cared more about such issues than its leaders did.

Movies about men and animals are always with us: see, for example, *The Journey of Natty Gann* (1983), the Australian *Phar Lap* (1984), and *Gorillas in the Mist* (1988). But only the last shares some of the rich environmental values of *Never Cry Wolf,* emphasizing the hidden worth of an abused species, the inaccuracy of its popular image, the danger posed by hunters and poachers, and the even more dangerous destruction of animal habitat. Even Ballard had made a more conventional animal adventure movie before, the stunningly photographed *The Black Stallion* (1979).

Never Cry Wolf goes beyond conventions: Ballard's skill in photographing scenes of pristine, minimalist beauty makes the screen shimmer and his story sing more wildly than any recent nature film. His style is content: his Arctic cinematography is fused perfectly with the story's theme of intimacy and bonding with natural forces. Pure images of the high, northern Rockies and barren tundra are complemented by long periods of silence and simple dialogue: the emptiness evokes the openness, solitude, and peace of such places. Using light Amerindian motifs, composer Mark Isham provides a near-perfect score that Ballard intersperses with wolf howls and an evocative solo bassoon. (In the story, we're shown that the biologist hero brought it along for nighttime diversion; in fact, as Ballard said, *he* needed it to provoke the production's crew of tame [but not trained] wolves to sing on cue). By such methods, *Never Cry Wolf* made the feeling, and value, of wildness palpable. Its style carries us far into the heart of elemental things, especially in the chilling, symbolic fall through the ice, its natural baptism (see opening).

The lake sequence is the turning point in the biologist's story, symbolizing how, in man's relationship with nature, we often act aggressively without really having cause. The film is based loosely on the experience of Farley Mowat, who was sent to the Yukon in the 1950s as a government biologist assigned to get the goods on wolves. But once Mowat's stand-in (Charles Martin Smith) is "reborn" underwater, he refits himself, thinking more carefully about his project. Again he goes out after wolves, but now ready to watch and learn. When he finds them, he discovers they are not gruesome hunters, but survive on mice, while humans (armed with high-powered rifles) are the ones decimating caribou. Smith studies a family of wolves intimately, and begins to understand their habits, playfulness, lifelong mating, shared puppy rearing, extended family life—in short, their likeness to that other gregarious killer, man. Wolves just don't kill each other. *Never Cry Wolf* is no animal movie; it is artful ethology.

The power of *Never Cry Wolf* is almost equaled by the movies of John Boorman, whose knowledge of nature is evident in *Deliverance, Excalibur,* even *Hope and Glory* (1987), with its woodland close, and most of all, *The Emerald Forest* (1984) a flawed adventure story that focused early attention on deforestation of the Amazon. But the main rival of *Never Cry Wolf* is the oddly titled *Koyaanisqatsi* (1983), a Hopi phrase for "life out of balance." The art documentary—directed by Godfrey Reggio with music by Phillip Glass—relies on some clichéd and extremist ideas, but still enriches them and raises them to a grand, prophetic level. With cinematographer Ron Fricke, Reggio sets out to film America, starting with slow pans of places like Monument Valley, picking up speed with aerial shots of the West Coast and Midwest farmland, then accelerating the film with time-lapse photography that catches the frenetic pace of New York and other Eastern cities.

Koyaanisqatsi has strong religious undercurrents. Reggio is a former Christian brother who turned late-sixties' activist with Santa Fe street gangs, founded a "Southwestern Institute for Regional Education," and began learning Hopi language and mythology. *Koyaanisqatsi* is filled with both primitive and Catholic religious feeling, at least the Franciscan kind. Glass's music adds depth to the religious images, especially at the end where he combines organ solo and chant of the title phrase in a quasi-liturgical mode. For all the novelty of Glass's music, one can't help but also hear in the piece one of the best modern allusions to a chorale prelude—of lamentation—by Bach. Few movies have ever been so one-sided so forgivably. *Koyaanisqatsi*'s extremism was understandable in the 1980s: our leaders certainly weren't listening.

The Shape of Things to Come, II

In 1989, George Bush changed the tune on the environment. The networks dutifully snapped to attention, making environmental reports nightly news features. The only drawback was that the stories (on recycling, protecting Alaska, acid rain) seemed ten-year-old reruns. Again, movies alone didn't neglect nature in the 1980s; the whole lost decade was a national undertaking.

Would filmmakers respond to the new mood? There was another film about environmental assassination due (a feature on the Brazilian killed for resisting Amazon development, Francisco Mendes Filho); some pessimistic city films (*Batman* and *Do the Right Thing*) seemed to mark an end to bold, boastful eighties' urban hype; coincidentally, Columbia released Jean-Jacques Annaud's *The Bear*. The spread of regional film offices means a continued supply of movies from multiple locations, and the preservation of idiosyncrasy on film against the gravitational pull of our coastal Babylons. Directors such as Barry Levinson (in late 1989, working on a movie about his immigrant ancestors in Baltimore), will always focus on the special places in their heart. And there are always our poets of landscape—Ballard, Reggio, Boorman, and Peter Weir—to sustain natural beauty on screen. Who knows: with great good luck, maybe no one again will ever have to endure another, single Soho movie. That, indeed, would be a breath of fresh air.

8

Patriotism

We were only fighting ourselves.

—*Platoon* (1986)

At first glance, the scene could be from any one of several wars: an American soldier stalks cautiously through an Asian jungle. As he scans the thickets around him, we hear his voice-over; in his mind (as soldiers do in so many war movies), he is writing letters home. Invoking images from earlier wars, his words help position him in time and place: from the looks of things, it's Vietnam. In his mind, the soldier tells "Grandma" he wants "to do my share for my country . . . to live up to what Grandpa did in the First World War and what Dad did in the Second."

The movie is *Platoon* and the soldier is its hero, Chris. The film has some real flaws, but two genuine strengths: first, the texture of a grunt's experience that had been missing from so many previous films about Vietnam; second, some short but potent passages that put Chris's experiences into wider perspective. Director and coscreenwriter Oliver Stone relies too heavily on the letters, which are wordy and overstated. They were done better in HBO's Vietnam documentary *Letters Home* (1987) or World War II films such as *A Walk in the Sun* (1943)—though even here the character who writes letters home is aptly named "Windy." Still, in this jungle passage, Stone uses the device for some key background on what moved some Americans to fight in Southeast Asia.

Stone—whose own experiences in Vietnam are embodied in Chris's story—stresses that not many soldiers were there for the reasons Chris spells out to "Grandma"; he is *not* supposed to be a representative GI. The other grunts know that he isn't; he has enlisted for idealistic

121

reasons (because too many poor people were being killed, he says; but as one black soldier tells him, "You got to be rich or crazy to think like that").

Chris's letters establish him not as a representative soldier, but a representative American—middle-class and college educated to boot—who believes in idealistic explanations of why we go to war. As his letters make clear, he wants to do his "share"; to him, Vietnam is part of an ongoing struggle in defense of freedom. Without put-down or approval, Stone presents Chris as a patriot, scholar, and spokesman for a national myth—not a lie, but an unconscious vision of history or mode of historic self-understanding.

Like many movies made since Vietnam (including Stone's *Born on the Fourth of July* [1989]), *Platoon* questions that myth, and treats with skepticism the related values it places on patriotism and heroism. Before Vietnam, American movies had generally sustained the myth; from the 1940s to early 1960s, movies had been one of the principal means of its transmission. Not all recent movies have dissented from the myth; indeed, *Rambo* spins some new myths of its own. Still, the growth of the antiwar film—and even the antipatriotic film *(Full Metal Jacket)*—contrasts sharply with the earlier tradition of American war movies.

As debates during the Bastille Day bicentennial illustrated for France in 1989, there are some events in a nation's past that even the best historians will never agree about. So too with America and the war in Vietnam. Hence the differences between *Platoon* and *Rambo,* or *Rambo* and *Full Metal Jacket.* Hence too the widely differing evaluations of such films, which often depend on a critic's view of that war or war in general; *no one* is exempt from such prejudices. But at least one thing is clear about recent films: because of Vietnam, we now have at least two ways of making war movies that mirror our divided national feelings not just about Vietnam, but about the use of force in national defense. Vietnam polarized America and our movies to some degree still reflect it. Between polar extremes of nationalist and antiwar moviemaking, what then do movies teach about patriotism and heroism?

Things were simpler once both on screen and in life. Imagine, for example, Stone's hero Chris as a child: a member of the first media generation, in some fifties' living room, he was glued to the TV, viewing reruns of *Gung Ho!* (1943), *Guadalcanal Diary* (1943), or NBC's long-running and masterful documentary serial, *Victory at Sea.* What he saw was dominated by heroic actions in World War II, "the good war." From *Twelve O'clock High* (1949) to *The Guns of Navarone* (1961) and *PT-109* (the tale of John F. Kennedy's navy exploits released just before his death), World War II provided the staple images for martial heroism: in our movies, Americans prevailed because of a combination of tactics and morality, true grit in a "just" cause. Armed with the best of arms and intentions, Americans outdueled everyone, even the "yellow peril" on its home turf. We could storm anything, just like John Wayne in *The Sands of Iwo Jima* (1949). But in Vietnam, as Chris discovers, things were different; in one analysis, as Rambo complains, we didn't "get to win." We didn't even get to fight on beaches, where we show our best stuff, the right stuff.

No one more represents the heroic tradition in post-World War II American movies than John Wayne. Wayne's career itself neatly circumscribes American history from Pearl Harbor to Vietnam, from *The Flying Tigers* (1942), *The Fighting Seabees* (1944), the elegiac *They Were Expendable* (1945), all the way to *The Green Berets* (1968), his patriotic rouser on the Special Forces first dispatched to Southeast Asia. Indeed, only several years separate *The Green Berets* and his last World War II movies, *The Longest Day* (1962), where he beats Nazis at Normandy, or *In Harm's Way* (1965), where he zaps Japs in the Pacific. Wayne personally links World War II and Vietnam—or at least the heroic images that Americans had of each—embodying the continuity that many, Chris included, saw as central to our war efforts. This sense of continuity remains strong for some today: when Fred Dryer sets up an antiterrorist consulting firm *(Death before Dishonor* [1987]), the picture over the desk shows Wayne from *The Sands of Iwo Jima*. The force is clearly with him.

The sense of continuity didn't stop with Wayne or World War II. In films about the cold war—or the hot one in Korea that seemed to derive from it—the American cause is presented again as part of one continuous, just, heroic struggle. It has become fashionable to be cynical about this movie tradition; we (or some Americans at least) have now become "enlightened." But at least some of the heroic images in the past, however glorified on screen—however evasive of some harsh truths about all wars—are based in fact. In World War II, Americans fought and won a "just war"—if there ever was one; it is also hard to imagine worse rulers than North Korea's. Many filmmakers (Capra, Huston, Stevens, Zanuck, and Ford) and stars (David Niven and Jimmy Stewart) took direct or indirect part in these wars; they knew our soldiers; they landed on beaches and tramped about in jungles; they saw happy crowds welcoming liberation by GIs. They sincerely *believed* in the myths that their films embodied; they had some reason to.

So too did many Americans who went to Vietnam, or supported the war, with images of World War II in their minds. Movies about that war led many to generalize from its lessons—an understandable process, to be sure, for some Americans, and to many still the correct one. But

World War II films may have provided the wrong lessons to apply to Vietnam. Movies about World War II seen by the Vietnam generation may have been truthful about a past "good war" but still may have misled it about what to expect in Southeast Asia. Saturated by such images, America faced Vietnam perfectly prepared to fight *the last war.*

In no other area are the partial truths of movies more dangerous than in movies about war. Movies—which by their nature simplify and sensationalize, which have such ready need for easily identifiable good and evil, which tend to place white and black hats on members of the two sides of any conflict—have by and large mainly expressed half-truths about war. Such films are especially dangerous given the lack of other sources of information on the subject. In other areas—sex, work and sports—viewers (and critics) have plenty of information from real life by which to judge what they see on screen. Except for vets who have survived battle and returned, actual experience of war is, well, foreign; most moviegoers and critics (me included) are mere armchair generals. In this vacuum, movies become a primary source of information or misinformation about battle. Indeed, many a Vietnam memoirist acknowledges that John Wayne films provided his primary expectations of what he would find once he got there (see "Notes," p. 206, middle).

But misinformation works two ways. Antiwar movies can also mislead audiences. Before Vietnam, most war movies glorified heroism; after, many lambasted it, turning American soldiers (and especially all officers) into ogres. But this is merely changing black and white hats on heroes and villains—and works no better than simplistic machismo in helping a nation sort out the complex issues in national defense. Indeed, some antiwar movies since Vietnam—*Coming Home* or *Apocalypse Now* (both 1979)—may have shaped a "Vietnam syndrome" so severe that some Americans are shy about defending our twelve-year-olds from being massacred by terrorists in foreign airports. We wouldn't want to upset anyone even if they blow some of us out of the sky at 31 thousand feet.

Pundits like to plague us with Santayana's remark that those who forget history are bound to repeat it. This is half true; it does explain the value of studying history (and making good movies about it [see chapter 3]). Still, the effects of war movies make the proverb cut like a two-edged sword. A war (or antiwar) movie may make its viewers remember *too well* and apply past lessons too quickly to new circumstances. Seared into the national psyche, such lessons are hard to counteract, especially when conveyed with the larger-than-life power of film imagery.

Platoon looks at Vietnam freshly. Its hero Chris slowly learns about new conditions which "Dad" and "Grandpa" had never encountered. The film's power derives not just from its close (and by many accounts) honest reproduction of the texture of Chris's experiences, but its attitude to history. Windy or not, Chris's letters allow Oliver Stone to examine belief in the continuity of our wars, a belief that movies about war have been a prime means of fostering. Through the letters, Stone implies that America wasn't as much wrong in Vietnam as mistaken. *Platoon* stands out among Vietnam films not just for its realism, but its acceptance of how a nation can mislead itself. It doesn't deny the value of patriotism or heroism: it questions their application. Neither antipatriotic nor even exactly antiheroic, it is *against* assumptions. Not all Vietnam movies are so subtle.

Going in Circles

The emergence of war movies that question national myths is rooted in more general developments in Western culture. Before 1914, the English-speaking world recited Tennysonian courage about war; "The Charge of the Light Brigade" ranked among its best-known poems. Even after the mass slaughter of World War I, heroic and patriotic images still dominated, as in silents like *The Big Parade* (1925); *The Charge of the Light Brigade* (1937) showed that the spirit of the Tennysonian knight was not dead on screen. New notes were heard in *All Quiet on the Western Front* (1931), with its horror at the slaughter in World War I; *Grand Illusion* (1937) bid a French farewell to arms, and Howard Hawks's *The Road to Glory* (1936) an American one. Sadly, these antiwar films could not prepare Europeans and Americans for the moral problem that would be posed by Nazi armies. With their "Great War" syndrome, many progressive-minded folks were perfectly prepared *not* to fight the last war. In 1939, with Hitler, they didn't get to choose.

Movies justified battle again after World War II. The heroic tradition was reasserted, albeit with more grit in Audie Murphy movies, or Sam Fuller's tough Korean War film, *Steel Helmet*. Modest dissent is evident in the Anglo-American *The Bridge on the River Kwai, The Caine Mutiny,* and certainly Stanley Kubrick's *Paths of Glory* (1957). But from the fifties to early sixties, only the rare film questioned the meaning or morality of heroic deeds by American armed forces. If anything, films about Korea reemphasized to Americans their role of defending freedom against barbarism, especially in Asia. The same theme is found in *China Gate* (1957), the first movie about Americans in Vietnam.

So what happens in the 1960s and 1970s? More pendulum swings.

Assertive enthusiasm for defense of American freedom in Wayne movies is answered by M*A*S*H, M*A*S*H by Stallone; a period of anti-war films gives way to a period that burnishes heroic images. Of course, this is understandable: the swings correspond to and foster liberal or conservative moods in the country. But one result of such swings is that no one ever maps a middle ground; rarely does a director not employ either right *or* left clichés about Americans at war. As a result, films seem to reduce our options to doing nothing or to overrespond—e.g., we become "a pitiful helpless giant" or we "nuke 'em". In the future, we may have to make complicated choices about the use of force; but few movies have built a constituency for such decision making.

Consider the swing away from Wayne's emphasis on heroism and nationalism in the mid-1960s. War films were still made, but so too "détente" films in which liberal filmmakers tried to blunt cold-war views, e.g., *On the Beach* (1959), *Fail-Safe* (1962), or *The Russians Are Coming, The Russians Are Coming* (1966). Kubrick's *Dr. Strangelove* (1964) treated the cold war with brilliant black comic satire. Books lambasting the military by Joseph Heller and Kurt Vonnegut found a quick route to films in *Catch-22* (1970) and *Slaughterhouse Five* (1972); *M*A*S*H* (1970) used the Korean War to satirize our military efforts in Vietnam; on TV, Alan Alda kept up the assault. *M*A*S*H*'s Hawkeye was not, like his Fenimore Cooper namesake, a hunter/warrior but a doctor/healer, an iconoclast of authority and tradition. *M*A*S*H* is not anti-American; still, it almost treats patriotism as (in Dr. Johnson's oft-quoted, misunderstood phrase) "the last refuge of a scoundrel."

The prevalent antimilitary tone of late-sixties' and early-seventies' movies is even more prominent in the first major movies about Vietnam, *Apocalypse Now* and *Coming Home* (both 1979). The latter was somewhat forced, and hardly about Vietnam at all; in the triangle of Jon Voight, Jane Fonda, and Bruce Dern, it plays out the cliché of "make love, not war." *Apocalypse Now* seemed mostly a rewrite of Joseph Conrad's *Heart of Darkness*, despite some searing scenes (e.g., the boat massacre) from Vietnam itself. Its Wagnerian images of oddball militarism (Robert Duvall's air cavalry as Valkyries) are campy, but may have more to do with Francis Ford Coppola's gift for overstatement than reality.

Did such movies about the horror of the war in Vietnam reflect and affect American values? In the late 1970s, President Carter was reluctant to use military force, and was often criticized for giving in to the "Vietnam syndrome," which the two movies seem to mirror. But a backlash was also building that made nationalism popular again. It is possible antimilitary filmmaking—and other antinationalist trends in the arts—fed the backlash. Post-Vietnam antiwar movies certainly affected American values to a degree. But they may also illustrate that, to generate constructive debate about war, something more than trashing of the heroic and patriotic tradition is required.

Romance with Rambo

The Deer Hunter (1978) was a partial sign of resurgent nationalism. Although limited in its view of Vietnam (with, at most, three minutes of combat), it manipulates the war in explosive ways, feeding American national myths and old, horrific images of the enemy as "yellow peril." The war is presented as a literal and figurative American suicide, first in prison cages where two Pittsburgh pals (Robert De Niro and Christopher Walken) are made to play Russian roulette by their sadistic Viet Cong captors (complete with Ho Chi Minh's mug in the background). Even when they escape, Walken cannot recover; he remains behind, engaging in Russian roulette in seamy side streets of Saigon.

America is seen in pastoral terms; even the opening shots of workers in steel mills have a knightly, chivalric glory about them. Although De Niro never quite rejoins the community, the movie often endorses its values, as at the end, when his friends sing "God Bless America" in their favorite hangout. Despite its heroizing of De Niro as a lone "existential hero," the movie also contains a moving tribute to the average Joes, "the blue-collar ethnics" who lacked college deferments to escape Vietnam. It also prefigures *Rambo*, Reagan, and the workers who voted for him because of concern about defense and the decay of American values.

In the early eighties, filmmakers celebrated America again, almost as earnestly as crowds at the 1980 and 1984 Olympics. The only anti-war movies came from abroad: the Australian *Breaker Morant* (about the Boer War), *Gallipoli* (about World War I), and *Das Boot*, a German view of its submariners in World War II. Interestingly, it was early eighties' foreign money that made possible the later antiwar films, *Platoon*, *The Killing Fields*, and *Full Metal Jacket*. The English *Gandhi* took many 1983 Academy Awards, which some saw as a reaction to renewed spending on American defense.

In American film production, trends were mostly opposite. As with images of nature, home, and racial relations, Hollywood turned conservative by osmosis; American movies emphasized old heroic images in what one critic called a "romance of militarism." *The Right Stuff*, for example, satirized space and military bureaucracy; but it also celebrated the test pilots who were willing to fly as "Spam in a can" in our first spaceships. Sam Shepard played "the best pilot in the whole world," former World War II ace Chuck Yeager who test-piloted X-15s yet was not allowed to become an astronaut because he lacked a college degree (hence, some satire on bureaucracy). Yeager, incidentally, showed up in the film as the smiling bartender at the pilots' dusty hangout; he seemed omnipresent on car and battery commercials at the time as well, and also produced a best-selling book. Aptly, Yeager's role in *The Right Stuff* was his first screen work since he did stunts for (who else!) John Wayne in *Jet Pilot* (1957).

Similar images dominate other films. Robert Duvall had "the right stuff" in *The Great Santini* (1979); Richard Gere trained for it in *An Officer and a Gentleman* (1982); Tom Cruise got it in *Top Gun* (1986), whose pilots compared dogfights to "sex in a car wreck"—a phrase truly worthy of the Age of Yeager. *Top Gun* sent its heroes, as *Dr. Strangelove* ironically put it, "toe-to-toe with the Russkies" over the Indian Ocean; but this time, with Mideast petro-tension, no one was laughing. Russkies threatened closer to home as well: *No Way Out* (1987) placed one at the top echelons of the Pentagon, and *Red Dawn* (1985) had hordes of Soviets and Latin-American Commies attacking Colorado, where our teenagers repelled them, Rambo-style, drinking blood to prove they had "the right stuff" too. Such movies and TV films like *Amerika* irked Moscow so much that Tass protested what it called our "warnography." The genre even included comedy—Bill Murray's *Stripes* (1981), with its jolly little incursion into Czechoslovakia. Also expressing chauvinism were the negative images of third-world countries in action-adventures such as *Indiana Jones and the Temple of Doom*.

Nationalism also permeated the symbolism of science fiction: *Star Wars* was not just a series but became a symbol of our anxiety over an "evil empire" and finally the colorful (if unofficial) name of a defense strategy; Darth Vader, of course, was helmeted to resemble our older enemy, the Nazis. Big-name stars enlisted against the Russians (Eastwood in *Firefox* [1982]) or against Russkie proxies (Eastwood in *Heartbreak Ridge* [1986], modeled on the 1983 invasion of Grenada). Resurgent American patriotism also led to films about returning to Vietnam to recover those thought by some to be still imprisoned there. "Would-Be Clint Eastwood" Chuck Norris went after them in *Missing in Action* (1984 [and sequel, 1985]) and Gene Hackman did the same in *Uncommon Valor* (1983).

Other films, however, manipulated social anxiety about the behavior of some of the returning vets, caricaturing them as maladjusted misfits beginning with *Taxi Driver* (1976). Vets became stereotyped psychos for sensationalist crime films—hardly a fair fate considering how much many of them had suffered, and how little many of us gave back. Even comedies traded on the caricature, as in Rodney Dangerfield's *Back to School* (1986), where a crazed history professor replays battles around Da Nang in classroom tantrums. The only film about a black vet, *Some Kind of Hero* (1982) with Richard Pryor, was almost ignored. But white veterans of Vietnam did not fare much better.

At least until Rambo—that is, a shrewd synthesis of two issues, the maladjusted vet and the return to Nam to find MIAs. The film is not exactly a sequel but a solution. *First Blood*, the original Rambo film, depicts the heroic vet's trouble on coming home; *Rambo: First Blood Part II* presents him channeling his martial energy back to the source—or the hell, since Rambo comes from Rimbaud, *poète maudit* of "Une Saison en Enfer"—where it was deformed. Once back in Vietnam, Rambo refights the war in a series of symbolic actions; through them, *Rambo II* presents a special view of Vietnam to fit heroic and nationalistic myths.

According to the plot, Rambo is sent in to find missing POWs, but only by bureaucrats intent on proving none exists; when he finds some being tortured, he has to be betrayed. This "stab in the back" in the film symbolizes the larger one in Vietnam; the message is that the whole war effort was undermined by politicians. Rambo is suspicious about his mission from the first because of this possibility. Hence the critical line Stallone spouts when first recruited by Richard Crenna for his mission impossible, "This time do we get to win?" By implication, the only thing that stood in the way of traditional victory in the original Vietnam War was lack of support of our fighting men.

Many dissent from this view, of course, but some Americans adhere to it; *Rambo II* supports them. It claims that the war was not won by the North Vietnamese, but the Soviets, who dominate their flunkies through a sadistic colonel from Nazi central casting (Steven Berkoff). Vietnam is seen as policymakers initially conceived it: a proxy war in an ongoing cold-war struggle against a monolithic Communism directed from Moscow, a kind of new Berlin. As a result, third-world issues are missing in action. There are few Viet Cong; enemies among civilians would mar the myth. The main local character is a heroine who supplies love interest; her killing only spurs Rambo to further vengeance.

This is a deft twist, since Rambo is not much for love; he's a machine for killing. But Stallone subtly manipulates key imagery about exactly what kind of machine he is, or relies on: his weaponry is all simple but deadly, user-friendly lightweight stuff, while the North Vietnamese are weighed down with heavy equipment and tromp about like clodhoppers. Indeed, despite being on their home turf, they are presented as incompetent in the jungle. But no one, not even the conservatives who claimed America could win in Vietnam, ever claimed that our enemy was so bad in combat.

But Stallone needs this nincompoop imagery for several reasons besides cartoon entertainment. First, it fits his case against politicians: *we* could only lose against such an enemy because *they* tied our hands. Second, it makes associations vital to Stallone's mythmaking. The North Vietnamese are helmeted and costumed to resemble the Japanese whom Americans always master in the many World War II films. The costumes and combat choreography imply we could have won in Vietnam, as we had in the past.

Caricaturing the enemy also allows Rambo to present himself as the true primitive. Despite his debt to Wayne, Stallone trumps him here; he is not one of the cavalry, but an Indian, a headbanded Geronimo. It is an odd but apt choice to depict the beset-upon white American males in the twentieth century who see themselves as victims—not just of politicians, but of taxes, government, pointy-headed bureaucrats, women, and affirmative action. Through such imagery, Stallone establishes his sense of the stakes in Vietnam: *we* were the real guerrillas who could have risen above victimization (cf. *Red Dawn*) if bureaucrats had only given us a chance.

No wonder *Rambo III* (1988) has him in Afghanistan "toe-to-toe with the Russkies" and allied with Islamic guerrillas. He plays the same put-upon primitive in *Rocky IV* (1986), training in a log-cabin wilderness and growing an Abe Lincoln beard before going toe-to-toe with a Russkie heavyweight (Dolph Lundgren), tall, blond, Nordic—your standard SS officer. Such imagery may help explain why, according to a 1989 poll, most high-school students think Hitler and Russia were allied throughout World War II.

Stallone's films have powerful appeal in part because they seem sincere. Sure, he made them to make money; but it is difficult to imagine him manipulating myths so well without feeling some of their power himself. Still, *Rambo* movies are more than one man's patriotism; they go beyond a "romance of militarism" to a passion for anti-Communist counterinsurgency. They prequel the efforts of Ollie North in what he saw as his patriotic duty to sustain guerrilla wars against Communism. On a cartoon level, *Rambo* (and *Rocky*) mirror the populism of President Reagan's attack on big government and his claim to be defending "little people." Silly or not, they reflect the force of a neoconservatism that sees itself as dynamic, antibureaucratic, and revolutionary. President Reagan was fond of saying how much he would like to have sent Rambo to several trouble spots around the world. But his most *Rambo*-like line was at the 1988 Republican Convention when he urged delegates never to let Democrats get away with talk of change as if they are its true originators: "*We* are the change."

Left, Right, Left

Not everyone, of course, went along with the change. Despite decline in irony on war during the Reagan years, an antiwar (or at least anti-military) work came forward from abroad, appropriately, from a film-maker who by this time had become an expatriate, Stanley Kubrick. Maybe that decision itself is symbolic.

After *Dr. Strangelove*, Kubrick eschewed politics for two other themes: man's instinctive violence and dependence on technology. In *2001* (1969) and *A Clockwork Orange* (1971), Kubrick contrasted high-tech sets and human beings who had no inner nature except the potential for kill-ing; his *Barry Lyndon* (1975) studied similar impulses in the luscious settings of eighteenth-century salons. Kubrick saw his characters com-pletely externally; in Kubrick, to quote Emerson, "Things are in the saddle and ride mankind." True, he allowed slight hope for a rebirth of humanity in *2001*, but that was under Aquarius, when, for a while, everyone believed in something. Kubrick's touch is most evident in the treatment of HAL in *2001*: as Pauline Kael notes, the computer's death is the saddest moment in any Kubrick movie. Only he could command the tone of HAL's last moments, a blackly comic tragic grandeur.

Given all this, Kubrick's treatment of Vietnam, *Full Metal Jacket*, is no surprise. A brilliant, daringly structured tour de force, it also seems mean-spirited, lacking in compassion, and mechanical. *Full Metal Jacket* exemplifies both the strengths in Kubrick's filmmaking and its weaknesses; it implies the two will always be inseparable. It also illustrates the way that a movie's weaknesses are forgiven, even swept under the rug, because of the hidden role of ideology in film reviewing. The media in general are not left-wing, but some film critics are, and often delight in ironic portrayals of America. Kubrick is an intellectual who addresses their intellectual predilections. So *Full Metal Jacket* got much automatic praise, and its possible faults were not only overlooked, but reinterpreted as signs of genius. But perhaps this mistakes a very good filmmaker for a guru.

Full Metal Jacket not only savages the American role in Vietnam, but the American military and nation. Kubrick's use of Thackeray's *Barry Lyndon* places him in the tradition of classic English satire, which normally aimed to balance harsh and constructive criticism. But his satire in *Full Metal Jacket* is monochromatic and negative. Many viewers took *Full Metal Jacket* as an antiwar film; it seems more anti-American. If it wasn't for its general misanthropy, it would seem (like the stupid 1988 satire *Walker*) the movie equivalent of burning the American flag.

The best part of the film was not in Vietnam, but at training camp, where a marine drill sergeant (Roy Ermey, who had been one before he became an actor) tortures his recruits, renaming them as part of his attempt to reduce their identities. The central figure is "Joker" (Matthew Modine); the sergeant's central target is "Gomer Pyle," a fat, dumpy recruit played by Vincent D'Onofrio. Kubrick's exterior style—his refusal to come close to the characters—has some basis in fact: basic training is designed to reduce the recruit into a killing machine. Few vets would deny the truth of what Kubrick depicts, but many would deny this as the total truth; there are also human feelings (besides the bloody ones that, Kubrick being Kubrick, eventually surface); there are the small but indispensable things that soldiers do to survive.

The lack of innerness in Kubrick's recruits separates them from the soldiers in HBO's *Letters Home* and other documentary works from Vietnam. The problem isn't that the sergeant forgets his recruits are people; the problem is that Kubrick does. Even when the characters emerge more fully, even in the strong scenes of fighting a sniper in Hue, the same external tone dominates: Kubrick is really involved only with one character, the aptly named machine gunner "Animal." Joker remains a set of poses, a vehicle for Kubrick to exploit for some loaded satire. He wears a peace symbol on his helmet next to the phrase, *BORN TO KILL*, explaining it as a "sign of the Jungian duality of man."

Other ironies are equally predictable. The inspired wit of HAL gives way to tiresome satire on American soldiers that you can see coming as soon as a new character appears on screen. A colonel shows up and says, "Inside every American there's a gook struggling to get out." A helicopter gunner answers a morally toned question about how he could kill women and children with a technical answer; you just "lead them more." It gets so you can call every shot, if not in particular, in general. When the survivors from the battle of Hue sing the Mickey Mouse song and the film ends, it's cute, sophomorically appealing, and cheap.

Of course at least some sadistic soldiers fought for America in Vietnam; the army was made of human beings. What Kubrick has done is reduce the whole experience and everyone involved to a cartoon. In doing so, despite the enormous differences in style, he shares some interesting affinities with Stallone. Both are single-minded, Kubrick from the left, Stallone the right. For one the USA can do no good, for the other no evil. Their movies thus attest to the polarization that the Vietnam War caused in America—a polarization that flares up anew with each international crisis.

Platoon: the Real Symbolism

Platoon maps out middle ground between Rambo and Kubrick. Perhaps this explains part of its appeal, but its success was not at all guaranteed. The movie was made only because of Oliver Stone's persistence; he had written the screenplay in 1976, but couldn't get it financed, and got zilch from American studios (Orion did finally pick up the distribution). The US military, which had made its carriers available for use in *Top Gun,* refused Stone any technical help. At the other extreme, at the Berlin Film Festival, the film was accused of being a whitewash of the American army. Having such enemies at both extremes is no sure sign of virtue. But it does suggest that *Platoon* may be more complicated than normally given credit for.

To be sure, its faults are many: contrived allegory and mythmaking, sentimental male bonding, Hemingwayesque romanticism, the wordy letters. Still, by many vets' accounts, it rang true: as noted, Stone served in Vietnam in the worst possible years, 1967 and 1968. His alter ego "Chris" (Charlie Sheen) enlists just as Stone did out of a mix of idealism and machismo. The first scene sets the tone: Chris's disembowelment from air transport into heat, dust, and body bags. Thereafter, it sticks close to Chris's experiences; despite mythmaking, it stays faithful enough to one man's story and point of view. Even the wordiness of the letters has to be seen in context: Chris says nothing while on screen for the first seven minutes of the film; the first sound he utters is a gasp in retching when he sees his first rotted body in the jungle. The movie has its tight-lipped moments. It also uses tight camerawork—close and medium shots—to match loss of perspective in jungle warfare; as in many reports of combat in Vietnam, Americans rarely can see the enemy.

Platoon is also fair in its judgments. One sequence is key, the one that follows Chris and his colleagues from a jungle bunker to a Vietnamese village. It dominates the center of the film—after Chris's first battle experiences, but before he really starts to mature as a soldier. Stone dates the sequences carefully—it is New Year's day, 1968, a month before Tet, the period of heaviest fighting by our ground troops. Guiding the operation are Chris's two father figures, Sergeants Elias and Barnes, "Hector" and "Achilles," or a Christ (the name Elias itself is suggestive) and "our Ahab" (as Chris calls Barnes on his way into the village). But allusion mongering is less potent than actual characterization: both Barnes and Elias are hunter heroes, Hawkeyes from the old tradition. The village scenes later separate them, but Stone uses the jungle to establish their combat fellowship.

Stone sets up the jungle sequences to reproduce the maddening terror of war against guerrillas. Chris is still learning the ropes; he doesn't see the bunker until Barnes warns him, after which the sergeant sends him and others in the group to reconnoiter. As Stone nicely cuts from one trooper to another, he also includes shots of Elias sliding into the bunker underworld, where he crawls around, and finds a body; moments before, it was being operated on in any enemy MASH unit. Quick editing works to raise tension: as Elias probes underground, two soldiers pick up a cache of maps—booby-trapped, of course. Just as Elias sees and shoots a guerrilla below, the bomb explodes; one of the soldiers staggers away, his arm in shreds. When the platoon regroups, they learn that a black trooper sent out a reconnoiter is missing: a thousand yards downstream, his body is trussed up, his throat cut.

In these jungle sequences, Stone has not only tried to be true to his experiences; he has given new life to some old gothic traditions. His wilderness invokes old Indian movies: Vietnam is a strange unknown where stealthy hunters of another race lurk undetected. American black/white conflicts are drawn quickly, economically, and truthfully, but are overshadowed by the conflict with the sleek, stealthy warriors who slip through the thickets, almost by magic. The difficulty of fighting such an enemy is fully conveyed, especially given their ability to blend into the native population. Stone is clearly trying to provoke understanding for those given the impossible task of rooting them out.

Stone also seeks to explain, but not excuse, how some soldiers took out frustration on local villagers. Even Chris, angered by events in the jungle, is tempted to excess, and when he routs out a VC suspect from a hole inside a village hut, makes him "dance" with gunfire, Western-style. But Stone also makes an effort to make distinctions. Just as Chris is calming down under the advice of one buddy, in walks another soldier—the homicidal Bunny. While he calls Chris wimpy, and while his colleague (Sergeant O'Neill) looks on, nervous, Bunny bashes the suspect's head in; later we see he also killed the man's mother as well.

Stone also uses wide-angle and reaction shots to individualize responses in the village center, making sure that we see how *different* soldiers react *differently;* no single truth encompasses them all. Stone provides no caricature here, only context and characterization. Barnes begins an interrogation of the village chief—but first sends an angry soldier away, it seems, as a precaution; only when he himself becomes increasingly frustrated and angry at a woman upbraiding him does he lose control and kill her. Stone pans to include the reactions of other soldiers who are clearly frightened; the translator is so shaky that Barnes then starts yelling at him. Just when further killing (of a small girl) is threatened, Elias returns, assaults Barnes, and the two have to be forcibly separated. Order is restored, the village is torched, the soldiers march off—not before Chris, affected by all he has seen, saves young girls from rape by Bunny and others.

Platoon combines narrative, moral fable, and complex social commentary to make several points at once: every army—being human—has its crazies, and the American army is no exception. In Vietnam, Stone shows, Americans were also subject to unusual stresses that also loosened moral restraints. Many soldiers withstood the stress, and tried to observe military law regarding noncombatants, hard as that was in such a context.

Stone intended these sequences to symbolize the whole war. They reflect the belief (going back to MacArthur) that Americans could *not* win, World War II style, a ground war against guerrillas on the Asian mainland. Japanese regulars, isolated on islands far from home, were tough enough to beat; guerrillas on native turf with hidden avenues of supply and retreat were harder. *Platoon* shows that you can't kill those you can't catch; you can't win the hearts and minds of those you kill. *This* network of traps was Vietnam; when Barnes and Elias fight, it's America at war over being there. As Chris says, "We were only fighting ourselves."

Chris's last letter concludes the film, but not before a fine penultimate combat sequence. Stone puts Chris and the platoon through a final battle, a realistic "Apocalypse now." After, in a rare long shot, a wounded Chris is evacuated by helicopter, a visual release from tension. As Chris ascends, we seem him wave to a surviving friend, Rhah (Francesco Quinn), who holds his hands wide, beats his chest, and whoops goodbye. Stone is a symbol hunting for both Tarzan and Jesus, but does better simply evoking hearty camaraderie. Stone is addicted to male bonding, which helps and hinders him in other movies, such as *Wall Street* where he so focuses on men that he turns his women into ciphers.

Like many good filmmakers, Stone's strengths and weaknesses are inseparable. Here strength dominates. He has too much respect (or perhaps guilt) over those left behind (the man on the ground is their living symbol) to treat them with cheapo irony. As a result, *Platoon* makes left (or right) politics take second place to a plain, sad sense of loss and regret. Stone doesn't wave the flag; he doesn't burn it either. Best of all, he won't play Mickey Mouse games with the memory of the dead.

La Guerre Est Finie?

Casualties of War showed the Vietnam film was not dead, but after Platoon, Hamburger Hill (1987), and 84 Charlie Mopic (1989), it sure seemed derivative. Despite a new focus on war atrocity, many of its framing incidents were clichés (the raw "cherry" needing rescue, a soldier shot just before the end of his tour of duty, a battle-scarred sarge with heroic associations, this time "Genghis Khan"). Based on a real incident, the film was more limited in range, never attaining Platoon's symbolic power. Director Brian DePalma is good at various parts of filmmaking—from his computerized storyboards and filmic allusions to his powerful visual and visceral style. But Casualties of War as a whole lacks depth of insight into character. DePalma may be too absorbed by his own technical skills and mastery of surfaces to probe as deeply as needed into the moral issues in the tale.

The central incident—the abduction and rape of a young woman— pits the sadistic noncom (Sean Penn) against the "cherry" (Michael J. Fox), who has a hard task of making good look appealing as he insists on reporting and prosecuting the incident. Fox does well, despite DePalma's saddling him with Hershey Bars, an idealized home life, and a lame scene with a chaplain. As in The Untouchables, DePalma's idea of good is lily pure; there are few of the shadows of Platoon; the evil characters are one-dimensional, and the movie's moral colors are black and white. At least the combat scenes have some verve; and Fox—like Stone's "Chris" when saving rape victims from Bunny—makes compassion convincing.

Combat films may be near extinct, but movies about Vietnam would continue into the 1990s, as in the Jane Fonda production, A Bright Shining Lie. Veterans would get their share—and a fairer shake, as in Oliver Stone's Born on the Fourth of July or the late-1989 releases Welcome Home and In Country, with its affecting end at the Vietnam War Memorial in Washington, perhaps the greatest work of public art in this country and the best art about the war in Vietnam to date. Would a single movie had half its power.

Glasnost permitting, arch-nationalism on screen will cool down in the near future, or take new directions. The Package (1989) vilified the would-be assassin of a Russian leader. Some at Paramount even thought that The Hunt for Red October (1990) based on Tom Clancy's "cold war" novel written during tensions of the middle eighties, should carry the disclaimer "Before Gorbachev." Indeed, one notices in a film like Black Rain, we have some new (old) enemies: it's not the Russians anymore, but, in symbolic crime "combat," the Japanese.

Clearly, it would be more fruitful to deepen understanding of other nations beyond celebrating their celebrities, and beyond putting white and black hats on anyone, including ourselves. But only the rare film-maker will resist quick formulas and achieve this.

9

Heroines

I was a better man to you as a woman than I could ever have been as
a man.

—Dustin Hoffman, *Tootsie* (1983)

A good strong woman is hard to find on film—or indeed, in many
of the arts. Good women, yes; strong women, yes; but rarely goodness
and strength *in the same woman*. Generally, women come in two sizes:
good/weak, bad/strong; rarely the twain shall meet.

Why are such stereotypes so powerful? Because of sexism com-
pounded by some askew emphases in traditional moral teaching. Good
has often been equated with passive, bad with self-assertive—a general
problem in our cultural history, but particularly acute for women,
victims of more than one double standard. To understand this, don't
start with films, or Freud, but romance writers such as Barbara Cartland
and her stock of damsels in distress and villainous vixens. Or go back
to Walter Scott, who first filled romance with innocent, fair-haired
virgins and mischievous black-eyed brunettes. Such stereotypes (color-
coded or not) are as ancient as *The Iliad*, in the richer forms of
Andromache and Helen. Indeed, like Helen, Homer's strong women—
the goddesses Hera, Athena, and Aphrodite—only spell trouble. For
a recent, vulgar version of such an unholy three, try *The Witches of
Eastwick* (1987). Or, for the good-weak vs bad-strong stereotype, rent
Gone with the Wind, and contrast wimpy Melanie and the tough cookie
Scarlett.

Assertiveness has been a hot topic lately; in the sports-obsessed 1980s,
people even went into "training" for it. Women got assertive in sports,
business, and in combining career, marriage, and children. But good,
assertive women were still hard to find in movies, many of which still

139

express the victim/villain (or angel/whore) dichotomy. Why should films be so limited? How have they not been?

Of course, fine actresses can enrich any role—the most pitiable victim, the most naughty villainess: see, for example, Meryl Streep in *Sophie's Choice* or Glenn Close in *Dangerous Liaisons*. Their star power and professionalism convey a force of character that evades stereotype and transcends particular roles. Still, not all such roles make good role models: the two noted are typical (if moving) victim and villain. It might be helpful if women could be seen in more varied ways, especially by the bulk of the audience, young male adolescents, hardly ever exposed to the likes of Streep or Close. Their favorite films rarely feature any female aside from a castrating Amazon or a doe-eyed bimbette—as, for example, Barbara Carrera and Kim Basinger in the James Bond fluff, *Never Say Never Again* (1983). Most of these viewers have simply passed from reverence to rape to slice-and-dice.

Assertive women were once plentiful on screen: Hepburn, Russell, Crawford, Davis, Garbo and lesser stars first showed actresses how to use personality to conquer clichéd roles; no one seems to have surpassed them. Perhaps only nostalgia confers this special glow; maybe the actresses will always resemble goddesses because they matured when films did—or when the American movie industry had more wit, when a large number of women were doing the screenwriting and when movies, so to speak, were still talkies. These stars of the golden era didn't have to play economically independent career women to convey inner strength.

Many of their roles fit the vibrant bad-girl stereotype; Bette Davis had a fine time at this in *Jezebel*—topping it all off with hammy repentance. Goodness was often restricted to the sacrificial formulas of the "woman's film," à la *Mildred Pierce*. Fast-paced comedies presented feminine strength better, albeit in formulaic "battles of the sexes": think of the buoyant Rosalind Russell dueling Cary Grant in *His Girl Friday*, or Hepburn teasing him in *Bringing Up Baby*. Hepburn was a prophet without honor ("box office poison" to the Catholic Legion of Decency); her popularity from the sixties onward directly reflects our changed public attitudes about women. In her best roles, she is both strong *and* friendly—never more than in her "marriage" films with Spencer Tracy, where interdependence does not exclude equality. The same mutuality spices the *Thin Man* films, where Myrna Loy shares snooping skills with William Powell with a sly, sexy strength.

Such assertiveness was not often in evidence in films of the fifties— or if it erupted, was often given a moral taint. Take the career of Jean Arthur. She could be a snappy, know-it-all reporter in both *Mr. Deeds*

Goes to Town (1936) and *Mr. Smith Goes to Washington* (1939); in both, she is touched by male naifs (Cooper and Stewart), but also has to use her street smarts to shepherd them to triumph. In the conservative 1950s, Arthur's most memorable role is in *Shane*—dependent out on the prairie, where she must be a good wife despite the call of the wild from Alan Ladd. As in other areas, eighties' images of women repeat the fifties: an insurance commercial used *Shane*'s homesteading imagery, with a bonneted wife even squealing "home" when muscular hubby steers their Conestoga into a picture-perfect happy valley.

Between the conservative fifties and conservative eighties came the icons of the age of dissent. In the sixties, old stereotypes broke down, but nothing certain was put in their place. Homes broke up, women wandered, and to a degree, were allowed to be shown as independent agents without stigma. An apt icon of the age was the popular Glenda Jackson, feisty queen for the decade in costumers such as *Elizabeth Regina* on PBS or *Mary, Queen of Scots* or battles of the sexes such as *A Touch of Class, Women in Love,* and *Sunday Bloody Sunday.* Elizabeth Taylor went from passive heroine to tenacious Maggie, *Cat on a Hot Tin Roof* (1958), to the fiery husband wrecker in *Who's Afraid of Virginia Woolf* (1966). In *Alice Doesn't Live Here Anymore,* Ellen Burstyn has the good luck to lose an obnoxious husband, launching her to explore life's new possibilities. In *Hester Street* (1975), *Carnal Knowledge* (1972), and *T. R. Baskin* (1971), Carol Kane, Ann-Margret, and Candice Bergen seek freedom and escape unpunished. Jane Fonda's power was first expressed in cartoon form in *Barbarella* (1968); in *The China Syndrome* (1979) she seemed to mirror her growth from fantasy bimbette to an activist political leader.

They Don't Make 'em Like They Used to

The eighties' emphasis on home represents, in part, a reaction against images in seventies' films. For women, this means a renewed value on motherhood, as in *Baby Boom, She's Having a Baby, Adventures in Baby-sitting, Raising Arizona, Three Men and a Baby, Parenthood,* and even *Cocktail* or *For Keeps* (two films involving early pregnancy in 1988). Motherhood returned in the the 1980s—for good reasons and bad, and too much seemed to ride on it (see "Home"). Apt symbols were the pseudoreligious *The Seventh Sign* (1988) and *The Terminator* (1984), both of which made motherhood a matter of apocalyptic importance. On TV, blonde and brunette stereotypes reached a zenith with *Dynasty*'s sweet Krystal and naughty Alexis.

The eighties' genre deluxe, sci-fi, especially emphasized constrained female roles. As feminist movie critic Kathy Maio noted, in *Back to the Future* Michael J. Fox can be active and do something about the relation of his past and future; by contrast, in *Peggy Sue Got Married*, Kathleen Turner is restricted to traditional female passivity about her fate. In *The Return of the Jedi* (1983) Princess Leia evolves through many stages of womanhood, but stays mostly a pleasing charmer; monsters like Jabba the Hut are used to conjure up horrific images of female castrators. As noted (see "Home"), no director more values the traditional hearth than Steven Spielberg; each of his homes is ruled by benevolent, often sentimentally idealized mother figures. And Spielberg's E.T. leaves a sexist message before he goes home: he touches Eliot's forehead and leaves him his power, but to his sister (Drew Barrymore) E.T. advises, simply, "Be good" (see "Notes," p. 207, middle).

Such phrasing clearly mirrors the backlash against feminism that partly explains the home phenomenon. Slasher films provided more grotesque examples, although the male sadism in this traditional genre hardly needed the aphrodisiac of female independence to be provoked. Still, it fits that Jason's first attack in many of the *Friday the 13th* movies often occurs after an adolescent girl has taken the initiative in exploring sexuality. As one critic noted of a junk horror film, *Out of the Dark* (1989) recent slasher films rely on a misogynistic formula that amounts to "forthright women are just asking for it."

Even sophisticated movies revealed some hostility to women. Bad or inadequate mothers are their special focus—the dark side of emphasis on having and caring for babies. *The Good Mother* (1988), in which Diane Keaton is accused by her ex-husband of allowing a boyfriend to molest their child, was simply the most glaring example of the trend; the same fear of failure at motherhood is evident in three Streep roles, *Sophie's Choice, Kramer vs Kramer*, and *Cry in the Dark*. Or consider the domineering images of Shirley MacLaine in *Terms of Endearment* (1983) and Faye Dunaway's Joan Crawford, marketed as "the biggest mother of them all" in *Mommie Dearest* (1981). The theme is also found in *Ordinary People* (1980) where Mary Tyler Moore plays a suburban mother whose mouth cut off unwanted comments as efficiently as her garbage disposer got rid of meals. But what do you expect when a film's fondest wish is to *Throw Momma from the Train* (1987)?

More subtle is the hostility toward an inadequate mother in *Kramer vs Kramer*. Like the later *Mr. Mom* (1983), it comically illustrates that men and boys can keep house even after Mom (Meryl Streep) acts out her version of the Beatles' "She's leaving home." The film was popular, and pushed a whole bunch of appealing buttons, but still has some serious problems. Perhaps some of the subtle twists and turns of the film explain why.

Meryl Streep leaves an unhappy marriage with ad exec Dustin Hoffman; the sharp opening scene of the film shows her tearful, affectionate farewell to her son, an Oedipal pietà. But while generating original sympathy for her against career-obsessed Hoffman, the film reverses sympathy by the end, where she is seen as vindictive and shallow. Her most subtly damning line in courtroom arguments over child custody is psychobabble about "finding myself in California"—we know what that means. Her lawyer entirely misrepresents how Hoffman has come to care for the child—caring that costs the job he had been obsessed about. Streep is also seen spying from phone booths at Hoffman when he takes the child to school; in such shots, director Robert Benton evokes stalker images, KGB tails, and a wicked witch of the Upper East Side. By the end of the film, even Streep realizes that she is inadequate, and gives back the custody rights she won in court. The fifties and eighties may be alike, but sometimes their conservatism comes from different sources. In fifties' films, men would show frustration at the limits that marriage imposes on them; in the eighties, they get angry at women for having the same feelings.

More opaque in *Kramer vs Kramer* is another sign of backlash, the frequent use of bathroom humor for comical effect. Not long after Streep leaves, the bathroom door gets left open for an audio of male urination; while Mom's away, the boys will play, it seems. But this occurs several times, and is used in a key confrontation. At work one day, Hoffman tentatively starts to ask career woman Jo Beth Williams for a date; she takes over, telling him, bluntly, "Yes," before he can finish. Benton cuts to night and bed, where we see Williams get up, naked, to go to the bathroom. But she is surprised in the corridor by Hoffman's child coming out of it. The contrast of a big naked, embarrassed woman (hands over vital parts) and the clothed, assured child makes for good comedy. But it also works as comeuppance, a male revenge fantasy against the image of a stronger woman: undressed and defenseless, she is subject to symbolic rape. Any viewer of slasher pix could have told Williams she was asking for it.

New Heroines: Film and TV

Still, put-downs are not the whole picture. Motherhood itself provided images of potent women who aren't punished. The 1985 farms triad, *Places in the Heart, Country,* and *The River* posed a kind of matriarchal populism, in which crises of farm life past and present were solved by enduring Earth Mother types. Even Meryl Streep "het a farm in Afreeca," and her portrayal of Isak Dinesen's powerful affection for land and natives approached the maternal. In *Aliens*, Sigourney Weaver emerges as a mother symbol, a feminine and feminist Rambo-like protector of young children against space monsters—an answer, on an unconscious level, to the anxiety about being a good mother pervasive in so many other movies. Weaver (whose chin God shaped to signal resolution) also embodied maternal macha as Dian Fossey in *Gorillas in the Mist*, or *Up in Africa*. Even her love scenes (with Bryan Brown) are shot in a subtle, punning way to convey a new sexual politics.

Images of powerful maternal protectors involve unusual settings: history, outer space, African wilderness, or farmland, and back-country America. But there have been heroines closer to home as well. Women have also been more powerful as sisters and buddies. Bette Midler has almost cornered the market on such roles with *Ruthless People* (1986), *Outrageous Fortune* (1987), and *Big Business* (1988) in which she plays a pair of twins with Lily Tomlin. In *Hannah and Her Sisters*, *Crimes of the Heart*, and imports like Margarethe von Trotta's *Marianne and Juliane*, "sisterhood," in this literal old-fashioned sense at least, was indeed powerful. *Shag* (1989) and *Mystic Pizza* (1988), celebrate sorority, if not actual sisterhood; despite some obnoxiously trendy clichés about city hipsterhood, *Desperately Seeking Susan* expresses sisterly sharing in symbolic form, with Madonna (playing a less-successful version of herself) passing on spunk to her secret sharer, Jersey housewife Rosanna Arquette. The best film about a woman finding herself through sisterhood was from Canadian director Patricia Rozema, *I've Heard the Mermaids Singing* (1988): here the fine Canadian comedienne, Sheila McCarthy, learns how to put spunk in her own life by freeing herself from worshiping other women. Rent it on video: there are few recent better "small" films.

Some of the best sports films of the decade featured strong women, as in the Canadian *Hockey Night* (1984) or *Personal Best* (1980). In *Heart like a Wheel* (1983) Bonnie Bedelia compellingly plays racing car driver Shirley Muldowney, who never gives up her career despite pressure to be a conventional wife or submissive girlfriend. In *Bull Durham*, Susan Sarandon is a groupie with a mind of her own; in *Compromising Positions* (1985), she achieves a real if tentative balance between home and free-lance writing.

Journalism films also provided powerful images of women, parallel to the rise of women within the trade. *Network* serves up the perfect ogress, Faye Dunaway's forte, but other films, even the awful *Switching Channels*, depict an alternative; in *Broadcast News* Holly Hunter personifies it best of all. But her role also shows the limits of women's progress on film. Despite the tremendous differences in size and demeanor, Hunter might become the next Eve Arden—the smart, wisecracking thirties/forties supporting actress who was doomed to isolation in careerhood. In *Broadcast News* Holly Hunter's high-powered work ethic inspires her production assistant (Joan Cusack) who tells her, "Except for sex, you're my role model." The line reflects the influence of superstars such as Diane Sawyer on so many young women; it also reflects the sexism in the plot. Hunter can't have both career and man, the screenplay insists. Despite being a far more attractive and intelligent person than fellow journalists Albert Brooks and William Hurt, Hunter is not allowed a spouse or kid at the end of the film, where both of them show up endowed with family.

Still, the movie marks some changes. Despite its adherence to sexist formulas, it can't help noting that the real issue wasn't what was wrong with Hunter, but her men friends. Hunter is not masculinized, as many career woman are in older films; in her party, blue polka-dot dress, she is very feminine and desirable; Hurt finds her energy highly attractive. That is, there is a contradiction between the formulas of screenplay and actual evidence of what Hunter presents: she is a lovable, sexy woman with a brain and enormous professional skills. Sadly, writer/director James Brooks doesn't let his insights into a modern career woman interfere with the ingrained sexism of movies about a type.

Women fared better on television—at least in terms of pure air time—for several reasons. As *Newsweek* noted, one reason for the larger role for women on TV was the sheer number of women directors, producers, and executives in the industry. Despite the rise of directors like Joan Micklin Silver, Susan Seidelman, Amy Heckerling, and Zelda Barron, Hollywood remained an old (and young) boy's network. The only woman to have sustained real power is Dawn Steel, rising through jobs of production chief at several studios to become head of Columbia from 1987 to 1989.

Television production involves less risk; TV shows simply don't cost as much as films. They have also become easier to market because of the development of programming slots designed for smaller, more select audiences than films can often find. TV execs can "narrowcast" to select markets in ways that movies, even in limited national release, cannot; TV can divide an audience by sex (or age, race, or class), film only by geography. For example, because of ABC's *Monday Night Football*, CBS in the early eighties geared its programs to the female audience that was assumed to be looking for an alternative. CBS went to an almost-exclusive woman's lineup with shows such as *Cagney and Lacey, Kate and Allie,* for a time *My Sister Sam* (still harping on those sisters!), and at last *Murphy Brown* and *Designing Women.* ABC made up for Monday's macho with Tuesday's *Moonlighting,* various "couple" shows, and ultimately *thirtysomething* and feisty *Roseanne* in 1988 (see "Notes," p. 207, bottom). Many of these TV shows are not high quality, nor are they without their own forms of stereotype. Still, women fare better on TV. On one *Designing Women,* Mary Jo even strikes back at films by saying, "Just once I'd like to see one of Jason's victims know when he was coming and kick him in the groin."

Images of comic role reversal also crop up in the movies. In *Mystic Pizza,* one heroine wants to have sex, but is unsure of marriage, prompting her boyfriend (Vincent D'Onofrio) to the outcry, "I want to get married, in a Church, in the presence of God, for Chrissakes!" The film is not vengeful; it uses role-reversal as a way of establishing equality and friendship. In *Peggy Sue Got Married* Kathleen Turner uses her knowledge from later life to tease her future husband Nicolas Cage about sex; he angrily drives away, screaming, "Woman! Humiliator!" Turner only humiliates the wimpy: in *Romancing the Stone* (1984) and its sequels, she may throw her body around with aplomb, but it is always *her* body, her zest for life—and her equality with Michael Douglas—that turns him on.

Smart Women, Limited Choices

Sexual equality is stronger in *Everybody's All-American,* where Jessica Lange plays a woman who becomes stronger than her man. Lange plays the girlfriend, then wife of Gavin Grey (Dennis Quaid), the "grey ghost" of LSU football. But Lange's character matures from domestic slavery to independence. In an early college scene she is asked what she majors in, answering in a drawl full of innocence and self-aware self-betrayal, "Gavin and me. I major in Gavin and me." She ranges widely here, from bellelike sweetness, submissiveness as an athlete's wife, obsession with maternity as compensation for being ignored, anger over Quaid's bad handling of money, and at last determination to save their home by starting a career in the eighties' South. But nobody wanted to see this film because they said it was an old story!

Lange's femininity fuses assertiveness and allure; she's big-boned and muscular, soft and radiant; in a blue denim jacket, as Pauline Kael writes about her in *Crimes of the Heart,* "She's everybody's favorite waitress." After *Music Box* (1989), Lange may become everyone's favorite female lawyer. She likes earthy, feisty roles, from *The Postman Always Rings Twice*

(1981), *Frances* (1983), *Sweet Dreams* (1985) to *Crimes of the Heart*, where wenchliness is, perhaps, laid on a bit thick. Her love of earth, if not earthiness, animates *Country,* which she produced as well as starred in.

Indeed, go back to the role that first earned Jessica Lange notoriety, ill fame, and a few extra years as a real-life waitress: the De Laurentis remake of *King Kong* (1976). Like many "starlets" in brainless movies, she got too much share of the blame for its silliness: when things go wrong, some critics look around for someone to call stupid, and a blonde beauty always serves best. In actual fact, Lange dignified the end of *King Kong* in a typical way, adding a (slight) note of earthy assertiveness when Kong falls from the World Trade Center and she has the grace to bid him a long, wailing ambivalent good-bye. A good, strong man has been hard to find lately; after all, the big lug cared.

Meryl Streep can also be feisty. According to conventional wisdom, her forte lies elsewhere, as our supreme suffering heroine. Many people look at Streep as "Class"; producers want her as a kind of Calvin Klein designer label that serves to stamp "prestige" on a mainstream film— with the result that they deny parts to other actresses who equal her power (not just Americans, but Kate Nelligan or Judy Davis, close to the best film actress in the English-speaking world). Streep herself rebels against this image making because it underplays her own vitality; consider *Heartburn* (1986), her early comic stage roles, or her new roles in *She Devil* and *Postcards from the Edge*.

In melodramas, Streep is famous for her accents, which illustrate her talent but also her problem. She is extremely studious, and can apply herself to mastering almost any style of speech; but a certain studied air has also been at the root of what many regard as a limit, a withholding of some kind, in some of her performances. Fortunately, her earthier roles (in *Silkwood, Cry in the Dark,* and to some degree, *Out of Africa*) have allowed her to get beyond a set of trademark mannerisms that she perhaps has found too easy to resort to when playing a neurotic, victim, or both as in *Still of the Night* (1982) or *Plenty* (1985).

In *Out of Africa,* her best scenes are not as a woman who can only sigh and pout over inadequate men (Klaus Maria Brandauer and Robert Redford), but with her black staff, with whom she reveals her spirit of play and command. In *Cry in the Dark*—really two films, on motherhood and journalism, out of whack—she is a mother who doesn't play the tragic heroine, doesn't conform to conventional standards of sentiment over the death of her baby, and must endure cruel misunderstanding as a result. In *Silkwood* she found depth in a confused, even shallow person by connecting powerfully with her resolve to become something more, even if she wasn't sure what it was. Rent it and wait until she says, "formaldehyde": now *there's* accent.

In *Silkwood,* Streep shared the stage with Cher, one of the most under-rated actresses of our time. In her music videos she can't shake loose the need to play the bad/strong stereotype to the hilt; there, she's enslaved to compulsive gestures of hiply defined freedom. In movies, however, her strength manifests itself differently; it is always allied to affection. The way she quietly nuzzles Streep on the porch in *Silkwood,* or kisses Sam Elliot in the funhouse in *Mask,* or falls into the arms of Nicolas Cage in *Moonstruck*—these are all of a piece with her blunt immediacy; her spontaneous but believeable emotionalism doesn't contradict her toughness, but is the flip side of her straight no-nonsense approach. She hates to audition; preparation is not to her taste; she hasn't studied acting and may never grow to expand her range. But that perhaps is a small price to pay for her ability to tap into certain emotions in so direct a manner. Intentionally or not, Cher challenges old stereotypes of good/weak, bad/strong; her (comparatively) late arrival in film may have let her shape a star presence independent of tradition.

Consider by contrast Glenn Close, whose roles reveal how hard it is for good actresses to escape stereotypes. After *The Big Chill,* and other early films, she frequently complained about being typecast as too sweet and wholesome; in *The Natural* her confined roles as an angelic prairie wife put her in peril of becoming cream cheese. Notice, however, how her "new direction"—as the wonderfully evil meanies in *Fatal Attraction* (1987) and *Dangerous Liaisons*—simply inverts the imagery of the good, sweet nurturer; that is, Close has mainly been good/weak or mean/strong. Near escapes came in as a strong-minded Mom in *The World According to Garp* (1982) and as a lawyer in *Jagged Edge* (1985)—a part undone when she is forced to go weak-kneed for her client (Jeff Bridges), accused of murdering his wife. Her latest film, *Immediate Family,* brought Close back to the good/weak stereotypicl role. Close's career shows not just how difficult it is to escape typecasting; it also illustrates how actresses are constrained by the restricted options that producers are ready to offer.

Still, who would trade away her perfomances in *Fatal Attraction* and *Dangerous Liaisons*? Despite the loose characterization in the former, Close made her role as psychotic lover come alive. If you thought about the loneliness and psychosis of her single career woman, the film was incredible; *if* you thought about them, which she didn't give you much chance to do. If you watched and listened, Close's delivery made everything about her character chillingly real: as she says in the film's most tingly line, "You're not going to *ignore* me!" Close's talent at making anger credible is also evident in *Dangerous Liaisons* especially when she comments about her experience of dependence in marriage. Most arguments and displays of anger on screen lately seem histrionic and false—a reflection, perhaps, of declining emphasis on the word and training with dialogue in movies. Close, who worked first in theater, knows how to keep hold of fierce emotion from take to take; she can release it rather than labor to dredge it up. She gives a human texture to temper; she seems *possessed* because she can embody strong anger without recourse to flailing and shouting.

No film caused more controversy over its images of women than *Fatal Attraction*. Was it, as some charged, another example of the good woman/bad woman stereotypes? Another eighties' counterattack on the image of a strong female? Close played a career woman who goes bonkers after a one-night stand with married lawyer Michael Douglas; after she gets pregnant, she harasses him, and demands he leave his wife for her. Many saw the movie as a caricature of a strong, independent woman; others claimed it was a warning about fidelity, or (some claimed) a symbol of fear over extramarital sex in an age of AIDS. Perhaps such analysis is to break a butterfly upon a wheel: thrillers reflect social issues, play off them, manipulate them, but don't necessarily hang together as coherent social comment. *Fatal Attraction* raised issues about character and motive that it didn't, or could not answer. Still, the film was compelling despite its looseness—a cheap, perfectly contrived, glossy provocation.

But its caricature of single career women remains a problem. Take as a partial parallel *Sea of Love* (1989), where Ellen Barkin (one of the smartest, sultriest of today's actresses) plays a single career woman suspected of using personal ads to date men and lure them to their deaths. Leave it to Hollywood to make a movie about the possibility of a woman using personal ads to entrap men: the movie was released just around the time an increasing number of news stories focused on the problem of date-rape and use of personal ads by men who molest women. Shortly afterward, cable TV featured another version of the same kind of story, *Personals*, starring Jennifer O'Neill.

Of course, suggesting that the villain may be a woman makes for a piquant twist; and in truth some women can actually be villains, despite the attempts of some feminists to ban the idea. *Sea of Love* does not, ultimately, endorse it; but like *Fatal Attraction*, the film (and its trailers) glibly manipulates certain male biases. Movies are always ready to crown characters with black and white hats; in sexy melodramas, strong women often seem to come equipped with black hat plus broomstick. Close's frizzy hairdo in *Fatal Attraction*—and her skill at cooking rabbit stew in a caldron—only clinch the association.

Still, the makers of *Fatal Attraction* showed less interest in what made Close tick, or in her career woman's life-style, than in depicting the shallowness of a man who starts a dangerous liaison for no obvious reason but the temporary absence of his wife (Anne Archer). Indeed, they intensify this by dropping the old formula that every betrayed wife is a weak, unsexy wallflower; paired against Close, Archer provides another strong female image. She is a mother, true; a homemaker as well, but, as noted above, so too have been a number of recent strong-willed heroines. Archer brought an added feistiness and independence; she also gets to give the best emotional fit in the film when Douglas tells her of his adultery. Her sensuality was so strong that it opened up a completely different issue: why should Douglas stray to begin with? In certain ways, *Fatal Attraction* is as much *antiman* as antiwoman; the hero is a wimp fought over by two strong women. Curiously, the motif governs *The Accidental Tourist* and other films.

The Good, the Strong, and the Feminine

sex, lies, and videotape (1989)—a good, but highly overpraised movie—also centers around the growth of feminine strength at the expense of two weak males. One, a lawyer, is a compulsive womanizer who sleeps with his sister-in-law; his ex-college buddy and alter ego (James Spader) traces his impotence to guilt feelings over once betraying a lover. It is the women who grow: Andie MacDowell starts as the lawyer's prissy wife and Laura San Giacomo is her naughty, bar-tending "bad girl" sister. At the film's end, both women share sensitivity and strength: the men represent two halves of a broken human wholeness.

Perhaps the best images of good and strong women in a recent movie come from *Tootsie*, for which Jessica Lange won her Academy Award as supporting actress. Teri Garr gave her best comic performance in the film; Geena Davis also shone in a lesser role. Still, the best woman in the film was Dustin Hoffman's Dorothy. Except for him, *Tootsie*'s women are comparatively passive; Garr accidentally locks herself in the bathroom; Lange floats about beautifully in sweatsuits two sizes too small. Garr gets one fine "exit" speech about taking control of her life, but the force is clearly with Hoffman, especially in his confrontations with the male chauvinist soap-opera director played by Dabney Coleman.

The film, of course, is partly a satire on male chauvinism; Hoffman clinches it with his final declaration (after revealing himself to Lange):

"I was a better man to you as a woman than I could ever have been as a man." The line seems simple, but underlines a message in the plot that conveys our ambivalent, equal/unequal attitudes to femininity and masculinity. On the one hand, the line suggests that men may grow stronger if they drop machismo. On the other hand, its phrasing about "better" reminds us how Hoffman's Tootsie is the only "woman" to deflate men—i.e., Hoffman was better as a woman than a woman could have been *because* he was a man; he even got the job Garr couldn't. If you want someone both good and strong, the movie sometimes implies, get a man.

That is, as in *Kramer vs Kramer*, one of the best performers in a "woman's" role in the 1980s was Dustin Hoffman. This is not his fault, but a credit to his shrewdness, packaging, and acting ability; by luck and skill and his strong corner on the "sensitivity" market, his career vamps off the women's movement. Like the roles still generally assigned to women, Hoffman's role in *Tootsie* thus suggests an old cliché about social progress: two steps forward, one step back. Given our history, this is not likely to change much very soon.

10

Justice

I believe in America. . . .
—*The Godfather* (1974)

"Go ahead, make my day," Dirty Harry dared a punk, and defined a decade. Crime annoyed most everyone; to adapt *Network*, people were "mad as hell" and didn't "want to take it anymore."

In the sixties, films sympathized with outlaws—witness *Bonnie and Clyde* (1967) and its imitators. In the eighties—with some exceptions, including one *very* major one—sympathy went to the prosecution, or at least figures inside or outside the legal system protecting "little people" against criminals.

Take, as a transition piece, a scene from *The Godfather* (1974). Like many late sixties' and early seventies' films, it glamourizes outlaws. But *The Godfather* is also the grandfather of more recent law-and-order films: its particular outlaws, the Corleones, live by stern codes of justice: intimate, personal, immediate. In effect, their family is their state. The opening of the movie, a fade-in scene just before the wedding, is key. An Italian immigrant (and now-successful undertaker) whose daughter was beaten while resisting rape and who sought justice in court comes to Don Corleone to tell him her attackers were let off. "For justice," the man reports he told his wife, "we must go to Don Corleone."

The Don first reprimands the man for trusting the impersonal justice of cops and courts; but eventually he agrees to help, sending some of his associates to adjust the matter ("Reliable ones," he says, who won't "get carried away"). Aside from the black humor of the Don's sense of restraint, we are left with a telling vignette about the breakdown of the social contract, and the appeal of smaller, more reliable units of

153

justice. In effect, the episode inverts the usual American pride in a government of laws, not men. The man appealing for help prefigures the rise of Dirty Harry; he wants Don Vito to go ahead and make his day.

Among the purposes of the United States is to establish justice. At least the preamble of the Constitution claims as much. That little gem of paragraph is a bit visionary: it sets out the ends for which the articles are specific means. Today its phrasing about justice seems utopian: the issue facing law enforcement has become, simply, maintaining national sovereignty. In large parts of the territorial United States, this no longer exists.

In such an age, the appeal of personal defenders, avengers, or equalizers such as the Don, Dirty Harry, Charles Bronson, Mad Max, walking "Lethal Weapons," or *Robocop* is easy to understand. Establishing justice is the new impossible dream. As a result, no movie genre, even sci-fi, has become more fantastic than the glut of recent movies in which tough guys protect innocents against criminals, even if the tough guys are mobsters themselves.

What do movies reveal about our attitudes to justice? They are, of course, wildly inaccurate; even a fine movie such as *The Verdict* (1983)—directed by the legal master storyteller Sidney Lumet—can easily be taken apart by experts in legal procedure; and TV's *People's Court* has also caused some jurists anxieties about what sort of lessons it may be teaching people. Films and television *dream* about justice, often inventing wildly violent scenarios and impossible courtroom events.

But are they dangerous in other ways, as many civil libertarians warn? The answer depends on how one defines the term *justice* itself. Ask lawyers what *justice* is and you will often get a technical answer. Their most common phrases testify to a life lived according to rules of procedure. They speak of justice as a mechanism, "the system of justice," the smooth running of which is critical to their set of values. Their catch phrases are "innocent until proven guilty" and "due process." When someone probably guilty gets off on a quibble or technicality, they shrug sadly and say, "That's the way the system works."

Lawyers have good reason for their emphasis on procedures. As shown in *The Thin Blue Line* (1988), justice is often served by nitpicky defense of a criminal suspect and repeated (often vilified) "time-consuming" appeals. The movie—described by its director Errol Morris as "the first nonfiction film noir"—is a gripping indictment of wrongful prosecution and conviction; it fortunately led to a reversal on appeal. According to the defense lawyer, the district attorney's office in question ran by the saying, "Any prosecutor can convict a guilty man; it takes a great prosecutor to convict an innocent." But knowingly trying to convict an innocent person isn't a prosecutor's job; at the very least it's wrongful prosecution. On a deeper level, it can even be obstruction of justice if it lets the guilty go free.

Justice means in part what *The Thin Blue Line* (or *An Innocent Man* [1989]) details: protecting the rights of suspects. But as many movies with sympathy for the prosecution suggest, a simple equation of justice with due process for the accused tends to leave out something critical. When people lose faith about establishing justice for innocents through the courts—innocents accused of crime and innocent *victims*—they look outside the system, and idolize real-life figures, or cultural icons, who make a better effort in defending innocence than the courts appear to be doing. Hence—despite *The Thin Blue Line*—Don Vito, Dirty Harry, Mad Max, a host of other avengers/"equalizers," or figures such as the young judge (Michael Douglas) in *The Star Chamber* (1983) whose frustration at watching criminals go free leads him to consider short-circuiting the judicial process. Sympathy for such figures reflects the growth of victims' rights in the last decade and outrage over the perceived neglect of such rights by the courts. Our movies, in short, have become and index of grave discontent with the system of justice. Somewhere in the system, our movies say, the *ends* of justice have been misplaced.

Yes, many of the "avenger" films are dangerous. They often equate being cuffed with being convicted, reversing the warning in *The Thin Blue Line* or a classic such as *The Ox-Bow Incident*. Often they use racial stereotypes as shorthand for suspected criminal activity, aggravating the racial divisions in our society that so often explain the underlying causes of crime. Worse still, such films rarely focus on the plague of crime committed against the mass of law-abiding citizens among minority groups.

But law-and-order films are not always so limited. Even *Dirty Harry/Death Wish* exploitation films may feed deep public needs, and perhaps the private psychological needs of many citizens (see "Notes," p. 208, top). Sympathy for the prosecution also extends beyond exploitation films to serious movies about the need to protect innocent victims from criminals, especially the need to use powers of prosecution to defend women and minorities. However much flawed, *Mississippi Burning* was still (at its release) the most frank movie about racial injustice since the 1960s; however much it misrepresented the case, it at least evoked sympathy for prosecution of crimes against blacks. *The Accused* was not the first, but the best of several rape movies whose common premise is the need for prosecution of sexual assault, and the defenselessness of women without it. Such films reflect the common perception that, pace the ACLU, it is not the police who go around raping people.

Movies about justice are always with us, and are part of no "trend"; they are a staple of film because they are a permanent staple of melodrama. They let a director round up the usual suspects—sex and violence, good and evil, and the reversals of fortune and revelations basic to classic theater.

Still, recent movies seem to reflect a shift in perception about who constitutes the greatest threat to the ordinary citizen. Libertarians talk as if the only threat to liberty is the government—a claim reflected in seventies' films like *Three Days of the Condor* (1975), *The Parallax View* (1977), and *All the President's Men* (1976). But in the eighties people had also acquired a lively fear of walking the street. Of course, the state always poses a danger to any citizen. But unless crime rates are government lies, fear of other citizens reflected in recent films is not entirely misplaced.

Consider even the work of Sidney Lumet: his first legal film, *Twelve Angry Men*, worthily recorded a victory for justice by an acquittal. By contrast, *The Verdict* records a victory for justice by a conviction—or at least, in its civil law setting, a finding for the plaintiff. *The Verdict* does not invalidate *Twelve Angry Men*, it merely shows that the jury system also functions properly when it convicts, or at least finds for the victim. The film provides heavy satire on lawyers, especially in the giant firm headed by a smooth James Mason; it also heroizes one lawyer (Paul Newman) as a comatose woman's personal "equalizer."

No scene better catches the weakness of the "system" than the moment when Mason, citing a legalistic quibble, asks that the testimony of one witness (a sympathetic nurse in Newman's corner, played with wonderful economy by Lindsay Crouse) be struck from the record and that the jury be instructed to act as if they never heard it. The episode illustrates how even a director sensitive to the need for precise procedure is ticked off by its abuse. Lawyers such as Mason live in a world of verbal quibbles; jurors, at least as shown in *The Verdict*, live in reality.

Like *Mississippi Burning* and *The Accused*, *The Verdict* implies a growing conviction by many citizens that maybe we need better defenses against criminals—corporate or street. Whatever their defects as accurate reflections of courtroom or police procedures, such *broadly conceived* "law-and-order" movies reflect our search for a kind of justice that goes beyond the mere "process" of a "system." Our movies are fiercer about this lately—even works by liberal filmmakers—precisely because many citizens perceive the system's plain failure to protect them. Of course, "avenger"/"equalizer" films manipulate the perception and sensationalize the failure; but they couldn't do so well if they didn't touch one of the most exposed raw nerves in American life.

Where's a Good Cop When You Really Need One?

Still, the problem of excessive violence by "avengers" is real, and many of the screen's "equalizers" (especially Eastwood and Bronson) strike sophisticated viewers as hardly different from the criminals themselves. Movies don't teach enough about real-life justice if vengeance alone defines our image of it. Hence the need for films about tough cops who don't go further than justice requires, or movies about law and order that do not wallow in bloody depictions of crime. Hence too the difference between two of the most important recent movies that go in search of one of our deepest social needs, the good cop.

Take *The Untouchables* (1987), which details the education of Eliot Ness (Kevin Costner) from naïveté to deeper knowledge under the guidance of tough cop Sean Connery. Ness comes to understand that violent, often extralegal means are necessary to destroy Al Capone (played with bravura strutting by Robert De Niro). The problem is the superficiality of Costner's development; director Brian DePalma is too in love with the glamour and energy of Capone to keep his other purposes adequately in mind. The intentionally comic-book and self-conscious, allusive style of the film conflicts with the seriousness of the acting and writing, especially when Costner leads a raid, declaring, "Okay, let's do some good." The comment comes across as stupid, not naive; saccharine greeting-card images of Costner's family life don't help. DePalma's vision of good is a sexless, joyless rectitude; as a result, he can't make loss of purity—and Costner's ultimate compromises— compelling. Except for Connery's performance, *The Untouchables* skirts the moral problems of establishing justice and how this eats at the insides of a good cop. Often the film is less about justice than body counts. When DePalma has Costner sigh regretfully, "So much violence," it sounds like crocodile tears.

Witness (1983) takes justice more seriously. It is comparatively chaste about bodies—with a gruesome killing in the bathroom of Philadelphia's Union Station at the opening, and a gunfight at an Amish corral at the end. Its romance is also chaste in its use of bodies, deployed only to heighten tension: precisely because Kelly McGillis plays a demure Amish woman, her relationship to policeman Harrison Ford has more of a chance than usual to develop, and accordingly has much more time to provoke suspense.

Amish groups complained about the film, but on the whole it fairly represented their special values. Indeed, it artfully incorporated them in a formulaic thriller/love plot that evolves when Ford has to take refuge in the Amish countryside. *Witness* is the closest thing to a meditation on the uses of violence in a mainstream movie in the 1980s—rivaled only in a cloudy way by *The Mission*. Its best scene has a quiet debate between the child who has witnessed the station murder (Lukas Haas, with his wide, wonderful, spooky eyes) and his somber, pacifist grandfather (Jan Rubes). With Ford's unloaded gun in hand, he tells Haas that killing with a gun means only evil—no matter the cause. But the child says that he has seen evil himself—the murder—and would rather stop it with a gun than watch it again. The old man gets the last word, but the filmmakers have the wit to examine this clash of values without neatly resolving it (as if anyone could anyway).

Ford is changed by his stay among the Amish, made not nonviolent, but less violent. Early on, we see him as the typical tough cop who has spent so much time pursuing criminals that he has begun to resort to their methods, and McGillis complains about his "whacking people." But his Amish interlude breeds a reluctance to use such means unless absolutely necessary—a reluctance first visible when, garbed in Amish black, he initially humors a young punk who harasses him, Rubes, and Haas in town. When this fails, Ford still is nonviolent; when this too fails, Ford finally has to whack him as a last resort. Director Peter Weir has filled the plot around options of excessive violence, nonviolence, and *just* violence—which is what Ford is led to discover in this scene and at the close.

The final sequence contains one of those Apocalypse/shootouts to which all Westerns, cop films, and now sci-fi must inevitably come. When the villains descend to kill Ford and the Amish family, he resists them, but does so in ways that show he has recovered his moral balance. For the shoot-out, Weir quietly borrows from an apt model, *High Noon*. Ford hides out among cows in a stable as Gary Cooper did among horses, picking off villains one by one. The echo of movies past is not simply technical. *Witness* echoes themes of *High Noon*—the heritage of Quaker nonviolence (represented by Grace Kelly and Kelly McGillis), the need to avoid violence if possible, and the final inevitability of violence if evil leaves you no options.

Ford, like Cooper, is a "good cop" softened by contact with nonviolence; like Cooper, he finally must stand and fight. But consider how Ford disarms the last villain (Josef Sommer): weaponless, Ford simply screams, "Enough!" at the carnage, and Sommer surrenders. The comment contrasts with DePalma's halfhearted "too much violence"; it also sums up *Witness*'s message on its central moral issue. A good cop relies on "enough" violence, but no more.

Justice and Sex

Recent movies about rape also examine the issue of how violent one might be forced to be to attain justice. Before *The Accused* came *Extremities* (1986) and the Australian *Shame* (1988), neither very successful. The last (with a female lawyer who motorbikes around the outback and brings sexual justice to a frontier-type town) exploited Western conventions, but perhaps in too playful a style. By contrast, *Extremities*, which originated in an off-Broadway play, didn't strike viewers as cinematic enough. It still posed a key question: would a woman be justified in avenging herself on a rapist after accidentally disarming him?

The movie made the question compelling by having the rapist threaten to come back someday, even if convicted, even if jailed, to murder her. He also brags about other rape-murders that he has committed. As the victim, Farrah Fawcett is tempted by his taunting: one blow and she can achieve the security that the system is unlikely to provide her (an earlier scene shows how unresponsive the police were after the villain's first assault on her, from which she escaped). *Extremities* failed to find an audience, but women who have lived in terror from rapists or abusive husbands who have been ordered to stay away from them might sympathize with Fawcett's dilemma about what to do when the law can't help you.

The Accused (1988) took a different tack, measuring how far law has come in defending women. Its plot was taken from a real-life gang rape in a Massachusetts bar, whose patrons cheered on the assault. The title is clearly meant to reveal a dark irony: rapists may be accused of a legal crime, but the victim is often accused of a social one, especially when the woman in questions drinks, smokes pot, and acts "sexy."

The Accused was not only a rape film, but partly a buddy movie, with the roles of friends/antagonists shared by victim and prosecutor. As the victim, Jodie Foster does a good job at portraying the victim's low-class habits and language, and for Academy Award voters, managed to compel full, outraged sympathy with her plight. Her costar was Kelly McGillis as the district attorney who must both prosecute on Foster's behalf and "defend" her from social stigma. Unfortunately, scenes between McGillis and Foster often fall flat, especially a key explosion when Foster accuses McGillis of abandoning her by settling for a conviction of the men accused on lesser charges of "reckless endangerment." Their chemistry is sub-Kelvin. At least, McGillis has more real work than her counterparts in *Jagged Edge* (1985), *Legal Eagles* (1986), and *Physical Evidence* (1989) where predictable love plots and tight-fitting skirts made the films resemble new, sexier ways of shooting *The Perils of Pauline*.

The Accused generated sympathy for victim, and finally, prosecutor McGillis, when she has the courage to bring charges of incitement against the bystanders who cheered on the assault. Like *Extremities* and *Shame, The Accused* reflects the desire by women's groups to increase public awareness of the evil of rape and to get people to stop blaming the victim. But more than the other two rape movies, it also stands as the perfect symbol of the new, more general trend in law-and-order films: the victim and prosecutor can sometimes be collaborators for justice.

Justice and Race

Sensitivity to sex crimes has been slow to come to movies. Sensitivity to race crimes—and the crime of racial discrimination—has been ever slower, reflected only in the fitful growth in screen pluralism. Indeed, beginning in the late 1970s, race was presented mainly in negative ways: as noted, many law-and-order films include members of ethnic groups only to stereotype them as animalistic criminals. There is no need for a movie version of affirmative action, nor for movies that whitewash minority group members of all signs of human frailty. But a little reality about their suffering would help. Until *Mississippi Burning* and *Do the Right Thing,* not much was forthcoming.

The two films are both flawed, but together pose the difficult question: from whom will the traditional victims of discrimination get justice? There was little concern with this issue until the very late 1980s; as *American Film* editor Chris Hodenfield writes, during the Reagan years Hollywood treated it with "benign neglect." Racial justice wouldn't be easy to achieve in any case, but lack of movies about it doesn't help.

Movie attention to racial tensions has a sad rhythm. In the latent but waning postwar liberalism of the late 1940s, race is dealt with honestly in movies such as *Gentleman's Agreement, Home of the Brave,* and *The Jackie Robinson Story.* Even an American Indian sports figure could be featured in a film—Burt Lancaster as *Jim Thorpe—All-American* (1951). But with Senator Joe McCarthy, Americanism got color coded, and demagogues (one, unfortunately, the head of the national police) equated civil rights workers and Communists. During the 1950s, frankness about racial problems, and indeed frankness about politics, died on screen.

It returned in the 1960s, in a spate of films that reflected and stimulated the civil rights movement: *To Kill a Mockingbird* (1962), *A Raisin in the Sun* (1963), *In the Heat of the Night* (1967), *Sounder* (1972), and *Claudine* (1974). Of course, the period saw "blaxploitation" too, as in *Drum, Mandingo,* and *Shaft.* Still, beyond crime and comedy, serious and important works pervaded the media, such as *The Autobiography of Miss Jane Pittman* (1974) and above all *Roots* (1975). In *Guess Who's Coming to Dinner* (1967) Sidney Poitier plays a sociology professor courting Spencer Tracy's and Katharine Hepburn's daughter; their parish priest makes them easier about it by greeting him, "Oh, you're the one who writes for *Commonweal!*" Those were the days.

In contrast, the eighties have been a period of blunted vigilance; by osmosis, movies took their cue from a national mood that placed racial subjects on the back burner. About the only film that dealt at any length with white racism was *Places in the Heart* (1984), when the Klan abuses Sally Field's farmhand (Danny Glover). Field herself led a "rainbow coalition"—women, children, the handicapped, and a black—representatively American enough to make James Watt smirk. *A Soldier's Story* (1984) and *The Color Purple* (1985) helped Hollywood accept the idea of large mixed audiences for films with black stars; still, while noting white racism, both movies focused much more on intrablack hostilities, the latter in an especially superficial way. Only Spielberg had the clout to get such a movie made; the inevitable result, albeit well-intentioned, is a Spielberg movie—minus his poetry of childhood. Oddly, in "adult" movies, he goes mawkish.

Signs of greater racial tolerance appeared in the mideighties, but didn't extend to the supersensitive area of white-black tension. Filmmakers began to realize the enormous potential of the Hispanic market and its buying and political power. The austere, independent *El Norte* (1984) detailed the harsh realities of escape from war-torn Central America; it paved the way for softer products directed at broader Hispanic concerns and mainstream audiences in *La Bamba* (1987), and, a year later, *The Milagro Beanfield War* and *Stand and Deliver.*

Other ethnic groups also got increasing attention. New England Portuguese Americans were featured prominently in *Mystic Pizza* (1988), and gypsies in Robert Duvall's earnest *Angelo, My Love* (1983). Asian-American experience was detailed in small, independent comedies like Wayne Wang's *Chan Is Missing* (1982) or *The Great Wall* (1986). Violence against Asian Americans was unevenly treated in *Alamo Bay* (1985) and more successfully in the PBS documentary, *Who Killed Vincent Chin?* (1989). Nearly every ethnic group was included in *Moscow on the Hudson* (1985), director Paul Mazursky's well-intentioned but shallow hymn to the ongoing life of the melting pot; naturally—in tune with the rest of the film—black-and-white issues are handled in comic fashion. But why could Mazursky not have given Robin Williams's refugee a black girlfriend, rather than a Spanish one?

The reason is simple: the taboo involved goes deep. Everything black-and-white in America is supercharged with a heavier weight of racial consciousness and heritage. This is not to derogate the problems of other minorities; but white/black tensions have plainly become a national tragedy—not least because of the inadequacies of the efforts to rectify them in the 1860s and 1960s. Movies mostly have tiptoed around this. Blacks were disproportionate among grunts in Vietnam; but few show up in *The Deer Hunter, Coming Home,* or *Apocalypse Now; Platoon* does a bit better. In sports films, black underrepresentation has been grotesque. Black athletes dominate some sports and are important influences in most, but there are few blacks in sports films except for *The Bingo Long Traveling All-Star and Motor Kings* (1976), whose title betrays its independent temper. Equally maverick was the ironically titled *The Great White Hope* (1970), with James Earl Jones as boxing champ Jack Jefferson.

The really popular "great white hope" has been *Rocky* (see chapter 5, "Sports"). The subtext of the first *Rocky* is antiblack, with Apollo Creed (Carl Weathers) a stand-in for Muhammad Ali. Indeed, Stallone conceived Rocky while watching an actual bout between Ali and a working-class great white hope, Chuck Wepner; Sly then went out and rewrote reality. Stallone manipulates the imagery of the pre-Reagan years (the first *Rocky* appeared in 1976) when his Rocky Balboa trains in a meat-packing plant and is condescendingly interviewed by a *black woman* news-caster. The scene neatly inverts the once-common crack by sixties' activists about racial and sexual equality, "I have seen God and she's black."

In the early eighties, TV did better than film, at least in giving blacks greater visiblity. With its lower costs and confidence about reaching small audiences, it has taken more risks, accommodating Bill Cosby and launching Eddie Murphy, who went on to become a star movie attraction, but in a comic, limited, and finally not very compelling way. In the early eighties, a few movies dealt with black-white tensions, such as *Say Amen, Somebody* (1982) and *Ragtime* (1981). John Sayles's *Brother from Another Planet* (1984) used sci-fi formulas to satirize racism, which was attacked more bluntly in *Betrayed* (1988), *Pink Cadillac* (1989), and *Lethal Weapon 2* (1989), which vilified apartheid.

Indeed, in the late eighties, the tempo seemed to pick up for black directors, actors, and black/white issues on screen. Spike Lee released his first films, and black actors suddenly seemed more prominent. Indeed, one of our best performers, James Earl Jones, came out from behind his Darth Vader mask and seemed omnipresent—in *Matewan, Field of Dreams,* and *Gardens of Stone* (1988). Danny Glover emerged in actioners such as the *Lethal Weapon* series; Morgan Freeman dominated

Street Smart (1987), *Lean on Me,* and *Driving Miss Daisy* (1989). He shared the spotlight in *Glory* (1989) with Denzel Washington, who also lit up *A Soldier's Story* and *Cry Freedom* (1987), and was called "the next Sidney Poitier." Poitier himself made a comeback in movies such as *Little Nikita* (1988).

Cops and Race

Mississippi Burning and *Do the Right Thing* seem to climax this trend. Despite differences in style and authenticity, they are heads and tails of one coin, the first strong movies in some time to depict the enormous problems in squaring justice and race in America. They represent a positive side of "sixties-something"—the search for social justice the eighties forgot. Their appearance (with some other films) at the decade's end suggests "benign neglect" is over. But what, if anything, will follow?

The former film had its defects, chiefly its misrepresentation—heroizing—of FBI agents, hardly the best friends of the civil rights movement. It underrepresented civil rights workers; indeed, no single black figure is well characterized, and none represents the many who struggled for their own freedom. The film also elides a key point: its Klan villains were never convicted in state courts, and got brief sentences in the federal.

What can excuse all this? According to director Alan Parker, he could only get financing if he made the FBI central and presented the tale in familiar Hollywood terms. His decision was to blend the stuff of social protest and the subgenre "buddy" fare now standard for all police-action dramas. Accordingly, after a brief but spookily terrifying sequence in which three civil rights workers are murdered, Parker focuses attention on the police. On one level, *Mississippi Burning* has as much to do with the civil rights movement as it does with *48 HRS* (1982) (see "Notes," p. 208, bottom).

Parker and screenwriter Chris Gerolmo's buddy team pairs Gene Hackman and Willem Dafoe, who plays a clean-cut, methodical, Kennedyesque special agent—about as close as any FBI man could get to the new frontier. There were, to be sure, officials in the Civil Rights Division of Justice like this at the time; Dafoe is their righteous incarnation. More knowing—and with a more winning part—is Hackman as a former Southern sheriff and drawling, all-around "good ole boy" who is ambivalent about racism, but knows a thing or two about how to deal with the Klan. Much of the film—sometimes too much—depicts the odd coupling of Dafoe and Hackman: they have to fight about methods, make up, find common ground, and go through standard buddy film rituals.

Did such formulas demean the story? Yes. Still, many who criticized the film remember the 1960s as a heroic age; for many born since, even many young blacks, the civil rights movement is ancient history. Even older members of the audience may not have recalled or *ever known* the story of the missing civil rights workers; they don't live in the newspapers as much as critics do.

Mississippi Burning got plenty of censure from liberals and radicals, but maybe they're just not in touch with the national audience. As Oliver Stone's *Talk Radio* (1988) dramatized—as any late-night spin around the dial would indicate—after years of education about civil rights, America doesn't suffer from excess tolerance. Whatever its flaws, *Mississippi Burning* was not without strengths in addressing this. Parker's terse tone and tight editing allowed him to re-create the tense atmosphere of the civil rights era and depict a kind of racist hatred that no one had gotten near the screen in two decades. The result is not pretty, but surely, sorely potent. The set—a backwater town, half-dust, half-swamp, with its shantytowns under constant threat—provides an American version of hell, where the Klan crucified mankind upon their cross of fire. This was bad to put on film?

Several blacks now represent Mississippi in Congress; they regularly get more local white support than white Democrats on national tickets. Still, racism remains a factor in the South; in the eighties, it reappeared in other regions, prestigious colleges, and big Northern cities. Parker knew this making *Mississippi Burning*; it's a protest against forgetting. The film ends on a long shot of Chaney's vandalized gravestone, with only it's bottom half ("1964 Not Forgotten") readable. "Not forgotten," no; but not always remembered clearly either, Parker implies.

Mississippi Burning implicitly protests against the "new federalism" that has been a code for deemphasizing national action to achieve racial justice. Whether or not the FBI helped enough, or at all, in 1963, is less important than the film's statement that they *should* have. The movie undercuts a dominant cliché of the Reagan era: federal government, the film says, can be good for you; goodness, even the feds can be public defenders.

Did Spike Lee Do the Right Thing?

Legal justice is also not always the same as social justice. The latter is not mentioned in the preamble of the Constitution; it derives more from the Declaration of Independence, its claim that "all men are created equal," and our populist heritage of social egalitarianism. Many Americans value it, especially those who complain that law sometimes works to keep society unequal.

Spike Lee's *Do the Right Thing* centers on the conflict of law and social justice. The movie is the major exception to the pattern of recent sympathy for the prosecution: Lee cannot imagine that the police can provide much for poor blacks beyond a nightstick. Its title is provocation: what can be "right," Lee asks, when legal justice and social justice are at odds? Lee values social justice above all, and sees property rights and the police as its enemies. Lee has little sympathy for the prosecution or cops because he sees them as enforcing social divisions. This is the reason, despite its defects, the movie is memorable: Lee forces us to examine what he sees as a painful clash of basic values. What's more, he throws in humor, style, and piquant characters. You need not agree with his answers to sympathize with his art.

Lee is now America's leading black filmmaker. In *She's Gotta Have It* and *School Daze* (made on shoestring budgets) and in *Do the Right Thing* (dropped by one studio, but supported by Universal) he provides an exciting but uneven blend of pop theatricality, comedy, and social realism. It's hard to combine them, and Lee doesn't always succeed. But (although criticized for omitting drugs from his slice of ghetto life), Lee is remarkably frank; he doesn't hide alcoholism, laziness, or the likelihood, on a hot summer day, of tempers rising into unreason and riot. He even adds a Jumbo blaster as one of the proximate causes. But like civil rights era comedians such as Dick Gregory, Lee succeeds in shifting blame away from the poor to the cycles of poverty. Some forget the humor in *Do the Right Thing* only because Lee is a *classic* artist who uses wit as stalking horse for bigger things.

The plot of the film centers on a Bedford Stuyvesant pizzeria owned by Sal, a middle-aged Italian (Danny Aiello, in his best role ever), who refuses to get out despite one son's disgust with the decay around them; across the street, a Korean has opened a fruit stand, and faces some of the same problems. Lee puts himself in the middle of the plot of *Do the Right Thing* as Mookie, Aiello's delivery man, who often tries to diffuse the simmering anger between him, his sons, and their customers. Mookie wears an old Brooklyn Dodger's T-shirt with Jackie Robinson's number, a set of frail threads holding Brooklyn together. In the battle to which the tensions of the film build, the teenager with the ghetto blaster confronts Sal, they fight, police arrive, and one brawny white cop (despite the pleas for "enough" from his buddy, à la *Witness*) puts him in a deadly choke hold. The kid dies. What surprises everyone is Mookie's response. As the cops pull away, he starts a riot by shoving a trash can in Sal's window. The use of undue force by one cop makes him lose all respect for legal justice.

But before the cops arrived, Mookie has been trying to keep peace by separating Sal and his combatants; if anything, he has been trying to protect Sal—a fact not discussed in debates about the movie. His change of sides is subtly revealing. Until the killing fuels his frustration at the powerlessness of the poor, Mookie values law and order, or at least observes it. Lee is caught between obedience to law and rebellion. With his closing quotes from Martin Luther King and Malcolm X, he brings us right back where the conflict first came to a head: the icons declare that the movie is another, more complex case of troubled "sixties-something."

Do the Right Thing is not wildly revolutionary, as many sixties' films were; in the figure of Sal, it celebrates hard work. Indeed, in its sympathy for white blue-collar ethnics, it is more generous than most recent movies made by whites on work-related subjects in our time (see "Work"). It even allows for the possibility of a good cop, however slow to control his partner. Still, the traditional values that Lee shares are upset by indignation about the plain fact that many minority group members can never hope to have what Sal has, not even pictures of their heroes on a pizza parlor wall.

And Justice for All?

In 1990, Sidney Lumet would be back with *Q&A*, and Scott Turow's *Presumed Innocent* would make the screen. Courtroom drama would rely for novelty on lady lawyers with Barbara Hershey in *Defenseless* and Jessica Lange in *Music Box*. Keeping old traditions very much alive will be *The Godfather, Part Three*.

But movies confronting racial issues mark a new trend. They included *Glory, Heart of Dixie,* and *A Dry White Season,* a protest against apartheid. The latter was directed by Euzchan Palcy, a young woman director from Martinique (a story in itself) whose *Sugar Cane Alley* (1987) presented third-world poverty without condescension. Of *A Dry White Season,* Palcy frankly said, "I made this movie based on the belief that movies can affect social change."

One hopes for even more—something like a glimmer of social enlightenment. Movies don't often focus on the way poverty fosters crime. As Allan Dershowitz has noted, recent films have not been good at getting at the roots of crime; we have no recent equivalent of *The*

Bicycle Thief or even *The Dead End Kids* and *The Hoodlum Priest* (1957), a decently made and affecting melodrama on the conditions (among poor whites) that breed criminality.

Although this was not the intention of *Do the Right Thing*, it is one of the results. We are left wondering how young people in such settings—without social reform—can ever *not* clash with police. The film implies that you cannot really establish legal without increasing social justice. You don't have to condone every aspect of *Do the Right Thing*, or its conclusion, to know that we could use a movie, and much more, about that.

11

Irony

Always look on the bright side of life.
—*Life of Brian* (1979)

Nine years before *The Last Temptation of Christ*, Monty Python's *Life of Brian* (1979) ignited a smaller version of the later controversy over movies about the life of Jesus. The film was picketed in the United States, banned in Ireland, and condemned by the Vatican. Yet its full significance was not simply an attack upon established religion. It exemplifies our broad attempt to substitute an odd kind of new one: the worship of Irony.

Irony has long been a resource of all drama. Its most basic mode is verbal wit (e.g., double entendres, antic malapropisms, witty wordplay). A second mode involves dramatic irony through foreshadowing; the audience acquires more knowledge of the plot than the characters themselves (e.g., when Desdemona's handkerchief falls and our anxiety rises). Artists also exploit Irony by juxtaposing unusual materials—a device that moviemakers, employing montage, have reveled in since Eisenstein. No recent example surpasses the scenes near the end of *The Godfather*, and their contrast of baptismal renunciations of Satan and mass murder.

In the 1980s, Irony has threatened to become even more important. Indeed, in modern and postmodern practice and ideology, it has emerged not as a mode *in* the arts, but almost the central value of all art, its most highly desirable characteristic, its crowning glory. This new, inflated idea of Irony pervades both pop and high culture; it encompasses the smaller verbal, dramatic, and situational modes of Irony, driving their central formulas to negative extremes: nothing means hat it says, no one can control one's fate, no single image can ьat it says, no one can control one's fate, no single image can ̤ ᴜᴛuth. It elevates these formulas to sacred truths, not only about art, but life itself. Such all-encompassing Irony can have the benign effect of teaching caution about being too certain about anything; art or films that exhibit it can be humbling and renewing. But this higher Irony can also lead to its own numbing certainty, a nihilistic gospel based on perpetual recourse to mock-heroic or other genres that travesty all values.

The new Irony is the intellectual black hole of our age. Traditional comedy undercuts pomposity to restore balance; the higher Irony undercuts for the sake of undercutting; a work of art (or film) is now judged to be cool if it validates the Ironic belief (and *belief* is all it is, no more provable than any other ideology) that nothing is valuable, or worth trying, or at least no human being is good enough to try. In film and literature, such negative messages are communicated through what the ever-trendy, *pseudo*nonconformist intelligentsia calls "anti-myths." In today's America, the formulation of such "anti-myths" is an apt complement to the "Vietnam" syndrome, implying not so much a reluctance to use force in military affairs, but to find hope in national, social, or personal ones. In short, the new gospel of Irony preaches blanket blithe cynicism; in pop media, Monty Python, *National Lampoon*, and *Saturday Night Live* are its prophets.

Life of Brian (1979) didn't exactly ironize the life of Christ; the Pythons took an indirect approach. Instead of a life of Christ, they depicted a parallel story of a fumbling and very reluctant "messiah" named Brian, whose mock-heroic activities in Judea are presented as periodically intersecting those of Jesus. As in the Sermon on the Mount scenes in many older religious epics like *Ben Hur* (1959) or *The Robe* (1953), the figure of Jesus is seen only in long shots. But this "distancing" is not created from reverence. Instead, it allows the Pythons to poke fun at how religious zealots, fanatically eager for any message, misunderstand or misapply Christ's beatitudes—e.g., after hearing them from a distance, they wonder what was meant by "Blessed are the cheesemakers."

Some of these scenes are hysterically funny, especially ones satirizing the fusion of religious and political fanaticism in ancient and modern Palestine. In general, there is no denying the merit of Python humor; it can knock you (or at least me) silly in skits such as the cheese shop, the dead parrot, and the Queen Victoria Handicap in *And Now for Something Completely Different* (1972) and *Monty Python at the Hollywood Bowl* (1982). Although too predictable, their swipes at stuffy curates aren't bad either. Lively send-ups of religious and other institutions provide valuable satires on pomposity. In this regard, Pythonism preserves the tradition of wackily irreverent English humor in Ben Jonson, Swift, Hogarth, and Dickens—some of whom the Pythons must have studied while students at college in the early 1960s.

The problem with Monty Python—and later ironists in our country—is how easily their brand of humor degenerates to mere put-down. Too often they pass from the value of humor to humor as the *only* value. *Life of Brian* crosses this line too frequently. It illustrates how satire against pomposity can easily become a new (if sly) form of pomposity itself: a knowing, know-it-all cynicism about *all* values. In this instance, *Life of Brian* is an apt prelude for a time when jokes become dangerous because nothing was sacred, except the urge to joke. *Batman's* Joker may have existed in cartoons and television long before the eighties; but his nasty humor certainly fitted the later 1980s like a mask. He wasn't the only Joker around in the decade; Kubrick celebrates one in *Full Metal Jacket*. But what did all all the jesting mean?

Don't Worry, Be Happy

First, it means holding nothing sacred, as in *Life of Brian*. According to the Pythons, the film was not antireligious, and was certainly not directed at Christ or Christianity. Really? As noted their TV skits certainly display a hefty diet of daft curates. Moreover, even if the film did not directly attack the Gospels, it shot so many holes through the desire to believe in something that its satire could be seen as implicitly universal. That is, while avoiding direct insult, *Life of Brian* called down a plague on most religious houses, with Christianity unquestionably the biggest one in the general neighborhood of the plot.

This hostility to belief reflects a new attitude toward religion by many Americans (see chapter 12, "Religion"). True, parts of America have experienced a religious revival in the eighties; but others seemed more than ever to enjoy the assaults in movies *against* religious values or images. Attacks on religion pervaded eighties' media, with caricature hypocritical ministers (*Footloose* [1984], *Light of Day* [1987], *Crimes of Passion* [1984], *Mosquito Coast* [1986]); fuddy-duddy church ladies (*The Witches of Eastwick* [1987], *Saturday Night Live*), stage lampoons of nuns (*Nunsense, Sister Mary Ignatius Explains It All for You*); muckraking on priests (*Mass Appeal* [1984], *Monsignor* [1982], and *True Confessions* [1981]); and fast-and-loose caricatures of Catholicism (*Agnes of God, The Name of the Rose* [both 1985]). Third-world religions were consistently misrepresented, typically through images of sadistic cults in *Indiana Jones and the Temple of Doom* and *Young Sherlock Holmes* (1984). Even Woody Allen's genial satire in *Hannah and Her Sisters* uses caricatures to knock kitschy Catholicism and Hare Krishnas. Yes: we've had plenty of "televangelist" frauds and ministerial mischief; yes, some Catholics worship fruity pagan idols. But most recent films on the subject imply, falsely, this is *all* there is to religion.

Life of Brian goes beyond satire on religion; it conforms to a more pervasive habit of mind in our time—a hip, smirking supercool Irony toward *all* forms of belief, religious, nationalistic, heroic, domestic. It trashes belief in anything at all. The end of the film is key. Brian has been crucified; his followers stand below his cross, jeering or offering little consolation. One of the other crucified (Eric Idle, a Python mainstay) tells him not to worry, and leads those dying with him in a self-consciously silly ditty, "Always look on the bright side of life." A chorus picks the lyric up, in a slyly grotesque version of a rousing number at the conclusion of an old-fashioned musical.

Idle's advice isn't unwise; it reworks the cliché that humor is the best therapy against depression. The setting is bizarre, however, and the tone blackly comic. "Always look on the bright side of life" might have ended a Norman Vincent Peale sermon or a Disney film. But the Idle number implies not so much joy or delight as a devil-may-care cynicism. It is a broad bit of jesting, a dismissive "what-do-I-care-about-anything-but-a-laugh."

Judging such humor is difficult. On one level, Idle's number is bound to offend anyone who cannot tolerate playfulness about a crucifixion. On the other, it rounds out the film's satire on political and religious zealotry. This is the way a movement ends, the film declares: not with a bang but a simper. But there is, perhaps, even more meaning in the song. Better not to get so serious about everything, it implies; as the pop song goes, "don't worry, be happy." In this case, such a message may have a dark side: don't worry; indeed, don't even get too concerned about anything much at all.

Why do we value such blithe spiritedness? Consider the world beyond film a moment. Stand-up comedians, masters of the ironic put-down, flourished in the 1980s; in May, 1989, HBO announced it was founding a twenty-four-hour comedy channel. Johnny Carson was rivaled not just in his own time slot but at live comedy theater "improvs" that sprang up around the country. The style of one-line zingers became contagious even beyond comedy clubs. Weathermen and sportscasters doubled up as wise guys on the local news. Politicians, so often targets of satirists, became masters of zingers too; campaigns degenerated into exchanges of "sound bite" insults where Don Rickles would feel right

at home. Given this "cant-agion" of comic insult (witness Lloyd Bentsen's cheapo, "You're no Jack Kennedy" treatment of Dan Quayle)
statesmanship degenerated into a version of *Gotcha!*, the campus game
that became the source of a spy film in 1984. Yes, such humor could
be fun. But what happens if a nation can put nothing in the put-down's
place?

Consider a parallel trend, what Joyce Carol Oates calls "pathography."
The term is applied to new biographies that recount all the past sins,
scandals, and neuroses of writers and artists whom previous
biographers had treated more gingerly—either through lack of information, generosity of spirit, capaciousness of judgment, or perhaps
the gift of understanding what a *whole* person is. In the arts alone,
Raphael, Rembrandt, Jackson Pollock, Picasso, and John Lennon were
all given the pathographic treatment in the later eighties—the latter two
in notorious biographies. As James Atlas writes, biography—initially
a genre to illustrate exemplary lives—now goes to an opposite extreme
and has become a major way to get back at them, showing "how little
is the happiness the great enjoy." Pathography is easy if you think about
it: what life, in all its aspects, could *ever* stand up to absolute scrutiny?
(Beyond the specific context of *Life of Brian*, pathographic put-down is
always at odds with the critical but humane understanding of personality in the best of religion; as unironic St. Paul once said, "No one
is righteous, no; not one.")

Amadeus provides an example of screen pathography—with one key
difference allowing for a more inclusive charitable vision (see below).
Clint Eastwood's film on Charlie Parker, *Bird* (1989), provides a similar
portrait of an artist—with sad insight balanced by generous judgment.
Indeed, most films do not take a direct pathographic route, since movies
have not become as sophisticatedly narrow-minded as letters; it is also
hard to imagine someone banking a biopic to destroy a reputation. Still,
the pathographic impulse now dominates a major form of film put-
down: the spoof.

The Put-down as Fine Art

Spoofs are the major mode of movie put-down in our times. The trend
is understandable: spoofs are needed to deflate hot air balloons, plenty of which have been launched recently. When so much folderol and
public relations pretension mark both a culture and counterculture,
spoofs become essential for satire, sources for good laughs and genuine
perspective; they are medicinal antihype vaccinations. Spoofs often

follow a time-honored tradition in literature, classified as "mock-heroic," in which either contemporary heroes are shown to be mere shadows of old ones, or old heroes are shown to be mere stuff and nonsense. Normally, movie or other media spoofs are more genial and bumptious than pathographic mudslinging. Still, they provide a parallel example of the current (and apparently desperate) need to deflate all heroic images. Individually often hilarious, cumulatively such spoofs may add to the corrosive cynicism of the age.

Monty Python specializes in mock-heroic spoof. Besides *Life of Brian*, consider *Jabberwocky* (1977), *The Missionary* (1982), and *Monty Python and the Holy Grail* (1974), a wildly uneven takeoff on Arthurian legend. Woody Allen also loves the mock-heroic, with spoofs like *Love and Death* (parodying *War and Peace* [1975]) and *Play it Again, Sam* (1972), where he measures his own heroism against Bogart's. Sometimes Allen just takes swipes at revered forms of heroism, as in *Radio Days* (1987), where he mocks sports legendmaking by depicting a "heroic" (or in his view, absurd) pitcher carrying on a career despite multiple injuries and loss of limbs—a takeoff on movies such as Jimmy Stewart's *The Stratton Story* (1949) and the "black knight" scenes in *Monty Python and the Holy Grail*. Allen's send-up of such legends may be viewed differently now that Jim Abbott, with one deformed arm, pitches in the majors. Nietzsche described Allen's attitude long ago: ressentiment.

A legitimate resource for art in every age, mock-heroic has become a universal crutch in ours. Consider the fate of old heroes in recent films, where few are untouched by revision. In *Without a Clue* (1988) and *Hound of the Baskervilles* (1977), Sherlock Holmes was shown as a foolish or inadequate detective; in *Young Frankenstein* (1974) the old tragic horror story is replayed strictly for laughs. Horror stories in general are spoofed in *Attack of the Killer Tomatoes* (1980). In films such as the fine *McCabe and Mrs. Miller* (1971) and *Buffalo Bill and the Indians* (1976), Robert Altman mocks the heroism of the Old West, and in *M*A*S*H* the US Army. The most popular history films of our times have been mock-heroic, as in Mel Brooks's *History of the World—Part 1* (1981). Westerns are spoofed in *Blazing Saddles* (1974), gangster films in *Johnny Dangerously* (1984), cop heroics in *Dragnet* (with *Saturday Night Live*'s Dan Ackroyd [1987]), and medieval heroism in *Eric the Viking* (with members of the Python crew [1990]). Movies such as *Mr. Mom* (a top money winner in 1983) find it easy to provide mock-heroic laughs simply through allusions to famous movie scores such as *Chariots of Fire* (in a corporate race) or *Jaws* (when a house husband is pursued by a voracious vacuum cleaner).

Or take the contrast of old-fashioned save-an-airplane films from

Zero Hour (1957) to *Airport* (1970) with *Airplane!* (1980) and its goofy send-up of sky-high heroism. *Airplane!* has an almost inevitable sequence: one of its heroes—the blond, macho pilot played by Peter Graves—turns out to be homosexual, and in one of the film's final scenes, is shown unconsciously trying to seduce a little boy. Woody Allen uses the same kind of humor to dismiss the ideas of Socrates in *Hannah and Her Sisters*. Albeit illiberal, some of this humor is funny; it is also cheap. Such mock-heroic reductionism could be written into any script, and against anybody; Monty Python did it repeatedly with the same kind of jesting in its skits with curates, policemen, and lumberjacks. In such an atmosphere, reductive Irony easily becomes a substitute for thought; instant iconoclasm becomes the lazy comedian's icon.

Even movie criticism turned spoofy, with "Joe Bob Briggs," the persona adapted by the *Dallas Herald Examiner* critic, John Bloom. "Joe Bob" allowed Bloom to express frank appreciation for many movies on the level at which they were made, getting off the throne of high-mindedness that he felt was boring and fake. So Bloom as "Joe Bob" took to the drive-in, providing lengthy reviews of kung-fu, slasher, and sexploitational movies in exuberantly lurid prose. The move was original and funny, but earned Joe Bob enemies among groups (religious and feminist) riled by his enthusiasms; Joe Bob wouldn't buckle and John Bloom left the *Herald*. Ethics aside, Joe Bob mistook a lark for a shtick. Few movie critics haven't felt the temptation to slum, but none has crusaded over it. But the god Irony demands full commitment; the one thing you can't be is ironical about *it* (see "Notes," p. 209, middle).

Anti-"Sixties-Something"

The eighties' "epidemic of Irony" has been long in festering. Irony has been the staple of modernism, dear to European and expatriate writers ever since World War I and the "lost generation." The roots of the new Irony go back even earlier—to the cynics and aesthetes rebelling against middle-class, late nineteenth-century culture: Flaubert in France, Wilde in England, and Joyce—the first patriot of Irony—in flight from Ireland to the Continent. Modernists (and now postmodernists) ache to repeat the Ur-gestures of these early heroes; consider the (legitimate) love of Flaubert in the works of Woody Allen, or the deification of Joyce and Flaubert in literary academia. On film, neo-surrealists practice a parallel ancestor worship in their never-ending efforts to make room for Dada—e.g., Alex Cox of *Walker* (1988) or ex-Python Terry Gilliam, director of *Time Bandits* (1981), *The Adventures of Baron Munchausen* (1989), and especially *Brazil* (1985). Naturally, when asked to explain his inspiration for the "Piss Christ" that so outraged conservatives during the National Endowment for the Arts controversies of 1989, Andres Serrano cited an early surrealist godfather from film, Luis Buñuel. In short, our hip avant-garde still equates originality with bold rejection of the nineteenth century.

In the past two decades, the higher Irony has seeped out from the ivory tower to contaminate pop culture even more pervasively. As social historian Todd Gitlin notes, even with its historical precedents, the recent Irony epidemic is "post-Vietnam, post-new left, post-hippie, post-Watergate," the product of a time when "history was ruptured, passions have been expanded, belief has become difficult, heroes have died and been replaced by celebrities." According to Gitlin, "irony and blankness are a way of staving off anxieties, rages, and terrors that have been knocked up but cannot find resolution." Irony is a sign of burned-out "cultural helplessness"; it forms the tone of enervated "postmodernism" with its "affectless" heroes and their refusal to trust in any strong focus of loyalty beyond the self. *In Country* provides a good illustration in the Vietnam vet played by Bruce Willis, who cannot find himself until the end of the film.

Is Irony so much an eighties' property? Rightly or wrongly, the sixties believed in the importance of being earnest. As *Spy* notes "the counterculture was virtually irony free: for every Firesign Theater, there were hundreds of Earth Day manifestors, Jane Fonda declarations of solidarity, John Lindsay depictions of earnestness, communal suppers of tofu and human placenta. But just as it became clear that John Lindsay and placenta eating were not going to transform the world, an irony industry sprang up to fill the void. In a few years, a generation's perpetual frown had become a perpetual smirk. One minute everything had been in deadly earnest. The next minute, everything was amusing." If you merge Gitlin and *Spy*, and add *Batman* and *Full Metal Jacket*, it seems that post-Vietnam cynicism turned our Jokers wild.

To be exact, the sixties did have their humorists, forefathers of today's ironists—such as Lenny Bruce and Dick Gregory. But their jokes at least had weight. Their bitter, driven, often-obscene comedy found a ready audience among the dissenting youth of Vietnam War years. Their targets were mainly establishment figures and manners, with their usual targets the army, church, schools. Early Python skits attacked many of the same targets. But in America and England the comic boom that began as satire on the status quo turned its guns on the "movement" to change it. *Life of Brian* again provides a key illustration, with satire aimed at both Christianity and left-wing, quasi-religous, self-righteous movements to reform or revolutionize the world.

In this context, the Monty Python song, "Always Look on the Bright Side of Life," takes on an even added significance. It provides a perfect symbol for the death of hope in political reform, however misguided, that permeated the 1960s and early 1970s and even tinged its comic spirit. The song is an apt symbol for a new, different, later sensibility that emerged in the late 1970s and early 1980s; it's not "good-bye Columbus," but "good-bye crusading." The song parallels the fate of "Alex" in *The Big Chill*, or of crusading in *The Last Temptation of Christ* (see "Religion"): we've all been too serious, the song says; better to chuck it all and look at the brighter side of life. In short, the end of *Life of Brian* marks yet another death and burial for the spirit of the sixties. Rebellion gets you killed, the movie says.

"Good-bye crusading" means "hello, comedy"—hence not just the Pythons but the wider coronation of comedy as king and Irony as god. (Even Bentsen's cheapo "You're no Jack Kennedy" line unintentionally reinforces what the eighties has been saying about *itself* all along: we are not the sixties). The closing chorus of *Life of Brian*, "Look on the bright side of life," thus explains in part the "feel good" spirit of the eighties: the need to "feel good" came from the disillusioned left as much as the right. The difference between conservative reasons for feeling good and left-wing ones is that the former are at least straightforward; the latter involve a defensive reaction formation against thinking about reasons for the failure of reform.

Consider *Saturday Night Live* and the films that derived from it. The best moments on the show, or in the many film vehicles for its cast, normally involved some form of mock-heroic. Some mock-heroic skits were hysterical: for example, John Belushi's takeoff on Japanese Westerns and John Travolta, "Samurai Night Fever." Broader social satire was also mock-heroic, with plenty of establishment targets. Politicians always got it in the neck, beginning with Chevy Chase's mimicking of Gerry Ford pratfalls with doors and staircases; religion got it with Dana Carvey's "Church Lady," and the army in movies such as Bill Murray's *Stripes* (1981). But radicals, or at least reformers, also received their knocks; Bill Murray spends almost as much time fighting an environmentalist from EPA in *Ghostbusters* as he does the ghosts. Even black activism was treated with humorous put-down—as in Eddie Murphy's caricature of the radical, "Shebaz X"; he also satirized ghetto life in "Mr. Robinson's Neighborhood." All these were typical eighties' good-byes to the ultraseriousness with which some "revolutionary" idealists of the seventies took themselves.

Humor was a natural response to disillusion caused by the crisis of the 1960s. At least it's better than other responses, such as depression or suicide, an option taken by numerous counterculture rock or folk singers and folk heroes. Humor aids in survival strategies, even perhaps a devil-may-care wildness. It's rare that humans can ever go without such humor; it's a basic form of defense against disillusion. The recent intensity of such disillusioned humor suggests just how strong the initial sixties' illusions were to begin with. Irony detaches, removes one from appearing too involved, frees from the heavy responsibility of fighting and losing on too many liberation fronts at once. Irony, in short, has functioned as a first line of defense against "The Big Chill."

The need for laughter is part of our search for healthy emotional balance. To a point, Irony helps. But overdoses (even of laughter) never produce healthy results. Humor, satire, and put-down—always legitimate against any and all targets—can become a tick; the attack on fashion *another fashion*. Satire as a weapon against pomposity becomes a comic crutch, a clichéd response, an enemy of alertness; it degenerates into satire for satire's sake. Rituals of knee-jerk Irony become so pervasive that everything unconventional becomes the new convention, and nothing is more predictable (or unfunny) anymore as a joke. Such jesting puts us exactly where we are today: trapped in a prison run by anarchists.

Comedy vs Irony?

The eighties will be remembered for some outstanding comedies that blended satire, mock-heroics, and out-and-out farce: *Tootsie,* Steve Martin's *All of Me* and *Roxanne,* some Robin Williams and Woody Allen movies, and the exquisitely paced *A Fish Called Wanda* (1988). Some quirky but excellent movies have used mock-heroic formulas quite heavily: mock-romances like *Choose Me* (1984); the mock-heroic film noir of the Coen brothers (*Blood Simple* [1984]) or their takeoff on baby movies (*Raising Arizona*); Rob Reiner's mock-rock documentary, *This Is Spinal Tap* [1984]); some satires by Paul Bartel (*Eating Raoul* [1982]); the Mafia satire in *Prizzi's Honor;* and the odd blend of "searching for America" and waiting for Godot in movies by Jim Jarmusch (*Down by Law* [1986] and *Stranger than Paradise* [1984]).

Bill Murray exemplifies something slightly different: a constant cool that doesn't always refresh. He can be funny. But sometimes you wonder if anyone really cool would be so relentless about it; in some films Murray's routines have become hilariously boring. He also illustrates the dangers of permanently affecting cool: little matters to him in his snappy, smarmy detachment from caring. A Murray vehicle such as *Scrooged* (1988) at first seems to satirize uncaring; his media mogul miser is even equated with eighties' egoism as opposed to his earlier (mild) idealism in the sixties. But *Scrooged* only pretends to update Dickens's *A Christmas Carol*; Murray's "Scrooge" is glamourously attractive in his nastiness, not repulsive and pitiable as in the original. *Scrooged* pays sentimental values only a closing, perfunctory mock-heroic tribute. As Vincent Canby wrote of Murray's cynicism after the film's release, "In a succession of mindless movies made without narrative intelligence, or a commitment to anything but their second-hand coolness, the attitude not only begins to seem stupid but as corrupt as the corruption it mocks." (Aptly, the only serious movie Murray ever made is *The Razor's Edge* [1982], which was based on a Somerset Maugham novel about post–World War I disillusionment. It is more ancestor worship from our leading "rebels").

As Oscar Wilde noted, only superficial people do not understand the importance of appearances. But a deliberately cool refusal to go deep or to credit insights of mind or feelings of heart—to play only at facades—aids and abets all those already strong tendencies in the entertainment world to stick to the surface and avoid depth. Whatever their intentions and intelligence, ironists disavowing seriousness are allies of those reducing movies into techno-displays, rock music, and camera angles. Ironic avoidance of depth also coincides perfectly with acting and directing styles that stress externals, not character or conflict. These trends are intensified by actors who keep things on the surface, often with a hip, knowing, ironic wink at the audience—not only Murray, but Mickey Rourke and Arnold Schwarzenegger, who has turned his strongman roles into camp mock-heroic.

Besides encouraging superficiality, Irony may have broader cultural and political impact. For example, what does the influence of reductive Irony do for hope of reform? (Yes, reformers as well as establishment types need spoofing; that is *not* at issue.) But Irony can weaken ability to hope in anything, however valid. Irony that shoots at all targets invariably weakens the new, most vulnerable ones most. As Richard Corliss says, overdosing on irony results in a "Who Cares?" attitude, a complement to benign neglect to social issues in recent years. "Always look on the bright side of life" is a recipe for giving in, not going on.

Irony can also corrode faith in any ideal. The higher irony is not only aimed at false belief; it implies that all forms of belief are false—with hope and love often thrown into the bargain. In doctrinaire Irony, every hero turns out to have feet of clay; there is no inkling that some people with feet of clay may also grow wings of desire to attain heroism despite or *because of* their weaknesses. But Irony cannot follow that; it wants nothing *really* complex: it craves simplicity; it merely exchanges hero trashing for hero worship. It insists there are no religions worth following, no myths worth belief, no joys worth pursuing, no teacher competent, no preacher sincere. Movie critics often worry about the effects of sex and violence on screen; they might worry instead about movies that—however funny or well made in themselves—cumulatively imply, as the *New Republic* warned, "that nothing is true and that everything is permitted."

The ancient Greeks believed that heroes had ruling spirits or "gods" whose gifts or advice explained their particular skill. One of the ruling spirits of many in our age is clearly the god Irony. Once a means in art, now an end in itself, it commands steady worship; those ruled by Irony act according to systematic disbelief in any value but debunking. Irony has become their only value, a kind of belief in nothing; for tax-exempt purposes all it lacks is self-consciousness of itself as a form of belief.

Among the literary intelligentsia, this Irony has its high priests; among lit and flick graduate students its acolytes, and among campy pop filmmakers, some of its most devoted followers. It gets amusing to watch them, all the "unconventional people," all the "freethinkers," all the liberated Bohemians in their repeated rituals of "individualistic" display as they march off in the same direction and to the same drummer. To paraphrase Lord Macaulay, there is nothing so ridiculous, or conventional, as the modern avant-garde in one of its periodic fits of value trashing.

Sympathy for the Devil

The most blackly comic forms of irony on screen in the 1980s come from Europe. Fassbinder's formally brilliant, cynical films are among the best example; he too felt a "Big Chill" (on a deeper level) with the decline of European revolutionary hopes after 1968. English left-wing films (e.g., *My Beautiful Laundrette, Sammy and Rosie Get Laid, Withnail and I*) still score points against Margaret Thatcher; but their satires often weaken into assaults on all "bourgeois" values, which are reductively equated with her sway. Despite their real flair, these films often get inflated praise from film journals because of their offhanded contempt for everything old and traditional—i.e., a major element in their artistic reputation is simply ideological zeal. This exemplifies reverse Victorianism in action: art is good if it's very, very bad.

In America, a related mode of black comic irony is reverse Disneyism, in which ironic filmmakers set out to assault belief in some traditional all-American image or symbol, and to reveal it as shallow, empty, and unstable. Small towns have been the most fashionable target as an embodiment of a mythic America of bygone wholesomeness, white picket fences, and ice cream sodas—a mythic view still alive in *Hoosiers*, *The Natural*, or *Racing with the Moon* (1984). Ironists accordingly shape anti-myths by deconstructing these images, as in "bleak chic" movies like *The Little Shop of Horrors* (1986), *Heathers* (1989), *Blue Velvet* (1986), *Something Wild* (1985), and *Gremlins* (1984), where the initial Christmassy, pretty-as-a-picture setup announces that the entire All-American scene is about to come apart at the seams. Of course, each of these movies has its funny or impressive parts; *Heathers* has a fine line from a high-school murderess, "I don't know if I'm going to the prom or to Hell." But the humor is often one note; even the witty *Heathers* goes heavy on the parental paté. There is nothing that serves ironists so well as a set of conventional images to deconstruct. Ironic formulas sure save thinking.

Blue Velvet at least had the distinction of consistent bleakness: after a voyage into a moral underworld beneath the surface of a "normal" American town, the smooth, clean-cut hero (Kyle MacLachan) doesn't even show any expanded awareness of moral issues. He sees a "heart of darkness" without the intelligence to realize "the horror, the horror." The result of all that experience is mere blankness; he's the affectless hero to the nth degree. It's not pretty, but possible, and director David Lynch has the courage to present the possibility. Still, critical praise for the film was wildly overdone; ignored, for ideological reasons, were its long-windedness, belabored wit with ironic double entendres, sloppy plotting, excessive violence, and incoherent end—not to mention the artificially contrived anti-myth costarring robins and bugs. If you rent the video, check for the bugs: the insect motif is as lightly executed as a thunderclap.

Even the Anglo-American *Dangerous Liaisons* served the trend to Irony. It relied on a complex screenplay, and even richer source in the novel by Choderlos de Laclos. It sparkled with splendidly authentic costumes, a gorgeous production design (complete with chateaux), and exquisitely mean acting by Glenn Close as the Machiavellian Marquise de Meurteuil. But it also suited our times by catering to lowest-common-denominator cynicism. Its intrinsic merit was heightened by the au courant ideological appeal of what Mick Jagger once knowingly sang of as "sympathy for the devil."

Delight in diabolism is a traditional (and often-legitimate) feeling that art evokes for purposes of vicarious participation. *Dangerous Liaisons* milked this tradition, but sometimes its deck seemed too stacked, its diabolism just a tad, well, *conformist*. The film's center was a contest of sexual chess, but often in dry, end-game variations. Meurteuil and her partner in crime, the Marquis de Valmont (John Malkovich), like to use sex to gain power, or at least to ruin others' self-esteem. To maintain his honor, Valmont aims to topple a virtuous married woman, the Marquise de Tourvel (Michelle Pfeiffer). When Close declares this impossible, he challenges her to bet her honor—or rather a night in bed— on his success with Tourvel. She accepts the bet, on condition he also beds her rival, the young Cecile de Volanges.

The screenplay by Chris Hampton (who wrote the play) contains some fierce exchanges. Meurteuil calls herself a "virtuoso of deceit"; she declares that life is a "war between love and virtue"; she lives by the battle cry, "win or die." As fiery as some of these lines are, her naughty bons mots and exchanges with Malkovich eventually seem to move like tired armies retrekking the same ground. The debates over which is better—love, revenge, betrayal, or cruelty?—became long-winded and theatrically abstract, degenerating at last into amoral sermons. But no hip audience will ever complain about *thus* being preached at; besides, the victims were either virtuous or virginal, or, in short, obviously repressed—to moderns, a fate worse than death.

Michelle Pfeiffer's performance (her best acting ever) did eventually alter these impressions; she made Tourvel's suffering compelling and pitiable. Even Malkovich grew in his role, and his Valmont became more interesting as he experienced doubts over his campaign of seduction, and as he sensed the pull of real love for Tourvel. But the acting was undone by the director, Stephen Frears, whose interests seemed to lie elsewhere. Indeed, Frears (also director of *My Beautiful Laundrette* and *Sammy and Rosie Get Laid*) didn't seem to care too much about the end of the film. In studio-produced interviews on TV around the premiere, he spoke glowingly on the evil machinations of Meurteuil and Valmont, not their mutual undoing at the end; he discussed the conclusion of the plot as if it merely involved tying up loose ends. As a result, the movie rushes through a closing as hurried as the buildup was lasciviously slow. In short, all the force in the film rests in diabolism, not the way the devils are finally hoist with their own petard.

Contrast this with *Amadeus* where Milos Forman used materials from the time of Laclos to fashion another diabolical tale of greater power and weight; he also orchestrated convincing, genuinely chilling irony *against* the ironic deceiver. *Amadeus* is "pathography" only to a point; its ironic view of Mozart was countered by a richer, deeper, more sophisticated Irony *against Irony*. It is Salieri who has the reductively ironic vision: like a modern pathographer, he can't see how such a low, vulgar man or "creature" such as Mozart can accomplish anything. The film allows us to see beyond the reality of Mozart's vulgarity (with its strong biographical base) into the reality of his genius.

Indeed, throughout the film version of *Amadeus*, Mozart grows in emotional stature. Modernist sympathy for the devil is undercut by sympathy for the "creature," particularly because of the glory of the score and the staging of Mozart's *Requiem*. Near the end, on his deathbed, Mozart is dictating to Salieri (pure fiction, but perfect here) several phrases from the "Dies Irae" of the Requiem Mass in which the soul asks God's forgiveness at the Final Judgment ("Confutatis maledictis, flammis acribus addictis, voca me cum benedictis"). Impressed by the phrases, and mistakenly believing Salieri to be his only true friend, Mozart asks him to forgive his earlier insults, quite a *dramatic* irony in view of the persecution Salieri is now completing. But Mozart's request also involves what the higher Irony, at its heart (or lack of heart), detests: avowal of weakness, final recognition of tragic flaw, and a generous response to the riches of music. For all his intelligence, Salieri can't ever respond that way. As Forman shows, some witty intellectuals live in deadly fear of being seen as inadequate.

In late 1989, Forman released his *Valmont*, another version of the Laclos novel, *Les Liaisons Dangereuses*. Again Forman attempted to use Irony against Irony, valuable heresy against an established god. In this case, Forman had the right impulse, but the wrong material. Laclos doesn't bend that much. But this is not necessarily to his credit, or Forman's blame.

Hope vs Irony

Humor, satire, and irony are always valuable; their worst enemies are often bad company. The Nazi propaganda minister Goebbels declared, "A joke is not a joke when it deals with the sacred goods of the nation." Goebbels obviously had his own special reasons for claiming this. But it is almost as dogmatic as Goebbels to claim there is nothing above a joke. Any "nothing" statement is pure doctrine, simplistic, mind-numbing, and rigid.

Classic satire aimed at the dismissal of extremes and recovery of balance. In Shakespearean comedy, in Pope, even in Swift (falsely labeled a misanthrope) satire begins as a corrective to pomposity or romantic pretension. But classic satire also aims at something beyond satire, a recovery of balance between humor and seriousness. Classic satire is satire for society's sake. It provides constructive—not destructive or deconstructive—criticism of social norms. Even armed with its weapons of wit and sarcasm, classic satire stays focused on one of the central duties of art, the responsibility of speaking positively, the importance of being earnest, once in a blue moon, about something of value.

Comedy often speaks in earnest terms; despite its excesses, even the sophomoric pop comedy of our times does so occasionally. But the higher Irony in various modes (pop cool, bleak chic, or European haute culture) is different. Many will say that it is apt for our age and that classic satire is "not possible anymore." But, to cite a central precept of modernism itself, this is only a matter of ideological choice. The literary high priests of Irony have been preaching this for years about belief in anything: they say that it's simply a reflection of personal ideology, which either conceals some form of personal interest (economic or gender bias, for example) or reveals some form of indoctrination in serving the interest of others. This is not necessarily true; but if they believe it, they could at least be consistent. What these priests never do is eye themselves in the mirror to examine how Irony serves their interests in perpetuating their sense of superiority and alienation from the rest of us. It is a very precious feeling, alienation: a kind of abstract property is involved, a sense of distinction and specialness. As a *thorough* Marxist might note, adhering to higher Irony is a way of conferring "class" on oneself, a way of being permanently one up on boobs who believe in anything. I just wonder how conscious the intelligentsia are, how genuinely self-critical. Of course, they are entitled to their beliefs; but it would be helpful if they recognized them as such. Anti-myths are just another belief system.

Walking out of a hip, classy theater near Lincoln Center on a brisk but pretty winter night in 1982, after seeing *Chariots of Fire,* I recall vividly hearing another moviegoer expressing puzzlement about the film: "It's so strange," she said. "That film actually has a happy ending. I don't know if I can remember another one." It's typical; as columnist Pete Hamill says, New York is "the last city before you get to Europe, the first city before you get to America." You can't be hip there and believe in hope.

But who really doesn't want a happy ending? To want one doesn't mean to be blind to the realities of life. But to be open to realities doesn't mean to give up—or never express—hope. And this is finally what Irony, a jealous god, demands as sacrifice.

This is, I know, so dreadfully bourgeois of me, and obviously reactionary. Take me away.

Religion

You talkin' to me?
— Travis Bickle, *Taxi Driver* (1977)

A gentle irony ruled the 1986 Cannes film festival. The three top prizes went to *The Mission*, *The Sacrifice*, and *Therese*, all high-quality, European-made films about religion. They were odd choices, given the usual treatment of religion by filmmakers in the last two decades— especially odd for such a glitzy festival, where quality has often been in but religion mostly out.

What had happened? Perhaps, as some said, it was the unaccustomed quiet at the festival: many famous stars and directors, paparazzi in tow, shied away from France in fear of terrorist reprisal for the American bombing of Libya earlier that spring. Cannes audiences, for once, could watch movies in relative quiet, and perhaps attend to the meditative, understated tone of all three films. In the case of *Therese*—which studied a portion of the life of St. Thérèse de Lisieux—the understatement led to one of the best films on a religious subject in many decades.

Such quiet contrasted with the controversy around *The Last Temptation of Christ* two years later (1988). To many people of different faiths, the movie seemed blasphemous for depicting Jesus as dreaming about having sex with Mary Magdalene. For some, it was the last straw in what they saw as a more-than-decade-old movie assault on religious values—or at least on images dear to religious believers (for a list of relevant films, see chapter 11, "Irony," p. 171).

The many ironic assaults against religion in recent films reflect the growing secularization in American society. They parallel recent negative treatments of other traditional sources of value—home, school, nation. But religion has really gotten it in the neck. The reverence that once dominated films with religious themes or characters has vanished. This is perhaps, in some ways, for the better; the exploitive mix of piety and prurience in De Mille epics is best forgotten. But what should take the place of old religious filmmaking? Today, as many recent movies that resort to vicious caricaturing of religion suggest, the main thing that filmmakers seem to be able to substitute is travesty.

There have been some exceptions: aside from *The Mission, The Sacrifice,* and *Therese* European movies continue to treat religion seriously: witness that gem of wit *and* affection, *Babette's Feast* (1987). Faith has also been presented strongly in *Tender Mercies* (1983), *Trip to Bountiful* (1985), and *Places in the Heart* (1984); all three are free from both sanctimony or condescension. The transplanted Australian, Bruce Beresford, who made *Tender Mercies,* even tried to make a new, tougher (and bloody) kind of biblical epic with the flawed *King David* (1985). *Field of Dreams* (1989) also had religious, albeit "new age" overtones. *Romero* (1989) replaced satire's caricature curates with the image of a real priest, assassinated in the cause of social justice.

Sci-fi also had its share of quasi-religious images: from the first *The Thing* and *The Day the Earth Stood Still* onward, rare have been the beings inside any spaceship who are not, in one disguise or another, angels or devils. As usual in recent sci-fi, Spielberg presented the most memorable images, not just with the glowing sacred heart of the dying E.T., but also with the most pathetic expression of hope in the spirit in any modern movie. In *Close Encounters of the Third Kind* (1977), Richard Dreyfuss piles mashed potatoes on his plate, surveys his astonished family, and announces anxiously, "This means something!" Dreyfuss is (unconsciously) thinking about Devil's Tower; consciously or not, Spielberg is voicing his own surburban animism; the phrase almost seems a prayer about matter itself. Still, the general trend of films has been to irony. *Shag* (1989) was an unusual, quirkily nostalgic teen romp; but it was perfectly conventional with its slap at one girl's father, a Baptist minister glibly dismissed as a "damned holy roller."

The Last Temptation has none of this dismissive irony. It has less in common with satire on religion than with the sensitive European treatments of faith rewarded at Cannes. The film was not made for profit; it only made money because of the notoriety that protests against it attracted. *Last Temptation* offended many, but it was *sincerely meant,* and had none of the cheapo sarcasm of so many other recent films featuring religious ogres. Just when *Last Temptation* ended its (controversy-prolonged) run, back came caricature with *The Chocolate War* (1989) about a Catholic school where priest/teachers are so eager to raise funds through selling candy that they encourage harassment of students who refuse to help. Such an obnoxious plot is far more troubling.

Still, despite its sincerity, The Last Temptation can't simply be excused because other films assault religious values more directly. Despite the extremism of many charges against it, it deserved its reputation as the most notorious movie life of Christ. The film's director, Martin Scorsese, claimed that, while it presents Jesus as God, "it comes at this from the human end." The film's final sequences, including Christ's dream of a last chance for earthly happiness through love of women, certainly went further than any movie before in depicting Christ's manhood. No one before had broken such a taboo. Was it worth it? And what does it say about the future direction of religious filmmaking?

At the very least, The Last Temptation revived the idea that one could make a serious film about religion—a taboo in Hollywood almost since the 1960s. Together with the Cannes films, it also represents a complex development in religious films—the emergence of individualized, argumentative statement not of, but about faith on screen. Unlike many recent film treatments that resort to caricature, the Cannes films and Last Temptation certainly have religious values and probe serious religious experiences. What's odd is the lack of old-style reverence; their makers follow their own lights. We are dealing with a new kind of religious film, in short—something beyond predictable sentimental reverence and the (now) equally predictable clichés of irony. Precisely because they are serious, such works are bound to cause trouble; indeed, they reveal how differences seem more offensive when they come from within a tradition, not from without.

They Don't Make 'em Like They Used to, II

Traditionally, filmmakers fashioned screen images of Christ and the saints in a worshipful manner. Like most religious teaching in the first half of this century, earlier films stressed the Christ's divinity, not humanity—not out of conviction, but a desire not to offend. The mere possibility of offending believers led studios to handle the subject of Christ's life with extreme care. Beginning with the silent Ben Hur (1926), Christ's figure was never shown directly, but only through crowds or in partial shots of his hands.

In the 1930s, under the influence of the Legion of Decency and the Hays Code, filmmaking about Christ maintained a perfect decorum. In over three decades of melodramatic biblical epics, Jesus was accorded a kind of "shadow" treatment. From The Last Days of Pompeii (1935) to *The Robe,* or *Quo Vadis?* (1951) and the second *Ben Hur* Jesus may have been a character in the plot, but was rarely if ever seen in full figure, or for very long. His role was limited to a kind of holy "cameo"—a momentary presence looking down on action, or seen from a long distance (reciting the Beatitudes in the 1959 *Ben Hur*) or only in a glimpse from the rear (*Quo Vadis?*). The camera angles literalized the humility of the woman in the Gospel who only desired to touch the hem of Christ's garment. Angelic choruses and tremulous violins suggested mystery and otherworldliness. Diffuse lighting added a holy glow around the barely seen figure of Christ. This kind of treatment, now reserved for benign extraterrestrials, lasted until the final biblical epic, *The Greatest Story Ever Told* (1965).

But the sixties, naturally, turned films about religion topsy-turvy, beginning with *King of Kings* (1961), the first full-length life of Jesus since the precode 1927 De Mille silent with the same title. The decision to present the whole story straightforwardly and the casting of youthful Jeffrey Hunter provoked controversy ("I Was a Teenage Jesus," *Time* termed it). Even with its reverential tone, *King of Kings* was the first act in the "humanization" of Christ in film that *The Last Temptation* took to such extremes.

This sixties' readiness to film the human face of the divine took on political overtones. In *The Gospel According to St. Matthew* (1965), Italian director Pier Paolo Pasolini provided a radical, down-to-earth image of Christ. Gone were the swelling musical climaxes and clichés of epic cinematography. In a style both neorealist and visionary, Pasolini filmed a grimy, disease-ridden Palestine where a swarthy Christ preached stern social lessons.

There was, however, no loss of the spiritual dimension, especially in scenes of the temptation in the wilderness. As in the Gospel, Pasolini's devil lures Jesus not with sex but power. Pasolini's Jesus is sure of his mission, another contrast to Scorsese's hero, who is neurotically anxious. The film, for all its humanization of Christ's context, still has its feet within tradition. For Catholics, it symbolizes the spirit of Vatican II and the church's renewed emphasis on social justice since that time.

Not all subsequent images of Christ in film or other media so neatly fell into the pace of reform in religion. More and more works attest less to institutional belief than a quirky, individual kind of faith. The Greek writer Nikos Kazantzakis's novel *The Last Temptation of Christ* (for which he was excommunicated by his own church, the Greek Orthodox, after its publication) was translated in 1960, and attained greatest popularity on American campuses in the late sixties, especially in divinity schools of liberal Protestant denominations. Rock "opera" provided similar popular humanizations in *Godspell* and *Jesus Christ Superstar* (which emphasized Mary Magdalene's love of Jesus). Both became films in 1973. In parallel, cinematic lives of the saints showed the human face of sanctity in *A Man for All Seasons* (1966) and Franco Zeffirelli's *Brother Sun, Sister Moon* (1973), with Francis of Assisi as a medieval flower child (a saint who talks to the stars is a natural for any director looking for a holy rebel). Such films matched the times and their diffuse religious enthusiasms, not just for new images of Jesus and the saints, but Hinduism, Zen, and the Great Spirit rather than the Holy Spirit.

Of course, the sixties involved revolt against many traditional values, including religious belief itself. The image of Christ—once treated so gingerly in film—was bound to become much less sacred. Rampant secularization meant the Bible or lives of the saints, if filmed at all, would be presented in a straightforward, down-to-earth or satiric manner. The possibility, or opportunity, of giving offense increased accordingly.

The best of the spirit of the sixties—sometimes delayed from fulfillment for several decades—has also resulted in new, individualized, private forms of religious statement on film. The uproar of the times created as many pilgrims as atheists. Many of those searching for religion imbibed a vague, sometimes mystical, sometimes misguided religious sensibility from its idealistic fervor. In this context Martin Scorsese matured—first in parochial school, then briefly as a junior seminarian, and afterward outside the church. From the early 1970s on, when he first read Kazantzakis's novel, he dreamed of adapting it to film. He did so, plainly, from a desire to express his own earnest religious beliefs. The book and Scorsese's film—offensive as they may be to some—are two from the heart.

Heart, unfortunately, doesn't mean all. Scorsese's heartfelt depiction of Jesus, for example, still cuts very close to the bone. To many believers, *Ben Hur* or *The Ten Commandments* (1956) might seem preferable. Indeed, to the orthodox, the difference between the new religious films and a nasty satire might seem rather slight; both, they believe, deserve damnation. This is, in truth, an old, too-traditional Christian story: one recalls how, in the Middle Ages, passionate sincerity landed many an individualistic believer or idealistic visionary at the stake. In *Brother Sun, Sister Moon* Zeffirelli implies Francis of Assisi brushed with such a fate. Maybe Scorsese could identify—with Francis, not Franco, who condemned *The Last Temptation* in vituperative terms.

Scorsese's movie had one precursor whose premiere anticipated some of the passion generated by *Last Temptation*. The film was made by a somewhat older man, but still a "sixties' personality," the radical filmmaker, Jean Luc Godard, whose freely sexual study of the life of Mary, *Je Vous Salue Marie* (1985), irritated some traditional Catholics. Yet it too was sincerely if oddly meant. The plot updated the virgin birth (with Mary the daughter of a French gas station owner who plays basketball). Godard's treatment of Mary's pregnancy came complete with gynecological exams and the girl writhing naked in bed in torment over her condition—at times, like Scorsese's Jesus, bemoaning that she's been chosen for anything. Godard, like Scorsese, claimed his film was religious, and pointed to its "Franciscan" affection for earth and animals—a mood "jump-cut" into the story in a subplot about scientists attending an environmental conference.

Godard's films are certainly from the heart—or at least from his cerebral melange of emotion and scattershot reason. But *Je Vous Salue Marie* struck some—including groups such as the Catholic Legion of Mary—less as personal poetry than plain sacrilege. The same kind of storm, at increased force, broke around *Last Temptation*. Storms like this (and later ones, as over *The Satanic Verses*) have so far only one result: like hell, far more heat and noise than light.

Sweet Reason

Still, the controversy is worth reviewing for the lessons it holds about the deep misunderstanding between the film and religious communities. Some of the latter's confusion about *The Last Temptation* results from lack of knowledge about how Hollywood works for artists like Scorsese. As noted, the film was made *absolutely not* because of any desire for profit through sensationalist sacrilege; the film was made against the best advice of many marketing advisers who said that a religious film just wouldn't sell. It was made only because Scorsese insisted that he be allowed to make one work from the heart in return for labor at studio-approved projects. Such negotiating is standard practice by a successful director—Clint Eastwood pulled off a similar deal for *Bird*. From a business viewpoint, *The Last Temptation* was indulgence of an artistic dream.

Not every member of an organized religion missed its sincerity. Some clerics from more liberal Protestant denominations praised the film, citing exactly what had been condemned elsewhere, its pioneering attempt to portray, as vividly as possible (even down to sexual matters) the full humanity of Christ. But many religious enthusiasts disagreed. American fundamentalists picketed against the film; in France, a theater was firebombed; in Ireland, the movie was banned. The film was labeled "blasphemy" by some religious groups, and "morally offensive" by the United States Catholic Conference of Bishops (but so too are many movies, often merely for lewd language—e.g., *Bull Durham*).

Far to the right, the most outlandish protestors snidely implied that *The Last Temptation* might cause a rise in anti-Semitism, a not so subtle insinuation that it originated in "Jewish" Hollywood. Of course, the idea that the film was "Jewish" in origin was absurd. As many critics noted, *The Last Temptation* originated in the minds of agnostics, or at least Christians, however much odd ones. Besides Scorsese's Catholic background, screenwriter Paul Schrader was raised in the Dutch Reformed Chruch, and novelist Kazantzakis in the Greek Orthodox. To foment anti-Semitism over their work was not just wrong, but also morally disgusting.

Still, this does not make *The Last Temptation* innocent. Biographical defenses of the film are as irrevelant as ad hominem attacks and racial slurs. How one or another filmmaker grew up can't make a movie less irksome. Blood has been shed about the meaning of the doctrine of the incarnation in the past, plenty of it Christian. Kazantzakis was excommunicated from his church for writing the novel; the fact that he had once been in the community made it no less annoying to its religious authorities.

Such fine points were irrelevant as debate about the movie raged in summer, 1989. The inaccuracy of some of the charges and protests meant large ticket sales and, in some quarters, mountains of moral prestige for the film. It became a case of social restraint against free speech, and many Americans value, or worship, nothing more than the latter. Universal got a big PR bonus when it became apparent that few of the protestors had actually seen the movie. *The Last Temptation* involves many ironies, but the best was that a studio almost had people feeling *sorry* for it.

Of course, the protests against the film went too far and were often unfair. But there is nothing wrong with being upset about a film without seeing it. Millions of people—including many who pride themselves on their tolerance and liberalism—have strongly negative opinions about, say, films such as *Friday the 13th*, or *Rambo*. Often they express these opinions without benefit of seeing the movies in question. Of course, no film critic should have; but what new law says ordinary viewers cannot object to something without seeing it? There is no point in arguing that Scorsese deserves better treatment than Stallone: how do you know if you haven't seen Stallone? Maybe *Rambo* is art.

Still, it is one thing to complain about a movie, another to seek to ban it on the basis of hearsay. But even this is partly understandable if one tries to understand the point of view of fundamentalist believers. For them, experiencing what they consider to be an "immoral" or "sacrilegious" film is as terrible as experiencing any other moral outrage. Are we forbidden from protesting against war without *experiencing* it? Many believers couldn't see *The Last Temptation* because they thought its evil was as great as war; they were convinced it profaned sacred images. A sure sign of liberal lack of understanding—*lack* is a weak term here—is the surprise of so many in the film and arts community that anyone was outraged at all. Not understanding why, they often brought ad hominem charges into the debate, claiming that religious people *feared* the film might upset their faith. That is, many liberals couldn't even accept at face value what the controversy involved, or the basic point of view of the protestors; like some protestors, they engaged instead in insult and insinuation, not argument. *Of course,* efforts to ban the film were wrong; but from one point of view, they were not totally illogical. What we have in the controversy is not just a "failure to communicate"; what we have is another example of polarization in American values that subverts any grounds for communication.

Defenders of the film argued that the sacred was never violated because the sex occurred "only" in a dream. This was a stunner. The whole film industry trades on the credibility of dreams, on its ability to generate belief in illusions on pieces of celluloid. Every movie is a fiction, and as such no better or worse than a dream. Every film still aims at a compelling semblance of reality; and as anyone waking from a nightmare can testify, dreams can seem very real. A dream inside a film seems no less true, or compellingly real, than the film fiction itself. Yet some defenders of the movie pressed their "dream" line as a credible rejoinder against the protests, and people, surprisingly, believed it.

Universal publicists also claimed that the actual lovemaking in the film was very brief and insignificant. But, of course, the length of the lovemaking was irrelevant; ten seconds would be enough to offend some viewers, and there is plenty more than that. The lovemaking is also followed by scenes in which Scorsese's Jesus is rather easily seduced into bigamy. Little of the debate focused on this latter episode. But when Scorsese discussed the sexuality in the film, he did not claim that the lovemaking or later bigamy were trivial; to him they were vital to his depiction of the full humanity of Christ. That is, the studio pooh-poohed the sex into never-never land; the director claimed it put the film on theological high ground.

Which is true? How should one consider the inclusion of sex: only as a harmless "dream," or as a reflection of something more serious?

If so, what? Does it just extend the "humanization" of Jesus evident in sixties' films? Does it reflect the general vulgarization of American culture? Could it involve both? Or could there be a third alternative?

California Dreaming

The Last Temptation has moments—only moments, mind you—of sublime spiritual grandeur. Scenes where Christ raises Lazarus from the tomb, the entire presentation of crucifixion, his final words of triumph— perhaps no director (including the European greats) has ever equaled their religious intensity. A master of gore in previous films, Scorsese makes crucifixion bone-crunchingly gruesome, as nailing a body to a cross no doubt must have been. At such times, you must at least *esteem* anyone who would volunteer for such a fate, especially someone with natural human anxieties.

These moments—sublime and inspired as they are—are often clouded by Scorsese's uneven dramatic touch. The film is filled with long exposition scenes stuffed with verbal gobbledygook and tedious passages; it also has a troubled view of sex. Take the infamous "dream" sequence. It's not merely weak dramatically; its content also raises several deeper questions. It begins well—with a childlike angel leading Christ (Willem Dafoe) down from the cross to a beautiful, lush landscape where he finds Mary Magdalene (Barbara Hershey). Did Scorsese need the explicit lovemaking that follows? It's not in the novel, where Jesus imagines domestic life, but not the actual act of sex; the sequence goes on far longer than necessary. It develops into other scenes where a domesticated Christ practices bigamy (see below).

Aside from the unease the explicit sex causes for some, these scenes weaken the original point. Both the novel and film pose a contrast between the cross and simple domestic joy, the kind of choice that might tempt a normal human being away from a dangerous crusade. But in the dream this contrast is displaced by one between the cross and promiscuity. A dream with a simple sequence of Christ with Mary Magdalene (even including a modest display of affection) would have served to make the simple point. Scorsese makes sex explicit, then follows Kazantzakis right into a double bed. The argument that these scenes show Jesus as fully human does not wash, unless it is fully human to be promiscuous. Is sexuality naturally indiscriminate? Is domesticity naturally bigamous?

The little angel tells us the real answer: all women are one. He makes no distinction between ordinary married sexuality and bigamy, or indeed faithful love and adultery. The angel is revealed to be a devil, but this only makes matters worse: at this point the film poses a contrast between salvation (only on the cross) and damnation (which begins with involvement with a woman, which almost seems the devil's doing). In short, the book and even more so the movie, express an implicit contrast between goodness and sexuality, a sexist opposition between a "macho" sense of mission and the "lure" of women. Once Christ loves one woman, *The Last Temptation* implies, all hell breaks loose. Both book and film view marriage, frankly, Mediterranean-style.

Behind this is the same obsessive puritanism about humanity that Scorsese ostensibly wants to attack. Puritanism is implicit in the Kazantzakis book: his last temptation involves sex alone, a typical modern reduction of sin to "sins of the flesh." As Saint Matthew describes the temptation scenes in his Gospel, sins of "the world" and "the devil" are also likely sources of evil; Satan tempts Christ with the lure of material wealth and false spiritual power. Scorsese depicts the temptations in the wilderness recounted in Matthew, but even in these scenes he collapses the broader temptations to a sexual one; the devil suddenly acquires Barbara Hershey's vocal chords. He almost *limits* sin to sex, a classic piece of modernist sex obsession. At times Scorsese admitted this, but claimed that he couldn't see things otherwise—except, for the fact that he already had, of course, in *The Color of Money*. If any age has been bedeviled by worldliness and false gurus, it's this one. Scorsese can be visionary; too bad he wasn't in *The Last Temptation*, couldn't look the eighties directly in the eye, and couldn't resist his own temptations to monomania.

There are more examples of reductionism, more central ones. No viewer of Scorsese's other films can fail to see in *Last Temptation* a new variant of his image of a tortured, suffering, conflicted hero; at times it seems that Scorsese's reluctant Jesus could quote Travis Bickle from *Taxi Driver* (1977, also written by Paul Schrader), and ask God, "You talkin' to me?" Reviewing *Taxi Driver* (1977), Stanley Kaufman wrote, "By now, I get the feeling that Scorsese burrows through scripts looking for the hysterical scenes." *The Last Temptation* provided a gold mine, the perfect climax to a set of Scorsese studies in madness and mission or both. Pauline Kael saw it coming, noting that Scorsese "instinctively tried to turn *The Color of Money* (1986) into a Jesus story"; he managed "to turn Eddie Felsen into himself; he even tried to turn Rupert Pupkin of *The King of Comedy* into himself." *The Last Temptation* completes the circle; if Scorsese heroes all resemble Jesus and/or Scorsese, sooner or later Jesus might wind up looking like the filmmaker too. Or vice versa.

Legends only come to life when we identify with heroic figures in some way. The central issue in *Last Temptation* becomes whether or not an artist has the right to blend his own private concerns with such a story, to find—so to speak—his story in history. When it does this well at certain moments, *The Last Temptation of Christ* takes its place square- ly in the long line of films, beginning in the 1960s, which humanize the image of Christ without reducing Jesus down to simply another regular guy.

As noted about history films, there is a difference between finding relevance in history and forcing relevance, between passionate iden- tification with a character and reduction of character to your own pas- sions. A careful artist avoids such solipsism; when you play a sym- phony, you interpret, not impose. *The Last Temptation* is unevenly careful; often it just wallows around in modernist anxieties and assumptions. Like many films about history, it projects today's attitudes into the past, flattening it into a dull mirror of the present. Scorsese relies on Kazant- zakis's treatment, which presents Jesus not only as very human, but very modern—at times a twentieth-century existential searcher, even an antihero (see the signature comment, "I want to rebel against everyone, against God"); at others, in his anxious uncertainty and passive neurosis, he conforms to the nineteenth-century vision of a paralyzed Hamlet. Under either category, the film could easily be re- titled *The Last Temptation of J. Alfred Prufrock*.

Scorsese's Christ also slobbers in petty neo-Romanticism, declaring with contempt of Jewish tradition, "The law is against my heart." This not only distorts Jesus' words ("I come not to destroy the law but fulfill it"); it shares vocal chords with Byron and legions of imitative rebels ever after. This confronts the established gods of the modern age? Give me a break.

Indeed, Scorsese's theology (minus the agony and Christo-centrism) at times even resembles Carl Reiner's in *Oh, God!* (1977) and its sequels ([1980 and 1984] *Oh God! Book II*; *Oh God! You Devil*). As played by George Burns in the first two, "God" is a sentimental deist's dream; he's not interested in religion, but faith—a valid distinction, in part, but one which Reiner and Burns exploit to empty all faith of all con- tent except confidence in a general, vague divine benevolence. "God" wants people to take charge of their lives, be nice to each other, stop war and pollution (in the seventies' original); in short, "God" endorses a sweetly liberal agenda—dear, say, to Carl Reiner, or even Jane Fonda. Naturally, the heart shows up: it's "the temple where all truth resides," Burns says. To whom? An ordinary Joe (John Denver), a supermarket assistant manager who'd rather (like Scorsese's Jesus) be at home with wife (Teri Garr) and kids. None of this is offensive exactly; it just turns faith into cotton candy.

Scorsese has far more depth. But his cheapo "relevance" and heart-based theology reduce the strangeness that is necessary to make any genuinely religious movie shock and sing to us: even if we're still in this world, we should be able to *feel* the border of another. We can't do so frequently in *The Last Temptation*; the feeling comes across best on film—witness *Therese* or *The Gospel According to St. Matthew*—via understatement, not exactly Scorsese's strong suit. As noted, his strong suit is hysteria.

The border of another world seems particularly distant when the supporting actors playing the disciples speak their peculiarly banal language. Their diction is not modern English or even American; it's Southern Californian, except for Judas (Harvey Keitel) who speaks Brooklynese. Other actors rely on clichéd acting ticks (raised eyebrows, piercing squints) to make points; shave the beards, change costumes, and it's the local sports and weather. Scorsese undercuts his efforts at authenticity and strangeness—the grimy shots of ancient Palestine, or the wildly ecletic, highly Oriental musical score—when he directs the actors (in the ultimate banality) to talk and behave "just like us." There is no greater obstacle to true universality than such triteness.

Another Home Movie?

Still, there is a deeper, richer "relevance" in the movie than these forced gestures at contemporaneity. Part of the relevance is timeless, the result of the strong performance of Willem Dafoe, the Christ-like sergeant in *Platoon*, as (at times) an inspiring Jesus. His explanation of nonviolence as "breaking the chain of evil" is compelling. He has no better moment—and Scorsese makes no better case for the "humanity" of this image of Christ—than, when challenged about apparent changes in doctrine, he explains, "God only talks to me a little at a time. He only tells me as much as I need to know." The line strikes home for anyone who has experienced the struggle to see through a glass darkly. Beyond a doubt, Scorsese has a real sense of that hard agony.

But there is a deeper root to the genuine relevance in the movie's content. Of course, the film derives from a novel written long ago. But it also builds from Scorsese's previous works, which are filled with references to Christ symbols and to anxiety over displacement from "normal," homey settings: see, for example, Griffin Dunne's prayer at the end of *After Hours*. In short, the movie details a universal dilemma that Kazantzakis first attached to the biblical story; but it also seems to have specific roots and resonance in Scorsese's life.

Recall the dream sequence: Christ (Willem Dafoe) is led by an angelic figure down from the cross into a beautiful, lush landscape where he finds Mary Magdalene (again, Barbara Hershey). They set up house, make love, Mary dies, after which Christ fantasizes marrying another Mary (the sister of Lazarus) and also her sister Martha, and raising with them a large number of babies. The sex scenes caused an outcry; less noted was the bigamy and multiple pregnancies, and how they perfectly fit our times.

Whatever one's views on the treatment of Christ in *The Last Temptation*, consider this implicit theme: its reimagined Jesus wants a home. He is anxious about his fate on the cross. According to the movie, he has to force himself into his mission, more like Jonah on the way to Nineveh. That is, despite its explicit sex, *The Last Temptation* ironically contains a neo-traditionalist "home" movie message: to paraphrase *Raising Arizona*, "Go on home and git yourself a toddler"—indeed get yourself a bunch, just like *Micki and Maude* (see chapter 6, "Home"). On one level, despite its offensiveness to many traditional believers, *The Last Temptation of Christ* is an unconscious, partly conservative tribute to the power of home in the 1980s. The buried wish of Scorsese's imaginary Jesus is to go on home and *cocoon*.

The choice of hero understandably angered some conservative commentators (including Catholics like Pat Buchanan at CNN). Nevertheless, its choice of temptation is vintage eighties. It reflects a reaction to and wrestling with the complex, ambiguous heritage of the 1960s in which director Martin Scorsese first matured—for one year, in a junior seminary filled with activist ardor. "Make love" (or at least babies), its temptation sequences say, "not war"—on poverty or other social problems. Crusade? Forget it. "That's history." It's the *wrong* thing to do.

In some ways, the movie reveals the depths of "sixties-something" in our culture. Of course, the desire to make the world a better place is by no means limited to sixties' forms; indeed, as the failures of the sixties showed, you can do a lot of Christ-like things by *not* being radical. You can even do them quietly.

Still, for Scorsese, the issue in *Last Temptation* seems to have a sixties' air and to derive from his own experiences at that time. On one level, the movie opposes the sixties and eighties, the spirit of service and sacrifice (however misguided) with privacy and personal fulfillment. It provides no alternatives to these hard choices; despite its secularization and even vulgarization of the biblical story, it takes them earnestly. What is a person to do, Scorsese asks, go home, or struggle to make the world a better place?

What luck or rather what Grace, Scorsese sometimes whispers, to find someone to mediate such hard choices for us. Or Someone. That, finally, is the majesty we sometimes see through his glass darkly.

The Fate of Faith on Film

Moviemaking on religious subjects will probably follow similar lines in the near future as the recent past. Rare will be an old-fashioned reverential film: Cannon Films had a wooden one ready about the Lourdes story in 1988, *Bernadette*, but (perhaps wisely) never released it. Less dated would be the whimsy of *We're No Angels* (1989) (with cons Robert De Niro and Sean Penn in priestly disguise), reminiscent of *Going My Way* and parallel to some new TV sitcoms such as *Sister Kate*.

Sure to continue will be mocking satires of low brain power, as in *Nuns on the Run* (with Eric Idle of Monty Python). *St. Francis of Assisi* (scheduled for release in 1990), with Mickey Rourke in the lead, also gives one pause. On the other hand, *The Handmaid's Tale*, based on Margaret Atwood's dark fantasy on theocracy, promises to raise satire on religion—or the intolerance of some religious bigots—to a genuinely prophetic level.

From Europe there will continue to come sensitive religious filmmaking in the mode of Gabriel Axel's *Babette's Feast*. While spicing that repast with French flavors, Axel also belongs to a Scandinavian tradition founded by grandmaster Carl Dryer and sustained by Ingmar Bergman even at his most agnostic. But in late 1989, plans were also announced by Danish director Jens Jorgen Thorsen to film *The Return of Jesus Christ*—with one of his appearances as a political terrorist. More reductionism? We don't need it. We need movies that ask probing religious questions, but also check themselves against temptations to trendy excess.

Such movies are not likely to have smooth sailing. They will always, per se, offend someone. But they may also help viewers gain a renewed sense of faith. Many today think faith means knowledge; better religious filmmaking might even help them understand it is not so certain. Faith means you *don't* know. Faith involves uncertainty, imagination, and hope at the core. "For we are saved by hope, but hope that is seen is not hope, for what a man seeth, why doth he yet hope for?" (Paul to the Romans, 8:24).

Notes

This book is not an academic work of research scholarship. Often passages in the chapters simply cite general critical opinion about a film or industry scuttlebutt. But I have at times referred to some specific sources for my comments. The following, which detail their locations, are arranged in a progressive order to follow my points as they are raised in each chapter. I especially want to note some books (see "Justice," "Nation," "Home") that have been very helpful in shaping my general argument. Several magazines and newspapers are also frequently cited; the list below includes their names and relevant abbreviations. The first two have been very helpful, though sometimes I disagreed with their writers:

American Film: (AF)
Film Comment: (FC)
Commonweal: (C)
Newsweek: (N)
The New York Times: (NYT)
USA Today: (USAT)

Chapter 1: Introduction

For the Paul Schrader quote, see *AF,* July/August, 1989, p. 19; for a sure view of one filmmaker's intentions, see Andrew Yule, *Fast Fade: David Puttnam, Columbia Pictures and the Battle for Hollywood* (New York: Delacorte Press, 1989). See also Bill Moyers's interview with Puttnam in *A World of Ideas* (New York: Doubleday, 1989), pp. 316–32.

I owe much of my thinking about the distinction between moralism and moral concern with movies to the work of Media and Values, directed by Elizabeth Thoman, 1962 South Shenandoah, Los Angeles, 90034 or 475 Riverside Dr., Suite 1370, New York, 10027. The magazine *Media and Values* is available on subscription.

For anecdotal links between media images and crime, see one story on a "Jason" mimic, *USAT,* November 16, 1988, p. 3A, and *NYT,* "The Jogger and the Wolfpack," April 26, 1989. On heavy metal videos and their possible influence, see Tipper Gore, *Raising PG Kids in an X-Rated Society* (Nashville: Abingdon, 1987), although many people prefer to damn Mrs. Gore's opinions without reading them. On the new film cartoons and their increasing violence: "Drawing on the Dark Side," Joe Queenan, *New York Times Magazine*, April 30, 1989, p. 32.

Some critics and scholars think there is far too much worry about sex and violence in the media. For a historical view of debates about the issue, see the study of the effect of movies on social behavior by I. C. Jarvie, *Movies and Society* (New York: Basic Books, 1970). For a negative view of the rating system, see Lois Sheinfeld, "The Big Chill," *AF*, June 1986, p. 9ff.

For a review of the whole debate about the influence of art and media images of sex or sexual violence, see Walter Kendrick, *The Secret Museum: Pornography in Modern Culture* (New York: Viking, 1987). For a recent study on links between images of sexual violence and violent behavior, see *The Question of Pornography, Research Findings and Policy Implications* (New York: Free Press, 1988) by psychologists Edward Donnerstein, Daniel Linz, and Steven Penrod. I am also indebted to a book by my editor Michael Leach, *I Know It When I See It: Pornography, Violence, and Public Sensitivity* (Philadelphia: Westminster Press, 1975).

There have also been two recent Presidential Commissions on Pornography, one in 1970 (Report of the Commission on Obscenity and Pornography) that recommended tolerance of almost all forms of expression (and that was roundly denounced by President Nixon and the US Senate); and the more recent Attorney General's Commission of Pornography, which issued a final report in 1986 in two volumes. Under the leadership of President Reagan's Attorney General Edwin Meese, it recommended new restrictions against pictorial pornography, not print, and also urged legislative action to prosecute pornography involving minors.

For the sighting of a zeitgeist, see Siegfried Kracauer, *From Caligari to Hitler, A Psychological History of German Film* (Princeton: Princeton University Press, 1947), which traces the rise of Nazism in expressionist film. Kracauer was sure that he had seen a zeitgeist; but then they are always more visible in retrospect.

Several recent books on arts and society during the sixties and seventies have been helpful: Todd Gitlin, *The Sixties: Years of Hope, Days of Rage* (New York: Oxford University Press, 1988); Tony Hendra, *Going Too Far* (New York: Doubleday, 1987); and, for England and Anglo-American exchanges, Robert Hewison, *Too Much: Art and Society in the Sixties* (New York: Bantam Press, 1987).

For the sixties as an influence on today's moviemakers, see "60's Chic," *FC*, August 1988, and articles on *Patty* and *Running on Empty* in *AF* (September 1988) and *Mississippi Burning* (December 1988).

In the early eighties' trend toward conservatism, not all media fell into step. Interestingly, television was better than movies in keeping some political themes alive on screen in the early 1980s; several early eighties TV movies (on the Kent State killings, or the murders of the four American nuns in El Salvador) clearly show that television did not become as conservative as film during that time;

movies on such subjects were only released in the later 1980s. As noted in the third chapter, history sometimes did better on TV than in the movies; so did women and racial minorities (see "Heroines" and "Justice"). Why did television—admittedly in small doses only—take more political risks? TV films and programs are cheaper to make, can be targeted more precisely at select audiences, and do not require the cost and effort of distribution. Of course, even the best of TV is dismal; but given the level of early eighties' films, that was better than brain-dead.

Chapter 2: Teaching

My thinking on this subject was originally stimulated by the op-ed essay by Richard Lodish, "More Dignity for Teachers in Film, Please" *NYT,* April 16, 1988, p. 31. Mr. Lodish is lower school principal at the Sidwell Friends School in Washington, DC. The original version of this chapter was printed as "Good-bye, Mr. Chips" in the *Journal of Religion and Intellectual Life* (ed. Nancy Malone, College of New Rochelle), Spring/Summer, 1989.

On the tradition of college films, see Wiley Lee Umphlett, *The Movies Go to College: Hollywood and the World of the College Life Film* (Rutherford, NJ: Fairleigh Dickinson University Press, 1984).

On the literary tradition of educational satire, see Charles Dickens, *Hard Times,* for the original Mr. Gradgrind; earlier satires include passages from Alexander Pope's "The Dunciad"; later, it pervades works by D. H. Lawrence, and made for the best scenes in Ken Russell's 1989 film, *The Rainbow.*

When *Lean on Me* was getting panned by critics for being too nice about Joe Clark, the *New York Times* (February 28, 1989, B1) ran a story about dangers in the schools that could make you think twice about the issue of just how far a principal should go to defend his law-abiding students against thugs. I doubt many of the critics who dismissed *Lean on Me* understand these conditions. For a word from the horse's mouth, see Joe Clark and Joe Picard, *Laying Down the Law: Joe Clark's Strategy for Saving Our Schools* (Washington: Regnery-Gateway, 1989). A positive review of the book by Elizabeth Lyttelton Sturtz, a public school educator, was in *NYT Sunday Book Review,* July 9, 1989, p. 14.

On the new trend to heroize schoolteachers, see Tracy Kidder, *Among Schoolchildren* (Boston: Houghton-Mifflin, 1989). See also the fine review of the book by Phyllis Theroux in *NYT Sunday Book Review,* September 17, 1989, p. 1. In a related interview, Kidder comments, "We need to get beyond the stereotypes of teachers either as dullards or miracle workers."

Chapter 3: Cultural Literacy

I am not sure who first used the phrase "the hidden curriculum." I first read about it in Neil Postman, *Teaching as a Conserving Activity* (New York: Delacorte Press, 1979). See especially his discussion of TV as "The First Curriculum," pp. 47–70. Postman's most recent book is *Amusing Ourselves to Death,* a study of how even "serious" television trivializes issues.

On the decline of history films, see Allen Barra, "The Incredible Shrinking Epic," *AF*, March 1989, p. 40ff. Barra's article covers both costs, issues, and cultural factors behind the decline of the history and "epic" spectacle. For a survey of the uses of movies for history teaching, see Robert A. Rosenstone, "History in Images/History in Words," in *American Historical Review*, December 1988. Rosenstone is right that movies can interest students in history and are valuable as an educational tool. But he assumes that there will probably be a continuing supply of such movies, an assumption that current trends do not support.

Regarding *A Man for All Seasons*, Allan Bloom notes in *The Closing of the American Mind* (New York: Harper and Row, 1988, p. 352) that the influence of models such as Thomas More's may not have always been for the best. Bloom has blind spots, goes too far in some of his arguments, but is acute in his insights about a kind of liberal close-mindedness. To my personal regret, he is often right on target about student reformers of the 1960s.

On *Drums along the Mohawk*, see John E. O'Connor, "A Reaffirmation of American Ideals," in *American History, American Film* (New York: Continuum, 1987), ed. John E. O'Connor, p. 97ff.

On the phrase "You're history," see Bharati Mukherjee's book review in *The Nation*, on Studs Terkel, *The Great Divide*, December 5, 1988, pp. 622–24. New connotations for old words do tell us a lot: consider, in a related instance, the modern connotation on the word *academic* as *pointless, abstract*, or *irrelevant*. This numbers among the great achievements of modern universities.

For Custer, see Evan S. Connell, *Son of the Morning Star* (New York: Harper and Row, 1985). Connell's novel on contemporary marriage, *Mr. and Mrs. Bridge*, was scheduled for release as a movie in 1990. Emphasis on the contemporary has even influenced production of toy soldiers, whose design now has to be ultramodern. See Cathleen Schine, "Floor Wars," *New York Times Magazine*, August 13, 1989, p. 28ff.

Janet Maslin, movie critic of the *New York Times*, I believe, coined the phrase *white flannel* movies, but I am not sure when.

On the distinction between history and nostalgia, see Robert Monaco, *Ribbons in Time: Movies and Society since 1945* (Bloomington: Indiana University Press, p. 124). Monaco makes a useful distinction: nostalgia films make their audiences feel about the past; history films make them think.

The argument for a dramatist's "poetic license" as opposed to exact history is made first in Aristotle's *Poetics*, chapter 9.

Princeton historian Natalie Zemon Davies was a consultant to *The Return of Martin Guerre*; she published her own version of the tale in *Le Retour de Martin Guerre* (Cambridge: Harvard University Press, 1983). The film also inspired the American-produced *Sorceress* in 1988, funded in part by the NEA.

Chapter 4: Work

On issues surrounding *Tucker*, see Jill Kearney, "The Road Warrior," *AF*, June 1988, pp. 21ff.

For a survey of movie satires on business, see John Taylor, "America, Inc.," *AF,* March 1988, pp. 59–61. For a view of recent satire, see William J. Palmer, *The Films of the Seventies: A Social History* (Metuchen and London: Scarecrow Press, 1987) and his emphasis on the omnipresent "corporate villains" in *The China Syndrome, Network, Apocalypse Now, Poltergeist,* and other films.

The theme of marrying rich in the eighties is noted by Pauline Kael in *Hooked* (New York: E. P. Dutton, 1989), p. 132.

For misrepresentation of medical work on screen, see Krim Grabbern and Glen O. Grabbern, *Psychiatry and the Cinema* (Chicago: University of Chicago Press, 1987), and Joseph Turow, *Playing Doctor: Television, Storytelling, and Medical Power* (New York: Oxford University Press, 1989).

On "discouraged workers," see Lawrence Shames, *The Hunger for More: Searching for Values in an Age of Greed* (New York: Times Books), p. 229. Shames is also good on the likenesses and differences between the 1950s and 1980s; on upscale workers, see his emphasis on their anxious rat race, p. 227. On unusually obnoxious business commercials of the time, see Shames's discussion of super-cool Wang computer ads and their specialized jargon, p. 110.

Advertising was satirized in two films, *Nothing in Common* (1986) and the English *How to Succeed in Advertising* (1989); in a more typical early-eighties, trendsetter *Kramer vs Kramer* (1979), Dustin Hoffman works for an ad firm; despite his difficulties with one, the business itself is treated very positively.

Lizzie Borden's *Working Girls* (1987) was one of the more ironic treatments of "discouraged workers" on screen. The film treated an elegant New York brothel as an industrial workplace in which the "working girls" go through the rituals of regular workers during their breaks—chats over lunch about (real) boyfriends, talk about going to college and clothes, etc. All the "glamour" of the world's oldest profession is reduced to clocking in and clocking out of the bedroom, ordering lunch, etc. Borden's madame is the prototype sweetly exploitative boss, who manipulates one of her workers into so much overtime she quits.

On women at work on screen, see Constance Rosenblum's feature, "Drop Dead Clothes Make the Working Woman" in *NYT Arts and Leisure,* February 26, 1989, II, p. 1. Rosenblum finds women at work are mostly treated in unrealistic ways.

For a feminist complaint against *Working Girl,* see Mona Harrington's "Working Girl in Reagan Country" in the op-ed section, *NYT,* January 15, 1989; for a response, see Suzanne Ramye Legault's letter to the editor, *NYT,* February 3, 1989. See also the complaint by James Greenberg, "Over 'The Rainbow' " in *AF* (May 1989), which attacked the movie because its heroine wanted to make money.

On the perils of "finance uber alles," see Robert Reich, "Leveraged Buyouts: America Pays the Price," *NYT Sunday Magazine,* January 29, 1989, p. 32ff. For a view of enlightened capitalism at work, see Thomas J. Peters and Robert H. Waterman, Jr., *In Search of Excellence* (New York: Warner Books, 1982). See especially chapters on "Man Waiting for Motivation," "Close to the Customer," and "Productivity through People." See also a piece on large, Tucker-like family-run businesses, "Renewing Traditional Values" *NYT,* June 10, 1986, D1.

Chapter 5: Sports

One of the best pieces ever written on baseball movies is Roger Angell's "The Sporting Scene: No, but I Saw the Game," the *New Yorker,* July 31, 1989, p. 41ff. Angell has always written well about baseball (e.g., "The [original] Mets were like France after the First World War; the very old and the very young, and no one in between"). I don't agree with all of his points about baseball movies, but share his love of *Bull Durham* and his dislike of *The Natural.* Mine extends to the book, for reasons noted in the text.

On college sports movies, see Wiley Lee Umphlett, *The Movies Go to College: Hollywood and the World of the College Life Film,* (Rutherford, NJ: Fairleigh Dickinson University Press, 1984). Umphlett notes the popularity of the genre in the 1930s and 1940s, and even some entrants in which winning was not the only thing (e.g., *Touchdown* [1931], *The All-American* [1932], and *Saturday's Hero,* [1953]).

Gene Siskel made the comment on *Listen to Me* as an imitation of a sports formula film on "At the Movies" May 7, 1989.

For the sports/media symbiosis, see Jay J. Coakley, *Sports and Society,* cited in *Media and Values,* ed. Elizabeth Thoman, Summer 1986. The whole edition covers "The Wide World of Media and Sports" from multiple angles.

For a recent book-length study of the Black Sox, see Eliot Asinof, *Eight Men Out* (New York: Henry Holt, 1987).

One good piece on the complexities of sports and race was by Jack Kroll et al., "Race Becomes the Game," *N,* January 30, 1989, pp. 56–59.

On *Rocky* and race, see Daniel J. Leab, "The Blue Collar Ethnic in Bicentennial America," in *American History, American Film* (New York: Continuum), ed. John E. O'Connor, p. 257ff.

For an attack on *Field of Dreams,* see J. Hoberman, "Shot in the Dark: Born-again Baseball," *FC,* May/June 1989, p. 78ff. But the piece is less a film review than a statement of ideological preference.

Chapter 6: Home

On the success of Wilford Brimley, see Sal Ruibal, "Pitches with the Most Punch," *USAT,* May 3, 1989, 6B. Brimley won the 1988 Star Presenter of the Year Award from *Advertising Age.*

Witold Ribcynski's two major books are *Home: The History of an Idea* (New York: Viking, 1985), and *The Most Beautiful House in the World* (New York: Viking, 1989).

For more neo-traditionalism in architecture, see the piece on new "old"-style baseball parks, "Field of Fancy, Field of Dreams," Jerry Adler, *N,* June 19, 1989, pp. 66–67. For neo-traditionalism in dress, see Barbara Kantrowicz and Karen Brailsford, "Victoriana Rules Again," *N,* January 16, 1989, pp. 60–61.

On a view of Woody Allen as a family filmmaker, see Richard Zoglin, *FC,* May/June 1986, pp. 16ff.

On baby boomers and the media, see Jeremy Gerard, "TV Mirrors a New Generation," *NYT,* 2, October 30, 1988, p. 1. For a brief, good treatment of *thirty-something,* see John O'Connor, "The Series for These Ambiguous Times," *NYT,* May 30, 1989. On sentimentalizing babies, see Molly Haskell, "Hollywood Madonnas," *Ms.*, May 1988, pp. 84ff.

Leslie Fiedler's study of male bonding in literature is the classic *Love and Death in the American Novel,* covering Hawkeye and Chingachgook, Huck Finn and Jim, Ishmael and Queequeeg. On the breakdown of heterosexual love in recent movies, see Julia Cameron, "What's Love Got to Do with It?," *AF,* April 1989, p. 30ff. Molly Haskell foresaw the antiwoman element in new male-bonding movies in the concluding sections of *From Reverence to Rape* (New York: Holt, Rhinehart, and Winston, 1973). See also Pauline Kael on the exclusion of women in *Stand by Me* and other male friendship movies in *Hooked,* p. 196.

For some relevant road movies, see Gerald Peary, "On the Road," *AF,* January/February 1987, pp. 65–67.

Negative treatment of the family movies of the last decade is common in liberal film journals. For a typical article that dismisses positive treatments of the traditional family, see Karen Jaehne, "Love in the Nineties: Coming Attractions," *FC,* January/February 1989, pp. 47ff. See also the less sarcastic piece by Marcia Pally, "Kin Con: The Family Goes Bananas" in *FC,* February 1988, p. 11ff.

Chapter 7: Environment

Farley Mowat's original book *Never Cry Wolf* was published by Atlantic Monthly Press in 1963; the same press also publishes many of Mowat's other fine works, and an anthology, *The World of Farley Mowat* (1980), ed. Peter Davison.

On hipster hyping of the city, see Joel Rose, "Lower East Side: Directors Love It to a Fault," *NYT, Arts and Leisure,*May 7, 1989, II p. 22.

Nature has been out in hip painting circles for some time. Indeed, modern painters do not even like the association when they work on *landscapes.* See Cathleen McGuigan, "Transforming the Landscape," *N,* December 26, 1988. Note the pervasive embarrassment of the artists in being associated with anything so "simple" as nature; they are all at pains to emphasize that their landscapes were purely "mental." In 1976, the Museum of Modern Art put on an exhibit of nineteenth-century American landscapes ("The Natural Paradise"), and justified it because the old paintings anticipated aspects of modern abstraction. Realistic landscape is of course passé.

I interviewed Ballard and Farley Mowat for the *Boston Globe;* the piece ("Wolf Man Mowat: At Last a Film Equal to the Book") appeared October 30, 1983, p. A8. I talked to Ballard at the Helmsley Palace in New York; there could be no more incongruous place to chat about *Never Cry Wolf.*

Besides *My Dinner with Andre,* another cult hit in New York was the British *Sammie and Rosie Get Laid,* an ultraironic bit of anti-Thatcherism. But it too catered to elitism or the urban superhip cosmopolitan sort: its hero and heroine love the joys of urban life (valid enough); the hero is especially proud of attending for pleasure lectures on semiotics; "Neither of us is English, you see; we're

Londoners," he says. How many of the avant-garde in this country would echo such feelings! Ironically, they think of themselves as friends of the masses.

At the release of *Powaqqatsi*, the uneven sequel to *Koyaanisqatsi*, I interviewed Reggio for the *Boston Globe* (May 8, 1988, p. 94) and *Commonweal*, May 18, 1988, pp. 304–5. Glass later wrote music for "Mattogrosso," an opera on the Amazon that premiered in 1989.

On the future film on the defense of the rain forest, see "Film Planned on Brazilian Ecologist" *NYT*, June 8, 1989, C15.

A few corporations also turned toward environmentalism in the later 1980s; Apple Computer even put up the money for a twentieth anniversary of Earth Day in 1990. See Anita Manning, "Big Business Puts Green into Environment" *USAT*, October 10, 1989, p. B2; see also Kevin Maney, "Companies Make Products Nicer to Nature," August 23, 1989, p. B1.

Chapter 8: Patriotism

Many of the insights in this chapter I owe to Albert Auster and Leonard Quart and their fine study, *How the War Was Remembered: Hollywood and Vietnam* (New York: Praeger, 1987). The Auster/Quart book is valuable for its survey of films about Vietnam and its close reading of the techniques of *Platoon*, to which the end of my chapter is indebted. No one interested in this subject can ignore their work; Quart and Auster, for example, show how influential were Wayne's films in the generation that fought in Vietnam (p. 79); they are also excellent on the films of Stanley Kubrick.

Other major works on movies and "the good war" are Jeanine Basinger's, *The World War Two Combat Film* (New York: Columbia University Press, 1986), and Bernard F. Dick, *The Star Spangled Screen, The American World War Two Film* (Lexington: Kentucky University Press, 1989). On the name "Windy," see Dick, p. 139.

On the debate in France, see Lynn Hunt, "It's Not Over till It's Over and It's Not Over," *NYT Book Review*, September 10, 1989, p. 12. See especially with its focus on the controversial antirevolutionary study, *Citizens*, by Simon Schama.

Some World War II movies were franker than others. David Denby wrote a nice article on the tone of John Ford's *They Were Expendable* (1945) in *Premiere*, August 1989. Denby claims the film looked back resentfully at some of the sacrifices and lack of preparation forced on frontline troops and sailors at the beginning of the war. Paul Fussell's 1989 study, *Wartime: Understanding and Behavior in the Second World War* (New York: Oxford University Press), more stringently focuses on the harsh battle realities of World War II that were buried under ultrapositive images on screen.

On the patriotic rhetoric of World War I and the disillusionment in literature afterward, see Paul Fussell, *The Great War and Modern Memory* (New York: Oxford University Press, 1975). See especially chapter 1: "Never Such Innocence Again." See Michael Isenberg, "*The Big Parade*: The Great War Viewed from the Twenties," in *American History, American Film* (New York: Continuum, 1987), ed. John E. O'Connor, p. 17ff.

For late-seventies' films about Vietnam, see Wiliam J. Palmer, *The Films of the Seventies: A Social History* (Metuchen and London: Scarecrow Press, 1987).

The phrase "the romance of militarism" was coined by Armond White in "Two Thumbs Down," *FC*, January/February 1989, p. 38.

On the death of HAL, see Kael, *Hooked*, p. 328.

For a good interview with Oliver Stone, see Pat McGilligan, "Point Man," *FC*, February 1987, p. 11ff.

For a (regrettably) neglected Vietnam film, see *84 Charlie Mopic,* a 1989 release by Vietnam veteran, Patrick Duncan. If anything, this movie (which fared badly in theatrical release) puts one even more in the context of the action than *Platoon;* Duncan used a hand-held camera, suggesting a cinema verité army documentary shot on patrol in the field. The camera choice put viewers close to the action, perhaps too close; it can give you a bad, but very convincing case of the nerves.

Casualties of War was criticized by some veterans groups for its portrayal of gang rape. See *USAT,* August 24, 1989, D1.

Chapter 9: Heroines

Many insights in this chapter I owe to the pioneering study by Molly Haskell, *From Reverence to Rape* (see notes on chapter 6) which covers female stereotypes in greater detail than I do here. On women screenwriters in the thirties, see p. 151. On Hitchcock's inversal of blonde/brunette formulas (often in plots with Grace Kelly), see p. 349.

On differences between *Peggy Sue Got Married* and *Back to the Future*, see Kathy Maio, *Feminist in the Dark* (Freedom, CA: The Crossing Press, 1988), pp. 192–193.

A good treatment of the backlash evident in early eighties sci-fi is found in Robin Wood, *Hollywood from Vietnam to Reagan* (New York: Columbia University Press, 1986), p. 177. See also the general treatment of *Star Wars*'s encouragement to sexual domesticity in Andrew Gordon, "The Power of the Force; Sex in the *Star Wars* Trilogy" in *Eros in the Mind's Eye: Sexuality and the Fantastic in Art and Film* (New York: Greenwood Press, 1986, ed. Donald J. Palumbo. The reading of the sink metaphor in *Ordinary People* is from Graeme Fuller, *Film as Social Practice* (London: Routledge and Kegan Paul, 1988), p. 48.

On television and women, see Harry F. Waters and Janet Huck, "Networking Women," *N*, March 13, 1989, pp. 48ff. In the mideighties ABC started using 10 P.M. as a "woman's hour," following Tuesday's *Thirtysomething* with *China Beach*, on Wednesday and on Thursday, *Heartbeat*, whose doctors could never dent NBC's *L.A. Law* (whose female attorneys fought it out much more realistically than in movies like *Jagged Edge, Physical Evidence,* or *Legal Eagles*— where Debra Winger and Daryl Hannah replay those dark/blonde stereotypes once again).

On Jessica Lange, see especially Kael, *Hooked*, p. 235.

Chapter 10: Justice

On law-and-order films, see the fine work by Susan Jacoby, *Wild Justice: The Evolution of Revenge* (New York: Harper and Row, 1983). I am much indebted to Ms. Jacoby's insights and observations in the first part of this chapter. See especially her view of the rise of images of vengeance as a response to the taboo on discussing the subject in polite society and therapeutic circles, "Revenge as Metaphor: The New Image Makers," pp. 150–82.

For a view of inaccuracies about law in *The Verdict*, see Thomas J. Harris, "The Verdict" in *Courtroom's Finest Hour* (London and Metuchen: Scarecrow Press). On TV images of the courtroom, see Harry Waters, "TV's Crime Wave Gets Real," *N*, May 15, 1989, p. 72.

On current frustration with the law, see Seymour Wishman's review (*NYT Book Review*, May 1989, p. 35) of lawyer Gerry Spence's attack on lawyers, *With Justice for None: Destroying an American Myth*. See also Meg Greenfield's outcry, *N*, August 1989, p. 68.

Sometimes even the dates of movies reveal trends. Most movies about rape, and with rape in the title, date only from the 1970s.

On "benign neglect" of social justice and racial tolerance on film, see Chris Hodenfield, editorial, p. 2, *AF* (July/August 1989). On the gifts and limits of Eddie Murphy, see David Ehrenstien, "The Color of Laughter," *AF*, September 1988, pp. 8–11.

Interestingly, there have been two movies of Richard Wright's *Native Son*— once in the pre-McCarthyite period (1950) and again at the end of the Reagan era (1987). But the sixties missed it.

On race in *Rocky*, see Leab, "The Blue Collar Ethnic in Bicentennial America," ed. O'Connor, 257ff.

Extensive coverage of the debate over *Mississippi Burning* can be found in *NYT Arts and Leisure* 2, December 4, 1989, p. 15 (an interview with Alan Parker); and in several stories in section 2, January 8, 1989. A critical op-ed piece by James Allen McPherson appeared January 14, 1989, p. A25; the letter of praise from Willie Brown is in *NYT*, February 27, 1989, 1, p. 18. It should also be noted that *Mississippi Burning* was part of the background when the state attorney general sought reconsideration of charges against the original suspects in spring 1989. On the danger of forgetting the civil rights movement, see Jonathan Alter et al., "Out of Sight, Out of Mind," *N*, January 23, 1989, pp. 52–53.

For *Do the Right Thing*, see feature articles on Spike Lee in *NYT Arts and Leisure*, 2, June 25, 1989, and July 9, 1989. For a negative response to the movie by a black woman, see Barbara Reynolds's column, *USAT*, "Not the Right Thing, Just the Same Thing," July 14, 1989, p. 13A. *AF* and *FC* were also filled with articles about Lee in summer 1989.

Dershowitz wrote on films in "Legal Eagles," *AF*, November 1986, p. 61.

Chapter 11: Irony

One of the best treatments of Irony in the larger sense of the term that I try to define at the beginning of this chapter is by Richard Rorty, *Contingency, Irony, and Solidarity* (New York and London: Cambridge University Press, 1989). Rorty emphasizes the value of Irony in breeding tolerance of others and understanding of mutual frailty and fallibility. He is right to a degree; a sense of irony certainly helps in not taking oneself too seriously and can thus foster sympathy and understanding of another's point of view. Rorty here emphasizes the positive side of enlightenment rationalism, and the way skepticism can breed tolerance. But as philosopher/historian/proto-deconstructionist David Hume noted in the eighteenth century, skepticism can also foster aimlessness. Historically, skepticism has led to greater respect for others, a helpful corrective to political and religious fanaticism. But twentieth-century celebrants of skeptical irony forget what the enlightenment foresaw: the inherent danger of taking nothing seriously. Such skepticism mocks not just human vanity but all human achievement.

On satire's losing its point in zaniness, see Tony Hendra, *Going Too Far* (New York: Doubleday, 1987); Hendra traces the new humor back to the sixties, but claims that, at some point, *National Lampoon*-type humor became not just tasteless but pointless.

My discussion of pathography is indebted to James Atlas, "Speaking Ill of the Dead," *NYT Sunday Magazine,* November 6, 1988, p. 40ff.

For the story of John Bloom's creation of Joe Bob Briggs, see David Chute, "The Fine Art of Red Neck Reviewing," *AF,* September 1986, 38ff. Joe Bob struck again in *AF,* July/August 1987, in "Kiss, Kiss, Bang, Bang" with retrospective capsule reviews of some slasher/nudie films on videotape—e.g., *Shogun Assassin, Make Them Die Slowly, Pumping Iron II: The Women, I Spit on Your Grave* ("ninety-four on the vomit meter"). Or try his review of *Eliminators:* "Great *Quest for Fire* ripoff scene where the entire cast is attacked by monkey suit extras. Kung fu. Laser fu. Transfusion fu. Throwing star fu. Thompson submachine gun fu. Toga fu. Monkey fu. Electric fan fu. Colored gas fu. Neanderthal fu. Lesbo fu. Hillbilly fu. Mandroid torpedo fu. Fire extinguisher fu. Laser-to-the-crotch fu." Joe Bob is not without a moral ideology, for all his slumming. As he notes, "I think the best critics, the ones who are read and reread, are always the ones who are slighted for not having enough moral content to their work." This statement is, of course, its own kind of moral judgment.

On the current rage for Irony, see Todd Gitlin, "Defining Postmodernism," *NYT Book Review,* November 6, 1988, p. 1. See also Paul Rudnick and Kurt Anderson, "The Irony Epidemic" in *Spy,* March 1989, p. 92ff. The apt cover ("Isn't It Ironic?") features Chevy Chase.

On the style and success of Bill Murray, see Vincent Canby, *NYT Arts and Leisure,* April 16, 1989, 2; see also Janet Maslin, "Under the Tree, the Laughs Are Scarce," *NYT Arts and Leisure,* December 11, 1989, 2, p. 13, where she says of Murray: "His may be the perfect comic sensibility for the eighties: casually cynical, serenely mean spirited, strictly out for number one." Maslin adds that she likes Murray's humor.

For the connection of ironic superficiality and acting styles, see Gavin Smith, "Actors Face the Truth," *FC*, January/February, 1989, p. 32ff. I am indebted to Smith for my details here. See also Pauline Kael on the style of one icon of surface, "Rob Lowe acts Rob Lowe acting" (*Hooked*, p. 178).

Richard Corliss complains about cynicism in film in "Who Cares?" *FC*, January/February 1989, p. 65ff.

On *Blue Velvet* et al., see John Powers, "Bleak Chic" *AF*, March 1987, p. 40ff.; for recent film images of small towns, see Richard Corliss, "Our Town," *FC*, December 1986, p. 9ff.

For the relation of Irony and the breakdown of love in recent movies, see Julia Cameron, "What's Love Got to Do with It?" *AF*, April 1989, p. 30ff, especially p. 58 on cynicism vs romance.

On the dangers of relativism and cynicism in the media, see the fine editorial on "The Culture of Apathy" in the *New Republic*, February 8, 1988.

Chapter 12: Religion

On *Therese*, see Annette Insdorf, "A Simple Movie That Wins Accolades," *NYT Arts and Leisure*, December 28, 1986, 2, p. 15ff; see also my own piece on *Therese* in the *Boston Globe*, B2, February 18, 1986.

Part of this chapter was originally printed as "Hope in the Movies," *Journal of Religion and Intellectual Life* (ed. Sister Nancy Malone, ARIL: College of New Rochelle), Summer 1988. For parallel trends in fiction, see Dan Wakefield, "And Now a Word from Our Creator," *NYT Book Review*, February 12, 1989, p. 1.

Much of the material on traditional filmmaking about Christ comes from my piece in the *Washington Post*, August 14, 1989, G1.

For *The Last Temptation*, see Andrew Greeley's piece "Blasphemy or Artistry" in the *NYT Arts and Leisure*, August 14, 1988, 2, p. 1; see also coverage of *The Last Temptation of Christ* in *AF* and *FC* in October 1988; see also the good Chris Hodenfield profile of Scorsese, "The Art of Noncompromise" in *AF*, January 1989, p. 46ff.

Many of the arguments for and against *The Last Temptation* that I discuss in this chapter were made on numerous television talk shows at the time of release of the movie, including *Nightline* (August 9, 1988), *The Larry King Show* (August 10, 1988), and *Crossfire* (July 27, 1988).

For Scorsese's acknowledgment of autobiographical touches in *The Last Temptation*, see the *Commonweal* interview with Scorsese by writer and filmmaker Mary Pat Kelly, September 23, 1988, pp. 467-70.

For "hysteria" in *Taxi Driver*, see Stanley Kaufmann, *Before My Eyes* (New York: Harper and Row, 1980), p. 204; the column is from the original review in the *New Republic*, July 23, 1977.

Debates of *The Last Temptation* are paralleled in part by other recent controversies over the relation of the arts and society. Many artists seem to think they not only have the right (which they do) to treat religious symbols ironically; they also seem to think that they deserve public money for doing so. For example, the 1989 controversy about National Endowment for the Arts funding for exhibits with the homoerotic photographs of Robert Mapplethorpe also touched on funding for works by sculptor Andres Serrano (e.g., his "Piss Christ," a crucifix in a jar of urine). During debates over a Jesse Helms bill to curtail funding for such exhibits in the future (including funding for works that might insult any religion), the arts community acted as if no one, at any point, could ever object to use of Treasury funds for works of art, no matter how much they might offend the public. Better still, they got mad at congressmen for daring to object. Of course, the NEA and its peer review panels should be free of political pressure; of course, Senator Helms's efforts should have been rejected. Nevertheless, it surpasses understanding how a National Endowment for the Arts funded by a nation of taxpayers cannot in some way be responsive to their viewpoints. The NEA is after all, the *NEA*. To assume an *NEA* should not at least take into consideration a *nation's* political, cultural, and religious values is pure, crackpot aestheticism, a perfect partner for a *danse macabre* with Puritan censoriousness. The mutual closemindedness of both sides in these disputes makes for a perfect dialogue of the deaf. Similar polarized battle lines were drawn over *The Last Temptation*. The unwillingness of all involved to concede even partial validity to the opposite viewpoint does not bode well for the future peace of the republic. The issues involved are not likely to disappear.

Index

This index is limited to movies released roughly within the time frame covered in the book. Dates of release are found in their first mention in chapters after the introduction. Naturally, some movies have to be listed under several chapter/subject headings.

Cultural Literacy (cont'd.)
The Return of Martin Guerre
A Room with a View
Sweet Liberty
Terror in the Aisles
White Mischief

4. Work

Absence of Malice
All the President's Men
All That Jazz
Baby Boom
Behind the Lines
Blue Collar
Broadcast News
Cabaret
Country
Gung-Ho
Harlan County, U.S.A.
Matewan
The Mean Season
Melvin and Howard
Network
9 to 5
Norma Rae
Places in the Heart
The River
Rollover
The Secret of My Success
Swing Shift
Switching Channels
Talk Radio
Tin Men
Tootsie
Tucker
Under Fire
Wall Street
Working Girl
Working Girls
The Year of Living Dangerously

5. Sports

The Best of Times
The Bingo Long Traveling
   All-Star and Motor Kings

Breaking Away
Bull Durham
Chariots of Fire
Eight Men Out
Everybody's All-American
Field of Dreams
The Great White Hope
Heart like a Wheel
Hockey Night
The Karate Kid
The Karate Kid II, III
Major League
The Natural
North Dallas Forty
Over the Top
Personal Best
Rocky
Rocky II, III, IV, V
Raging Bull
The Slugger's Wife
Stealing Home

6. Home

About Last Night . . .
The Accidental Tourist
Adventures in Babysitting
Alice Doesn't Live Here Anymore
Another Woman
At Close Range
Baby Boom
Back to the Future
The Big Chill
Big
Big Business
Coal Miner's Daughter
Cocoon and sequel
Country
Crimes of the Heart
Cry in the Dark
Dad
The Dead
Divorce American Style
End of the Line
E.T.
Everybody's All-American

7. Environment

Environment (cont'd.)
Mountain Family Robinson
Never Cry Wolf
New York Stories
Phar Lap
Places in the Heart
Poltergeist
The Poseidon Adventure
Quest for Fire
Radio Days
Return of the Wilderness Family
Roar
The Secret of My Success
Silkwood
Slaves of New York
Soylent Green
Tin Men
To Live and Die in LA
The Towering Inferno
Watership Down
Wilderness Family
Wolfen

8. Patriotism

Apocalypse Now
Born American
Born on the Fourth of July
Breaker Morant
Casualties of War
Coming Home
Das Boot
Death before Dishonor
84 Charlie Mopic
Fat Man and Little Boy
Firefox
First Blood
Full Metal Jacket
Gallipoli
The Great Santini
Heartbreak Ridge
The Hunt for Red October
In Country
The Killing Fields
The Longest Day
Missing in Action

No Way Out
An Officer and a Gentleman
Platoon
Rambo: First Blood II
Rambo III
Red Dawn
The Right Stuff
Some Kind of Hero
Star Wars
Stripes
Taxi Driver
Top Gun
Uncommon Valor

9. Heroines

The Accidental Tourist
Aliens
Baby Boom
Big Business
Broadcast News
The China Syndrome
Cocktail
Country
Crimes of the Heart
Cry in the Dark
Dangerous Liaisons
Everybody's All-American
Fatal Attraction
Frances
The Good Mother
Gorillas in the Mist
The Handmaid's Tale
Hannah and Her Sisters
Heartburn
Heart like a Wheel
Hockey Night
Immediate Family
I've Heard the Mermaids Singing
Jagged Edge
Kramer vs Kramer
Legal Eagles
Marianne and Juliane
Mask
Mr. Mom
Mommie Dearest

11. Irony

Agnes of God
Airport
Airplane!
All of Me
Amadeus
And Now for Something Completely
  Different
Attack of the Killer Tomatoes
Bill and Ted's Excellent Adventure
Blazing Saddles
Blood Simple
Blue Velvet
Buffalo Bill and the Indians
Chariots of Fire
Choose Me
Crimes of Passion
Dangerous Liaisons
Down by Law
Eating Raoul
Eric the Viking
A Fish Called Wanda
Footloose
Ghostbusters
Gremlins
Hannah and Her Sisters
Heathers
History of the World—Part 1
Hound of the Baskervilles
Indiana Jones and the Temple
  of Doom
Jabberwocky
Jaws
Johnny Dangerously
King of Comedy
Life of Brian
Light of Day
Little Shop of Horrors
Love and Death
M*A*S*H
Mass Appeal
McCabe and Mrs. Miller
The Missionary
Mr. Mom
Monsignor

Monty Python and the Holy Grail
Monty Python at the Hollywood
  Bowl
Mosquito Coast
The Name of the Rose
Play It Again, Sam
Prizzi's Honor
Radio Days
Raising Arizona
Rancho Deluxe
Roxanne
Sammy and Rosie Get Laid
Scenes from a Class Struggle in
  Beverly Hills
Scrooged
Sherlock Holmes' Smarter Brother
Something Wild
Strangers in Paradise
Stripes
This Is Spinal Tap
Tootsie
True Confessions
Valmont
The Witches of Eastwick
Withnail and I
Without a Clue
Young Einstein
Young Frankenstein
Young Sherlock Holmes

12. Religion

Agnes of God
Bernadette of Lourdes
The Chocolate War
Crimes of Passion
Field of Dreams
Footloose
Hannah and Her Sisters
Indiana Jones and the Temple of Doom
Je Vous Salue Marie
King David
The Last Temptation of Christ
Light of Day
Mass Appeal
The Mission